Imaginary Philosophical Dialogues

Kenneth Binmore

Imaginary Philosophical Dialogues

between Sages down the Ages

 Springer

Kenneth Binmore
University College London
Monmouth, UK

ISBN 978-3-030-65386-6   ISBN 978-3-030-65387-3 (eBook)
https://doi.org/10.1007/978-3-030-65387-3

© The Editor(s) (if applicable) and The Author(s), under exclusive license to Springer Nature Switzerland AG 2021
This work is subject to copyright. All rights are solely and exclusively licensed by the Publisher, whether the whole or part of the material is concerned, specifically the rights of translation, reprinting, reuse of illustrations, recitation, broadcasting, reproduction on microfilms or in any other physical way, and transmission or information storage and retrieval, electronic adaptation, computer software, or by similar or dissimilar methodology now known or hereafter developed.
The use of general descriptive names, registered names, trademarks, service marks, etc. in this publication does not imply, even in the absence of a specific statement, that such names are exempt from the relevant protective laws and regulations and therefore free for general use.
The publisher, the authors and the editors are safe to assume that the advice and information in this book are believed to be true and accurate at the date of publication. Neither the publisher nor the authors or the editors give a warranty, expressed or implied, with respect to the material contained herein or for any errors or omissions that may have been made. The publisher remains neutral with regard to jurisdictional claims in published maps and institutional affiliations.

This Springer imprint is published by the registered company Springer Nature Switzerland AG
The registered company address is: Gewerbestrasse 11, 6330 Cham, Switzerland

To Danny and Christina

In memory of Albi, where much of this book was written.

Preface

What would Charles Darwin have said to Karl Marx about his claim that dialectical materialism is an evolutionary theory? This book explores such questions by inventing imaginary dialogues between pairs of sages down the ages who were alive at the same time, beginning with a retelling of the Platonic Dialogue between Protagoras and Socrates. My intention is not to give potted accounts of the whole philosophy of the protagonists I have chosen, but to have them discuss some specific issue intended to illustrate the wider differences of opinion at the time at which they lived. It was always tempting to say more, but I thought it best to keep each dialogue to just a few pages.

Nobody should regard these imaginary dialogues as either comprehensive in their coverage of the philosophical issues that were relevant at the time, or even accurate in the views they attribute to different philosophers. Sometimes my protagonists give voice to ideas that I feel sure they would have understood and endorsed if they had been proposed at the time they lived, but were not actually formulated until hundreds of years later. Occasionally I have found it necessary to invent very unlikely expedients to get philosophers who were historical contemporaries together at the same time and place.

I hope my various fictions will not be judged too harshly. My intention is that the book should be an amusing diversion for those who think exploring intellectual issues is fun, rather than yet another worthy tome weighed down with scholarly references and learned footnotes. For those like me who try to make their own mind up about things rather than accepting whatever views are currently popular, there is also the prospect of hearing heretical opinions about philosophers who are normally mentioned only with great reverence. Adam Smith, for example, is allowed to be almost contemptuous of Immanuel Kant's famous categorical imperative when they are imagined to meet in Königsberg.

The dialogues are loosely held together by a common theme that comes across most strongly in the early dialogues. Where do we get our ideas from? Are they built into the fabric of the universe waiting to be discovered, or do we make them up as we go along? This issue is as ancient as philosophy itself. The ancient Greeks saw the problem as choosing between *physis* and *nomos*.

The distinction between *physis* and *nomos* can be troublesome for us because our word physics is derived from the Greek physis, but we are not talking about the world itself when we distinguish between *physis* and *nomos*, but about our models of the world. Since everybody agrees that the models of modern physics are human constructs, their study therefore comes under the heading of *nomos*. The same is not true of mathematics, which many philosophers nowadays treat as a branch of *physis*, although it is not so long ago that it was routinely thought to be a branch of *nomos*. That is to say, philosophers no longer take for granted that mathematicians invent their axioms and theorems; it is fashionable instead to proceed as though their axioms and theorems are discovered in the course of exploring a pre-existing mathematical universe.

One might reasonably respond that it does not matter much what philosophers say about physics or mathematics, but the same is not true of ethics, where the *physis* or *nomos* controversy has raged on and off since ancient times—and continues to rage today. Are the so-called natural laws propounded by moral philosophers genuinely natural? Are they part of the natural universe awaiting discovery by those who think hard enough about ethical problems? Or are they really artificial, and all that is natural about them is that evolution has made it natural for the human species to invent such laws?

In ethics, orthodox philosophy has largely come down on the side of *physis*. It is common to argue that modern philosophers have no more to offer than footnotes to Plato, in whose dialogues Socrates is dismissive of those who put the case for *nomos*. My own view is more in line with the views of modern philosophers of science, who are unsurprisingly empiricists, who take the same attitude to all models as physicists take to quantum mechanics or relativity. They ask whether there are genuine reasons to favor one metaphysical model over another. Are the opposing philosophers who call themselves rationalists really gifted with insights that provide a hot-line to the absolute truths of the universe? Or do they deceive themselves when they imagine their ideas are more than elaborate models they have invented for themselves? The modern imaginary dialogues between Lakatos and Popper, and between Harsanyi and Rawls, illustrate that such divisions have persisted for more than two thousand years, and it does not seem likely that they will be settled in the near future.

At different times and places, the philosophers who debate these issues might have summarized their differences as:

> physis versus nomos
> realism versus nominalism
> idealism versus materialism
> tradition versus enlightenment
> faith versus science
> rationalism versus empiricism

but I am uninterested in the fine distinctions between such philosophical positions. What is gained, for example, by placing mathematics on one side of a sharp divide and physics on the other? Is it really useful to call Spinoza a rationalist for reasoning like a geometer? Is Berkeley's attempt to justify religion genuinely empirical?

The dialogue style is particularly appropriate for talking about issues like the physis versus nomos debate, because it allows the author to remain nominally neutral. But it is not easy to emulate Plato. Whatever one may feel about his own philosophy, there is no doubt that he was—not only a crucial figure in western intellectual history—but a master of the dialogue style. I cannot aspire to match either his literary skills, or his feeling for the intellectual spirit of the times in which his dialogues are set. I hope, however, that my attempt at writing dialogues will make it possible to regard my protagonists as real people—creative but fallible—rather than as the superhuman heroes of philosophy textbooks, all of whose thoughts are to be treated only with the greatest of respect even when they contradict each other. On the other hand, we must try not to forget that our philosophical predecessors were giants in their time, even though we can nowadays sometimes see further than they could. To paraphrase Isaac Newton, when we see further than our predecessors, it is because we stand upon their shoulders.

Acknowledgments

I had much help from many people. I would like to make a special note of the following friends, who could not always persuade me to keep to the strait and narrow path:

Hartmut Kliemt
Manfred Holler
Heinz Kurz
Larry Samuelson
Haris Shekeris
Brian Skyrms

Contents

1 Protagoras versus Socrates   1
2 Diogenes versus Plato   7
3 Aristotle versus Plato   11
4 Eudoxus versus Aristotle   15
5 Epicurus versus Zeno   21
6 Sextus Empiricus versus Marcus Aurelius   25
7 Augustine versus Hypatia   29
8 Anselm versus Abelard   33
9 Thomas Aquinas versus Roger Bacon   39
10 William of Ockham versus Duns Scotus   45
11 Thomas Hobbes versus René Descartes   49
12 Blaise Pascal versus Pierre de Fermat   55
13 John Locke versus Thomas Hobbes   63
14 Gottfried Leibniz versus Baruch de Spinoza   69
15 David Hume versus Jean-Jacques Rousseau   77
16 Immanuel Kant versus Adam Smith   83
17 Edmund Burke versus Thomas Paine   89
18 Jeremy Bentham versus John Stuart Mill   95
19 Friedrich Engels versus Karl Marx   101
20 Charles Darwin versus Gregor Mendel   107
21 Karl Marx versus Charles Darwin   115
22 Georg Cantor versus Bertrand Russell   123
23 Bertrand Russell versus John Dewey   129

24 Ludwig Wittgenstein versus David Hilbert	135
25 Oskar Morgenstern versus John von Neumann	141
26 Karl Popper versus Ludwig Wittgenstein	149
27 Jean-Paul Sartre versus Simone de Beauvoir	155
28 John Nash versus John von Neumann	163
29 Rudolph Carnap versus Leonard Savage	169
30 Imre Lakatos versus Karl Popper	175
31 Robert Nozick versus David Lewis	181
32 John Rawls versus John Harsanyi	189
33 Derek Parfit versus John Rawls	197
34 Index	203

Chapter 1
Protagoras versus Socrates

Context

Our first imaginary dialogue sets the scene for the whole book by retelling Plato's account of a meeting in ancient Athens between a youthful Socrates and the ageing sophist Protagoras.

My version of their debate is a lot more fictional than Plato's, although experts argue that Plato's *Protagoras* must also be fictionalized to some extent, since the historical evidence suggests that the audience of distinguished intellectuals who supposedly listened to the debate could not all have been in Athens at the same time. Since the issues discussed are only loosely connected, perhaps Plato joined together several accounts of meetings between Socrates and Protagoras.

In Plato's later dialogues, the Socrates who leads the discussion is plainly altogether fictional, but the Socrates of the *Protagoras* was probably based on the real Socrates. If the *Protagoras* were totally invented as in the case of the *Republic*, presumably Socrates would have been more successful in trouncing Protagoras. But Socrates actually comes across as a mere gadfly, employing what we would nowadays call sophistry to score debating points against a reluctant Protagoras, who understandably seems to care more about retaining the respect of his wealthy potential clients than putting Socrates down.

In any case, I follow Plato in being casual about matters of fact, and about possible anachronisms in particular. For example, any actual encounters between Socrates (469–399 BC?) and Protagoras (490–420 BC?) almost certainly took place before the Delphic Oracle pronounced that Socrates was the wisest man in Greece. Where I do not follow Plato is in his downplaying the fact that Protagoras was the leading exponent of the sophist attachment to the *nomos* side of the long-running dispute between *physis* and *nomos*, in which Plato remains a leading exponent of *physis* to this day. However, in my version of their dialogue, Protagoras holds his end up just as well as Socrates when he is the target of the questioning for which Socrates is famous.

But we begin, as Plato began, with Hippocrates calling on Socrates to tell him that the famous Protagoras has just arrived in Athens. Their first and last exchanges are abbreviations of Jowett's translation of Plato's actual words.

Dialogue

Socrates is awoken one morning by Hippocrates banging on his door in great excitement. The famous sophist Protagoras is in town! Socrates urges caution:

SOCRATES: Is not a sophist, Hippocrates, one who deals wholesale or retail in the food of the soul? To me that appears to be his nature.

HIPPOCRATES: And what, Socrates, is the food of the soul?

SOCRATES: Surely, knowledge is the food of the soul; and we must take care, my friend, that the sophist does not deceive us when he praises what he sells, like the dealers wholesale or retail who sell the food of the body; for they praise indiscriminately all their goods, without knowing what are really beneficial or hurtful.

Socrates is particularly concerned with Protagoras's claim that he teaches virtue to his students. Does Protagoras really know what virtue is? Is virtue something that can be taught? So they agree to go together to the house of Callias—where Protagoras is staying—to find out whether his reputation for wisdom is sufficiently well-founded to justify Hippocrates paying to become one of his students. After some difficulty with a surly doorkeeper, they finally gain admittance, where they find Protagoras holding forth to an admiring audience of Greek intellectuals. Socrates is introduced to Protagoras, and the audience gather round to hear who comes out on top in the dialogue that ensues.

SOCRATES: You once said that man is the measure of all things. Do you therefore hold that each man makes up what to count as virtue for himself?

PROTAGORAS: I continue to say that man is the measure of all things. But it does not follow that each individual man makes up what to believe for himself. Communities share their beliefs about what it is appropriate to count as virtuous. Nor do individuals or communities think out such beliefs from scratch in a cold-blooded way—they largely inherit their beliefs from their ancestors.

SOCRATES: To what definition of virtue does this way of thinking lead?

PROTAGORAS: Your question implies that you think virtue is an absolute—that it has a definition that can be given without reference to what community we are talking about, or anything else. But the sophist position is that virtue—and much else—is a relative concept. Herodotus tells us of a tribe of Indians who regarded it as virtuous to eat the dead bodies of their fathers, and were shocked to learn that there are Greeks who burn them. Perhaps a time will come when your relationship with the youth Alcibiades will similarly shock our descendants. Perhaps women will one day be held equal to men. Perhaps slavery will come to be thought abhorrent.

SOCRATES: So you think that truth is relative—that the truth for one community may differ from that of another.

PROTAGORAS: What is truth? It is coherent to imagine that there are propositions that a universe might or might not satisfy, and that the propositions that our universe satisfies are true, and those that it does not satisfy are false. But perhaps the universe transcends the kind of propositions that we humans can imagine. However, let us nevertheless proceed on the assumption that we know what we are talking about when we talk about truth.

SOCRATES: I am pleased that we have found something on which we can agree. Let me then repeat my question in different words. How can truth be relative, if the nature of the universe depends on what propositions are true and what propositions are false? Surely sophists do not hold that the nature of the universe is just a matter of opinion?

PROTAGORAS: You are correct that we do not hold that the nature of the universe is a matter of opinion. There are propositions that are true because people believe them to be true—for example, that it is moral in Sparta for young women to exercise naked, as young men do in Athens. If the Spartans believed what Athenians believe about what is moral, then it would be false that it is moral for women to exercise naked in Sparta. However, there are other propositions that are universally held to be true in that they are believed by everybody—for example, that Sparta is in the Peloponnese, and Athens in Attica. As for the true nature of the universe, that lies beyond our knowledge. The best we can do is guess.

SOCRATES: I notice, Protagoras, that you distinguish between something being universally held to be true, and something actually being true. But surely something is either true, or it is not true.

PROTAGORAS: One might say, Socrates, that the difference lies between our knowledge of the objective, and our knowledge of the absolute. It is illustrated by your own response on learning that the Oracle of Apollo in Delphi had named you as the wisest man in Greece.

SOCRATES: It is true that when Chaerephon told me of the answer the Oracle gave to his question, I was puzzled. Why me? The answer I came up with is that I am no less ignorant than others, but I know that I know nothing.

PROTAGORAS: You will perhaps think that what I shall say next is the kind of tiresome sophistry to be expected of sophists like myself, but it cannot be true that a person knows nothing if he knows that he knows nothing. So you must have been using the concept of knowledge in two different senses if you are to be absolved from uttering a contradiction.

SOCRATES: I should perhaps have been more careful to exclude trivial everyday knowledge—like the location of Sparta or Athens—on the grounds that such knowledge is better described as belief. But I am interested to hear the different concepts of knowledge you are anxious to distinguish, since the works of Protagoras are closely associated with careful attention to the correct use of words. I attach much importance to what knowledge means because I hold that nobody would fail to act virtuously if they really knew what virtue means. It is their ignorance that leads people astray rather than their intrinsic ill-nature. So what is your definition of knowledge?

PROTAGORAS: As with virtue, knowledge doesn't have a definition that is somehow independent of the way human beings organize themselves. To understand what people mean by words, we have to explore how they use them in real life. In the case of knowledge, Socrates, I agree that it should be distinguished from belief. Belief is open to revision but knowledge is not. If our host Callias were to change his mind about something, we would say that he was mistaken in thinking that he knew it in the first place. Philosophers therefore usually take for granted that knowledge implies certainty.

SOCRATES: So we agree in distinguishing knowledge-as-certainty from mere fallible belief?

PROTAGORAS: We do agree on distinguishing knowledge-as-certainty from fallible belief. But empiricists like myself regard knowledge-as-certainty as unattainable. We think that when people speak of knowledge in ordinary life, they are really talking about knowledge-as-commitment. They are telling us what propositions they regard as axiomatic in their approach to living their lives. This is what my mentor Democritus meant when he taught that people who are very sure of their knowledge are no less ignorant than the rest of us—they are usually just repeating the principles on which their community believes itself to be based. Who, for example, is more sure of anything than their religion? But different communities honor different gods.

SOCRATES: You speak of Democritus of Abdera in Thrace, which is also your own home city. He is certainly worthy of much respect if only for his mathematical work. How did he become your mentor?

PROTAGORAS: When I was no more than a porter, Democritus was impressed by my mathematical precision in tying up the bundles of wood I was carrying, and so took me on as an apprentice. I am forever grateful to him for singling me out, and for the training in philosophy with which he gifted me.

SOCRATES: So you learned your notion of knowledge-as-commitment from Democritus. How does he handle the problem of contradiction? What happens if something held to be knowledge-as-commitment is contradicted by matters of fact?

PROTAGORAS: In practice, contradictions or denials are ignored or explained away as irrelevant anomalies. For example, it seems to me, Socrates, that you proceed as though the proposition that virtue is an absolute concept—necessarily the same for everybody everywhere—is self-evidently true. Those who do not share this piece of knowledge-as-commitment are explained away as being inadequately philosophical.

SOCRATES: What then is your final definition of knowledge? Or perhaps you and your mentor prefer to dispense with talk of knowledge altogether?

PROTAGORAS: Democritus is famous for saying, "By convention sweet is sweet, by convention bitter is bitter, by convention hot is hot, by convention cold is cold ... in reality, only atoms and the void." But he can no more have knowledge-as-certainty of such things than Socrates can have knowledge-as-certainty of the absolute nature of virtue. In saying that our perception of flavor or temperature lies in our minds, and would be different if our minds were different, he expresses beliefs about how our minds work. When he speaks of atoms and the void, he expresses beliefs about the external world. If he acts as though these beliefs are true for certain, he makes them into knowledge-as-commitment.

SOCRATES: Is Democritus unaware that Parmenides of Elea has shown that to speak of the void is to utter a contradiction?

PROTAGORAS: I follow Democritus in believing that what the Eleatics show—particularly Zeno in his paradox of Achilles and the Tortoise—is that the language we are accustomed to using when trying to make sense of the world around us is inadequate. It is not only our models of the universe that we need to improve, but the language we use when talking about them. However, I would prefer not to be diverted from our discussion of the nature of knowledge.

SOCRATES: Please forgive me, Protagoras, for my digression. I agree that we should revert to our discussion of knowledge, on which subject you were saying that Democritus treats knowledge in general no differently from the axioms that mathematicians use when proving theorems. They act as though they are true without knowing for sure that they are true. I see now, Protagoras, what you mean when you say that man is the measure of all things. Your view of things is indeed bleak. Virtue does not exist. Our souls are imaginary. Truth is a chimera. There is no point in my trying to define them because there is nothing there to be defined.

PROTAGORAS: We sophists don't say that that it is pointless to proceed as though such absolutes exist. It is not for us to put limits on the endeavors of others. We only say that experience shows that one can live a fruitful and satisfying life without committing oneself to the kind of metaphysical foundations that you think essential.

SOCRATES: Perhaps you are right that one doesn't need to be a metaphysician to live an adequate life, but Athenians are unlikely to take kindly to your teaching our youth that foreign religions and customs are as good as our own.

PROTAGORAS: Your advice, Socrates, is good. I shall not teach my Athenian students to observe foreign customs. I shall teach my students how to take their place as useful and respected citizens according to the criteria currently regarded as virtuous in Athens. Nor shall I teach them how to make the lesser argument seem the greater in public debates. I shall teach them how to make the best case possible for or against whatever proposition is in question. It will be for others to decide which side of the question to support. It is true that I take money for these services, but I do not cheat my students any more than an honest butcher or baker. I do not pretend to knowledge-as-certainty of an absolute notion of virtue or anything else.

SOCRATES: I think to the contrary that a philosopher ought to operate on a more sublime level than a butcher or a baker—that the unexamined life is not worth living.

PROTAGORAS: And who better than Socrates to understand the value of the examined life! I cannot but applaud your energy and your conduct of an argument. I admire you above all men whom I know, and far above all men of your age; and I believe that you will become very eminent in philosophy. Let us come back to the topics of our discussion at some future time; at present we had better turn to something else.

SOCRATES: By all means, if that is your wish; for I too ought long since to have kept an earlier engagement, and only tarried because I could not refuse the request of the noble Callias to prolong our dialogue.

Chapter 2

Diogenes versus Plato

Context

Plato (429–347 BC?) was a scion of the aristocratic elite of ancient Athens. He founded the Academy to maintain the philosophical tradition of Socrates (470–399 BC?) of whom he was a fervent admirer. All of his written work is believed to survive, nearly all of which is in dialogue style with Socrates as the leading speaker. As in the *Protagoras*, the early dialogues are thought to be fictionalized accounts of genuine encounters between the real Socrates and a wide spectrum of debating partners, ranging from *Parmenides*, who instructs him on the nature of being and not-being, to *Euthyphro*, who is no competition at all. However, the later dialogues feature an invented Socrates, who arguably becomes merely a mouthpiece for Plato's own opinions.

Diogenes (404?–323 BC) is the philosopher who famously lived in a barrel, and made fun not only of Plato's pretensions at having penetrated the mysteries of the universe, but of the conventions of normal life in the Athens of his time. He apparently made a show of his contempt for the system of rewards and punishments with which societies sustain such conventions, by openly defying them. He is said, for example, to have publicly masturbated in the Agora.

However, the stories that have come down to us of his living a totally minimal life sustained by begging, cannot be the whole truth. He seems to have been a popular character in Athens, and acceptable at the Academy in a manner that would have been impossible for a common beggar. The fact that such behavior was tolerated or even admired suggests that his philosophical talents were thought to outweigh his personal idiosyncracies. Plato is said to have described him as a "mad Socrates". In any case, he went down in history as the prophet of the cynicism movement in philosophy—so-called as a result of his describing himself as Diogenes the Dog.

Diogenes was born in Sinope on the Black Sea, where his father was in charge of the mint. They were both expelled from the city for debasing the coinage. Some reports attribute the crime to Diogenes himself. Diogenes then settled in Athens, living at least some of the time in a ceramic wine tub that tradition calls a barrel. However, he seems to have nevertheless been able to travel like other Greek intellectuals of the time. In fact, a trip to the island of Aegina proved to be potentially disastrous, since he was enslaved by Cretan pirates, who sold him to a wealthy burgher of Corinth. (Being sold into slavery was a standard hazard of the time—even Plato apparently had to be rescued after being sold as a slave when an adventure in which he sought to make the tyrant of Syracuse into a philosopher-king went wrong.) He was employed as a tutor for the sons of the family, at which task he was a big success. He must have been gifted with much charm, since he is said to have become beloved not only of the family but of the whole city of Corinth, where he died at the age of perhaps eighty.

The story of his encounter with Alexander the Great says everything about him that makes him admirable. When Alexander was reestablishing Macedonian hegemony over Greece after the assassination of his father, he looked up the elderly Diogenes, who was sunning himself in a Corinthian gymnasium. Alexander asked Diogenes what he could do for him. Diogenes supposedly replied that Alexander could stand out of the sun!

The imaginary dialogue that follows is more plausible than many that follow in this book. Diogenes and Plato would certainly have exchanged views, and Diogenes was famous for his skepticism. I doubt, however, that Diogenes would have anticipated the version of the Turing halting problem with which he challenges Plato's claim to have superior self-knowledge. He certainly would never have guessed that Plato's Academy would one day become a champion of the skeptic branch of philosophy.

Dialogue

Chrysippus had just finished delivering a long and very dull lecture at the Academy. It had been livened up towards the end when Diogenes cried out, "Cheer up, guys, there's land in sight!" as he saw the blank end of the speaker's scroll coming up. But neither Plato nor Chrysippus were amused. Fortunately, Chrysippus was briskly carried off for dinner by Theaetetus and Archytas, and so Plato was spared the task of smoothing the incident over.

We join Plato as he begins to retreat to his private apartments for a well-earned rest. But he is intercepted by Diogenes, who wants to take up the question of the immortality of the soul. What is the soul? How do we know it is immortal? Suppressing a sigh, Plato gives Diogenes his attention.

Even at a better time, Plato would have preferred to avoid an argument with Diogenes—whose debating skills are said to have rivalled those of Socrates himself. But Aristotle and other students of the Academy have gathered round, and Plato sees that his dignity as head of the Academy requires that he defend his position, although he may have to tolerate impertinences from Diogenes that he would not have been expected to tolerate from anyone else. Diogenes obliges by blowing his nose with his fingers to show that he is unimpressed with his fancy surroundings, and gets straight to the point.

Diogenes versus Plato

DIOGENES: Orpheus entered Hades to rescue his beloved Eurydice from the miserable fate that awaits the dead in the myths with which we Greeks torment ourselves. But need we really fear such an awful fate? Why do we not accept that death is the end? What reason do we have to believe that we have immortal souls fated to wander forever in a dreary underworld after we are dead? What is a soul anyway?

PLATO: I recall a similar discussion between us, Diogenes, in which you remarked that you had seen my cups and tables, but not my cupness or tableness. I responded that you must look not only with your eyes, but with your intellect as well. The same is true in the case of the soul, except that only the intellect is then available. Your soul is what perceives my cups and tables. Without a soul, you would not be able to perceive anything at all.

DIOGENES: Your definition does not distinguish between the soul and the mind. I certainly believe that I have a mind that thinks my thoughts, but when I use my intellect to think about myself, I am unable to find a soul. I have thoughts; I think about my thoughts; I think about thinking about my thoughts, but when I turn to the "I" that is supposedly doing the thinking, it recedes into the distance. You perhaps identify the soul with this mysterious "I"? In doing so, I think you confuse a name you call yourself in an internal model of how your mind works with how your mind really works.

PLATO: The fact that you fail to encompass your true nature when you attempt to examine your inner self does not imply that others may not succeed.

DIOGENES: How can a thinker fully understand himself? If he could, he would be able to predict his future thoughts—to predict his own predictions. But the resulting theoretically infinite regress is what I experience in trying to make sense of the "I".

PLATO: Your argument is subtle—worthy of Socrates himself. Knowledge-as-certainty of our inner selves is perhaps beyond our reach. But there remains a large gap between what I see as your obstinate refusal to concede the obvious, and the enlightenment possible for those who follow Socrates in accepting that the unexamined life is not worth living.

DIOGENES: We both follow Socrates in accepting that the unexamined life is not worth living. We differ on whether examining one's own self with sufficiently close attention necessarily leads to identifying a soul that somehow transcends the mind that thinks one's thoughts. But perhaps we can agree to disagree, and move on to the question of how we know that some part of our inner selves is immortal. Is this belief not merely wishful thinking by those who foolishly fear death?

PLATO: Why do you say that it is foolish to fear death?

DIOGENES: If no part of our selves survives death, Plato, then we will not be there to experience being dead. What is there then to fear about being dead? We do not experience being dead when alive, and cannot experience it when dead because we will no longer be there to experience it.

PLATO: Another argument worthy of Socrates! But it depends on the presupposition that the soul dies with the body. In my *Meno,* Socrates offers a proof to the contrary.

DIOGENES: I follow Socrates in denying that I know anything for certain. The Socrates of your *Meno* is more sure of himself. As I recall, he asks a slave boy a series of questions to which the boy's correct answers provide a proof of a simple version of the famous theorem of Pythagoras. But the boy had no opportunity to learn geometry. So his soul must already have known geometry when it came into the world. Therefore souls are immortal!

PLATO: A beautiful argument, is it not?

DIOGENES: I find it quite unconvincing. The story of the slave boy is certainly very plausible, but the notion that he could not have learned enough geometry in his daily life to answer Socrates' questions accurately is not. After all, Egyptian surveyors who know nothing of Pythagoras have learned to make right angles using rope triangles whose sides are 3, 4, and 5 units long. In fact the story illustrates our basic difference. You believe the world is a mere shadow of an ideal world of perfect forms. I believe that your ideal forms are no more than simplifications of what we see in the real world. In particular, the geometry of mathematicians is simply an invented idealization of the geometry of the world around us.

PLATO: I see no prospect of breaching your skepticism. You are determined to regard our existence as mean and empty. Let us abandon this discussion for an occasion when we are both less tired.

Diogenes accepts his dismissal gracefully, feeling that he has established that Plato's belief in the immortality of the soul is a case of what Protagoras might call knowledge-as-commitment, and religious folk call faith. Even if such a belief were shown to entail a contradiction, it would not be abandoned. He can see, however, that Plato's students for the most part think the debate evenly balanced. Only Aristotle appears uncomfortable with its outcome.

Chapter 3

Aristotle versus Plato

Context

Plato and Aristotle are the two great figures of western philosophy. Raphael's famous painting—used as a cover for this book—shows them surrounded by the intellectual elite who followed in their footsteps down the ages. It is therefore close to hubris to imagine a dialogue between them, especially since it covers only one small aspect of their contributions to philosophy.

Raphael's picture indicates the issue they discuss by showing Plato gesturing at the heavens above, while Aristotle focuses on the earth below. The Aristotle of my dialogue fits this paradigm, but the real Aristotle resists all attempts at classification. He was a polymath, whose work ranges across the whole range of philosophical enterprise. The practical, scientific line of questioning attributed to him in the dialogue is only one aspect of a life of intellectual endeavor that escapes any attempt to tie it down. It is breathtaking to learn that it is only by a fortunate chance that his many surviving books came down to us intact.

Aristotle (384–322 BC) joined the Academy at the age of seventeen, and remained a student in Athens for twenty years. It is significant that Aristotle came from Stagira, which was a Greek town close to ancient Macedon. Aristotle's father was court physician to the grandfather of Alexander the Great, and Aristotle himself became tutor to the teenage Alexander after leaving the Academy around the time of Plato's death. Aristotle later returned to Athens, and used Macedonian money to found a parallel institute to the Academy at the Lyceum, which was an established public space at about the same walking distance to the north-east of the walled city of Athens as the Academy was located to the north-west. But he become unpopular in Athens when it sought to reestablish its independence after Alexander's death, and spent his final year or so in quiet retirement elsewhere.

Our imaginary dialogue concerns Plato's theory of forms, which are ideal concepts that Plato thought embody the true reality, of which the world of our senses is a mere shadow. At the time of their imaginary dialogue, Aristotle probably already thought that the reverse is the case—that the world we perceive imperfectly though our senses is what is real, and that Plato's ideal forms are merely attempts to model our perceptions in a simple enough form that we can manipulate our environment to some degree. However, although Aristotle came to differ from Plato on a number of other points too, he was always very respectful of his mentor, a feature of their relationship that I have tried to retain in their dialogue, in which I have foreshortened history by eliminating the two years or so that Aristotle spent abroad after Plato's death before he received his invitation to tutor Alexander. Here and in the remaining imaginary dialogues, I am more interested in the philosophical issues discussed than in strict historical accuracy.

It is a pity that we don't know more about the day-to-day events at either the Lyceum or the Academy. There was probably no formal organization at all. However, Aristotle's followers called themselves Peripatetics, which derives from Aristotle's preference for walking up and down while discussing philosophy—a habit which I assume without any authority that he inherited from Plato.

Dialogue

When Aristotle had matured into a philosopher in his own right, and his mentor Plato was sinking into old age, he realized that the time would soon come for him to strike out on his own. An invitation to act as tutor to the teenage heir to the throne of Macedonia—the future Alexander the Great—provided a pretext to find an opportunity to be alone with Plato to discuss his future. They met in an olive grove called the Akademia that gave its name to the adjacent Academy that Plato had made the center for intellectual life in ancient Athens. We join them as they walk together amid the olive trees in the cool of an evening in late summer.

ARISTOTLE: It is twenty years, Plato, since I came to Athens at the age of seventeen to study at the Academy. I wish to express my deep respect for your achievement in founding such an institution without which my philosophical talents, such as they are, would have withered on the vine. But the time has now come when I must make a decision about my future. My family in Stagira has a long-time association with the royal house of Macedon, as a consequence of which I have been invited to take the position of tutor to Alexander, the thirteen-year-old heir to the throne. Would it be wise for me to accept this invitation?

PLATO: I thank you for your graceful tribute. Not all my students have been so respectful. You will perhaps recall the antics of the young Eudoxus. His mathematical talent was not enough to outweigh his lack of good breeding. But you, Aristotle, have been a worthy student in the best traditions of Socrates.

ARISTOTLE: And what of my invitation to Macedon?

PLATO: I believe we have a duty to put our philosophical discoveries at the disposal of our fellow men, for which reason I wrote both my *Republic* and my *Laws*. I am therefore positive about your opportunity to expound the views of the Academy at the current center of political power in the Hellenic world. But I must remind you of the personal disasters that followed my own attempt to make a philosopher-king

Aristotle versus Plato 13

of Dion when he became Tyrant of Syracuse. Do you feel you have the courage to take on a similar task at a court more barbarous even than that of Syracuse?

ARISTOTLE: I do not doubt my courage. It is my ability to pass on the traditions of Socrates adequately that I doubt. So I am hoping, Plato, that you will be patient with me if I question you in the Socratic style about some features of your theory of forms that I do not properly understand how to defend against a skeptic.

PLATO: Nothing will persuade obstinate skeptics like Diogenes of Sinope, who had the impertinence to say that he had seen my cups and tables, but neither my cupness nor my tableness. How can it make sense to deny the existence of something you cannot envisage in your mind's eye? However, I will be pleased to answer questions that more reasonable doubters may raise.

ARISTOTLE: In your *Republic,* you have Socrates tell the fable of the cave, to illustrate that all we see are shadows cast upon a wall by whatever reality may be. Empiricists respond that if nothing is left unmodeled by the fable, then we can say no more of reality than that it must be capable of casting the shadows that we see. In particular, how do we know that your theory of ideal forms truly represents ultimate reality—that the objects of the physical world are mere shadows of ideal counterparts that occupy a metaphysical universe available only to the intellect beyond what we perceive as space and time—that cups are not really real; that what is really real is the concept of cupness?

PLATO: How do philosophers like Democritus of Abdera—who fancy themselves empiricists that pay attention only to the evidence of their senses—come to be so certain that the real world consists of nothing but atoms and the void? They need their intellects if only to distinguish between the evidence of their senses and other thoughts they find themselves thinking.

ARISTOTLE: I see that naive empiricists have foundational problems too. But it is the foundations of our own philosophy that I am anxious to defend from critics. Where do metaphysical models of reality come from? Are there shadows cast in the cave of human experience that are commonly overlooked, but which provide a potential hot-line to the absolute truths of the universe?

PLATO: The shadows on the wall are not the only feature of the fable of the cave that are significant. The intellects of the observers imprisoned in the cave are what really matter. They seek to make sense not only of the shadows they see on the wall, but also of what they they think about the shadows, and about their own thoughts. This is true, Aristotle, not only of followers of Socrates like you and I, but also of the most naive of empiricists. They may pretend not to be influenced by their own thoughts, but it is their thoughts that are genuinely real. We know nothing for certain but what we think—and we think in terms of the ideals of the theory of forms.

ARISTOTLE: Nobody is likely to deny, Plato, that we think in terms of ideals—that our models of the world are put together from concepts that you place in your intellectual world of ideal forms. But what do we say to a critic who argues that we just make these models up? That philosophers from different traditions might make up different models, and that there are no absolute criteria to distinguish between them?

PLATO: Are we to say similarly that there are different geometries? That it is a matter of opinion whether the angles of an ideal triangle sum to two right angles?

ARISTOTLE: I see how to defend geometry from relativists, but what of ethics? I recall that your lecture on the ideal form of the Good and its relation to the One created a certain consternation among the audience. How are we to respond to critics who argue that humans are unwise to look beyond the kind of mundane happiness to be found in living a useful life as part of a close community of friends and colleagues? That the Good and the One are mere inventions? What indeed are we to say to such as Aristippus of Cyrene who regards unconsidered indulgence in the pleasures of the flesh as the only good worthy of our attention?

PLATO: Diogenes called himself a dog. Aristippus might equally be called a pig. It is an insult to the memory of Socrates that a student of his should express such base opinions. To all such critics, I say again what Aristippus failed to learn from his teacher—the unexamined life is not worth living. We have minds, so let use them to improve the way we live. Let us look beyond the daily round of humdrum life to find transcendent meaning and purpose in human existence.

ARISTOTLE: Those who do not seek will certainly not find. Thank you, Plato, for this edifying conversation, and for your approval of my Macedonian venture. Thank you, for your hospitality and care during the twenty years of my tenure at the Academy. Your influence on philosophers will last as long as philosophy itself survives.

Chapter 4
Eudoxus versus Aristotle

Context

It seems odd to us that Aristotle did not succeed Plato as head of the Academy. Perhaps his differences from Plato on matters of philosophical doctrine made him unacceptable to Plato's more orthodox students, but the respect he retained for Plato extended to his establishing an altar to Plato's memory at the Lyceum. In the imaginary dialogue that follows between the mathematician Eudoxus and Aristotle, I have taken the liberty of allowing Eudoxus to be less respectful.

Tradition has it that the entrance to Plato's Academy featured a notice forbidding entry to any but geometers, and the academicians certainly included some notable Greek mathematicians. Theaetetus, for example, is credited with the discovery of the five regular polyhedra that are nowadays called the Platonic solids. It is a pity that Plato's *Theaetetus* has more to say about Protagoras's supposedly secret support for Heraclitus than Theaetetus himself. (Heraclitus taught that nothing is ever the same—Plato preferred Parmenides, who taught that nothing ever changes.)

Eudoxus of Cnidus in modern Turkey was twice a visitor at the Academy. He is regarded as the greatest of the Greek mathematicians—barring only Archimedes himself. Eudoxus learned his mathematics in southern Italy where he was doubtless exposed to the semi-religious outlook of the Pythagoreans, who held that everything is number. He then travelled to Athens at the age of 23, where he enrolled at the Academy, but his tenure as a student lasted only a few months. The imaginary dialogue that follows invents possible reasons why he might have fallen out with Plato. He then spent time in Egypt studying astronomy, before setting up his own school in Cyzicus on the Sea of Marmara. Although the school was successful, he abandoned it, and returned to Athens with some of his students. Perhaps he was expelled from Cyzicus, as Epicurus was later expelled from Mytilene.

It is doubtfully said that Eudoxus headed up the Academy while Plato was away in Syracuse. Eventually, he returned to his home city of Cnidus, where he became a leading citizen, as much respected for his civic virtues as his scientific achievements. His extensive travelling was by no means unusual for Greek intellectuals of the time.

Eudoxus was famous among the ancients for explaining how the observed orbits of the planets—notably the occasional retrograde path of Mars—can be reconciled with the Pythagorean notion that only uniform circular motion is perfect. His ingenious solution in terms of multiple interlocking spheres centered on the Earth was taken up by Aristotle in his *Metaphysics,* and reached its final form in Ptolemy's system of epicycles within epicycles. We credit Copernicus with correcting Ptolemy's geocentric system to a system centered on the sun, but it is plausible that Copernicus moved the center of the system to the sun only because Ptolemy's system failed to explain the orbits of the planets in terms of *uniform* circular motion. If so, he abandoned the geocentric assumption—not because he was committed to the heliocentric alternative—but because the geocentric assumption and uniform circular motion can only be reconciled by a system so enormously complicated that it defies analysis. Did Copernicus believe that the planets really orbit the sun, or did he think that his system merely simplified the necessary calculations, as the Church preferred to argue? It is a pity that the rules of my dialogue game do not allow Copernicus to be paired with the Greek Aristarchus, to whom the idea of a planetary system centered on the sun should actually be credited.

Modern mathematicians value Eudoxus most for his work on quantifying the notion of length, as later immortalized in Euclid's *Elements*. When providing firm foundations for the notion of a real number, the German mathematician Dedekind observed that all the hard work had already been done by Eudoxus. So why did the invention of real numbers have to wait two thousand years? In speculating on this question, my imaginary dialogue attributes the views of early German mathematicians like Dedekind and Weierstrass to Aristotle. Eudoxus responds by anticipating Kronecker's remark that "God created the integers; all else is the work of man."

Eudoxus will have met Aristotle when he visited Athens for the second time, but the imaginary dialogue that follows is set in the Lyceum at a later date when many of their respective achievements were already in place. It is a total invention that Eudoxus brought his son Aristagoras to be a student with Aristotle, and took the opportunity to seek Aristotle's influence with Alexander the Great in his treatment of Cnidus. The anachronisms involved will not bear close examination.

The Lyceum was located at a site that had been used at one time for meetings of the Athenian Assembly. It was notable for its gymnasium and a wrestling school. Plato mentions the Lyceum in his *Lysis*, in which Socrates meets his friends Hippothales and Ktesippos by the Ilissus river at its southern boundary. At the time of our imaginary dialogue, it is envisaged that the buildings of Aristotle's school were still under construction using money amounting to many millions of dollars donated by Alexander. Archeologists have unearthed what was probably a small covered walk or stoa that is the putative location of the conversation between Aristotle and Eudoxus that follows.

As in all the imaginary dialogues of this book, the characters mentioned are historical. Theophrastus succeeded Aristotle as the head of the Lyceum. He is remembered nowadays chiefly for his pioneering scientific work. Aristotle's son Nicomachus was immortalized by the *Nichomachean Ethics*. Theophrastus and Nicomachus reportedly became lovers. Eudoxus would have been unworried that Theophrastus might seduce Aristagoras, since the ancient Greeks took human bisexuality for granted. Eudoxus himself apparently made his first trip to Athens in the train of his lover Theomedon.

Dialogue

Aristotle is resting after giving his customary morning lecture at the Lyceum, when Theophrastus brings the news that Eudoxus had arrived with his son Aristagoras, who wants to enlist as a student. Aristotle asks Theophrastus to size Aristagoras up while introducing him to the other students, so that he can have the opportunity of catching up on old times with Eudoxus. After the standard greetings and expressions of good will, Aristotle and Eudoxus stroll together in the grounds of the Lyceum, as had been their habit at the Academy a good number of years ago.

ARISTOTLE: Theophrastus was very excited at the arrival of Eudoxus of Cnidus at the Lyceum. He gave me an unnecessary run-down of your mathematical achievements. I did not interrupt, because I learned long since that common courtesy requires allowing others to tell you what you know already. However, I hope that you will remain long enough at the Lyceum for us to be able to discuss some of the philosophical implications of your discoveries.

EUDOXUS: There is no time like the present! But first I must carry out the duty entrusted to me by my fellow citizens, and ask that you use your influence with Alexander to deal gently with my home city of Cnidus

ARISTOTLE: Alexander is an enlightened monarch. Some of my students travel with him, and send home scientific samples for my collection. He has donated the enormous sum of eight talents toward developing my center here at the Lyceum. You can see the work still in progress. You need not fear that he will not know of the greatest mathematician the world has yet seen. It is not necessary that I use what influence I have on behalf of your home city, but I shall comment on your concern in my next letter, although now that he holds the fate of the world in his hands, we cannot hope that he will have much time to spare for our small troubles.

EUDOXUS: I am deeply obliged by your kindness. Would it be possible to see something of the work on which Alexander's munificence is being expended?

ARISTOTLE: Let me first show you the memorial stone I have erected in honor of Plato. My students call it an altar.

EUDOXUS: I was never able to sustain the same deep respect for Plato as yourself. We did not get off to a good start when I first came to Athens at the age of 23. I had expected to find a mathematician following up the Pythagorean ideas to which I had been introduced in Tarentum, but Plato turned out to have no mathematical talent of his own. On his part, he could not conceal his contempt for somebody so poor that he could not afford a place to stay in Athens, and so trudged seven miles back and forward every day from the Piraeus. My welcome at the Academy was much warmer on my second visit as a result of my having solved the problem

Plato proposed of explaining the wandering of the planets without departing from the Pythagorean ideal of uniform circular motion.

ARISTOTLE: Your solution is one of the great achievements of our times. I have incorporated it into my *Metaphysics,* in which I envisage the planets as being embedded in a system of interlocking crystal spheres whose joint rotations explain their sometimes reversing their paths.

EUDOXUS: I have always wondered, Aristotle, what status you assign to your theory of the movement of the planets. My own possible explanation of the retrograde movement of Mars was intended merely as a mathematical exercise to demonstrate that it is not inconsistent with the assumption of uniform circular motion. You, on the other hand, seem to assert the reality of your crystal spheres.

ARISTOTLE: It is a delight, Eudoxus, that you should raise the thorny question of how we know things, so famously discussed by Protagoras and Socrates. Is man the measure of all things? I think perhaps I shall find you more in support of Protagoras than Socrates. Let us stroll in the shade of the portico that I have had erected with Alexander's money while you consider your answer.

EUDOXUS: I do not care for Plato's misrepresenting Protagoras in his dialogues, but I share Plato's view that we can have knowledge-as-certainty of at least some aspects of an absolute world accessible only to the intellect—the world of number in particular. How could it be that different people might invent different concepts of the integers 1, 2 and 3?

ARISTOTLE: Do you then share the Pythagorean view that everything is reducible to number?

EUDOXUS: Such leaps of the imagination are too much for a mathematician like myself. I am even reluctant to grant the same status to geometry as to the integers. I have made a point in my geometrical work of stating my assumptions as axioms. For example, my proof that the volume of a cone is one third of the volume of a cylinder with the same base and height is a matter of logic. Those who might have occasion to use this fact in the real world, might be said to be treating my axioms as knowledge-as-commitment—to be proceeding as though the axioms are true without being able to properly justify doing so.

ARISTOTLE: I would like, Eudoxus, to press you on your concept of number. One of your great achievements has been to bring clarity to the problem raised by the Pythagorean discovery that the hypotenuse of a right-angled triangle need not be commensurable with the other sides—so that no matter how many times we lay copies of the hypotenuse end-to-end and no matter how many times we lay copies of a side end-to-end, the results need not be equal. One might have thought of expressing this by saying that the sides of the triangle need not be exact fractions of the hypotenuse—so treating fractions as though they were numbers like integers.

EUDOXUS: The length of a side is then squeezed between all the fractions of the hypotenuse that are too big and those that are too small. Since I have shown that

Eudoxus versus Aristotle 19

there can only be one such length, you will now perhaps say that length itself should be regarded as a number.

ARISTOTLE: You anticipate my next question. Why not treat length as though it were a number?

EUDOXUS: My answer returns us to Protagoras. We can invent new kinds of entities and call them numbers, but they will be the work of man, and not absolutes like the integers. One may buy half a fish in the Agora if one has enough money, but the fraction one half is then a relative concept. My calculation of the volume of a cone as one third of the volume of a cylinder with the same base and height is similarly relative to the volume of the cylinder.

ARISTOTLE: Could one not, Eudoxus, regard one third in absolute terms as a fraction of the absolute integer one?

EUDOXUS: I think one would then just be playing with words to give a relative concept the appearance of being absolute. The sense that mathematicians have that they are discovering facts built into the underlying reality of the universe is more powerful than any intellectual conviction that Plato could advance for his general theory of forms The loss of certainty that would follow from your suggestion would be too heavy a price to pay for the convenience that would follow from abandoning my admittedly complicated theory of proportions for an invented notion of absolute fractions.

ARISTOTLE: I suspect that Protagoras would have argued that even the integers are the work of man—that knowledge-as-certainty is altogether beyond our reach—that all the knowledge claimed by mathematicians is really knowledge-as-commitment. He would doubtless also have said the same of the principles of deductive reasoning I describe in my *Logic*.

EUDOXUS: He would not have found many takers for such a revolutionary idea! However, I am more open to Protagoras's more general criticisms of Plato's theory of forms than I take you to be.

ARISTOTLE: Perhaps not. I should certainly have been more cautious when generalizing your theory of interlocking crystal spheres. The idea that only uniform circular motion is possible for the planets does indeed come under the heading of knowledge-as-commitment. I think perhaps that we are even closer on personal and social issues.

EUDOXUS: My experience as a citizen of Cnidus is certainly consistent with your own observations on what makes people happy. To run after some absolute notion of the Good as Plato recommends is to chase after a chimera. Whatever your notion of the good may be, it is enhanced if you take pleasure in pursuing it. A notion of the Good that treats our feelings of pleasure and pain as insignificant cannot therefore be adequate. On the other hand, those like Aristippus of Cyrene who argue that only the pleasures of the senses are worth pursuing have failed to learn the lesson that the unexamined life is not worth living. As Socrates argued, we should use our reason to plan our lives so that we can flourish as human beings.

It is important to love and to be loved; to have good friends; to be a useful part of a community in which people respect each other. I think that to be virtuous is to do what is necessary to this end. But perhaps I stray too far from you in the Protagorean direction in this regard.

ARISTOTLE: I am certainly nearer to Plato than you on the nature of virtue, and why societies like Cnidus can work so well, but we are very close on what it is reasonable to count as a good life. However, I see Theophrastus returning with your son. It is evident from his demeanor that he approves very much of Aristagoras, and I hope that Aristagoras feels the same about his introduction to the Lyceum. In a few years I plan to enroll my young son Nicomachus in the Lyceum, and I hope Theophastus will befriend him too. We would both have reason to be proud if our sons grew to emulate Theophrastus, to whom I plan to entrust the Lyceum when it is time for me to retire.

EUDOXUS: I cannot adequately express my gratitude, Aristotle, for your kind welcome and your willingness to take my son as a student. The pleasure in having the opportunity to converse with you is even greater. But it is true that I have not yet fully recovered from my journey, and you are right to guess that the time has come when an older man like myself needs to rest.

ARISTOTLE: Till tomorrow then, when I hope that you will instruct me and my students on your ingenious method of exhaustion in finding the areas and volumes of difficult shapes.

Chapter 5
Epicurus versus Zeno

Context

Epicurus (341–270 BC) first came to Athens from the island of Samos when he was 18 to serve the military apprenticeship necessary to retain his Athenian citizenship. Xenocrates was then the third head of the Academy; Aristotle was still alive but in retirement abroad. Epicurus was a follower of the down-to-earth philosophy of Democritus of Abdera, of whom we heard earlier as the mentor of Protagoras. As such, he was a life-long opponent of Plato, against whose ideas he rebelled at the tender age of 14.

Although his origins were humble, Epicurus eventually established a philosophical school in Mytilene on the island of Lesbos, but he and his followers were expelled as a result of the civic unrest to which their teachings apparently led. The school moved to Lampsacus, where he acquired Metrodorus as a friend and disciple, and then to Athens. In Athens, Epicurus bought a house with a walled garden—on the road from the Agora to the Academy—where he established a school called the Garden set up in explicit opposition to Platonism. Perhaps as a result of his unpleasant experiences in Mytilene, his followers in Athens played little or no role in Athenian social and political life.

Epicurus was a hedonist, a materialist, an empiricist, and a relativist. He was most famous in the ancient world for espousing the doctrine earlier attributed to Diogenes that our souls do not survive our deaths—so that we need not fear the miserable afterlife in which the Greeks believed. Nor do we need fear any gods there may be, as they take no interest in human affairs. Perhaps it was this feature of Epicureanism that made it the leading philosophy in the ancient world for some six hundred years—but it was not the epicureanism of modern dictionaries. The idea that he revelled in gluttony and lust was an invention of his philosophical enemies, enthusiastically adopted by the early Christian Church in their urge to find reasons to discredit their major opponent.

Zeno (334?–262 BC) of Citium—the founder of Stoicism—is sometimes confused with Zeno of Elea, whose Paradox of Achilles and the Tortoise was mentioned earlier. Our Zeno was of Phoenician origin, born of a wealthy merchant family in Citium on Cyprus. He is said to have been dark-skinned and gaunt in appearance. He famously came across Xenophon's memoir of Socrates in an Athenian bookshop. He asked the bookseller where such philosophers were to be found today, and the bookseller pointed out Crates the Cynic who happened to be passing by.

Someone less suited than the introverted Zeno to the extravagant rejection of conventional mores practiced by the followers of Diogenes would be difficult to find, but he persevered in his philosophical studies with a variety of other mentors in addition to Crates, and eventually founded a fourth school of philosophy in Athens alongside the Academy, the Lyceum, and the Garden. It met in a portico in the Agora called the Stoa. For this reason, Zeno's followers eventually became known as Stoics.

Only fragments survive of the actual writings either of Zeno or Epicurus. In the case of Epicurus, this is not very surprising since his many books were sought out, and systematically destroyed by the Church. Since the teachings of both Zeno and Epicurus advocated a similar ascetic life-style in which adepts learned to treat the vicissitudes of life as largely irrelevant to their equanimity, it seems odd that Stoicism should have escaped the same kind of persecution. Perhaps the fact that it became the standard philosophical position of the elite of the Roman Empire has something to do with this (although its best exposition is to be found in the works of Epictetus, who was a freed slave). In any case, there is a good reason why we nowadays refer to the virtues espoused by the Stoics as Roman.

Dialogue

Hearing of the fact that Zeno of Citium had recently established a school of philosophy that met in Athen's Agora, Epicurus unusually joined one of his freed slaves on a marketing expedition, accompanied by Metrodorus, his most faithful follower. There they found Zeno in the Stoa debating philosophical issues with a bunch of his students. After some awkwardness, Epicurus and Zeno fell into conversation, strolling up and down in the shade of the famous colonnade in the classic style of the time. We join them as their followers listen with bated breath, although it takes the two great minds some time to get around to serious issues.

EPICURUS: I do not often come to the Agora, but having learned of your habit of meeting with like-minded thinkers in the Stoa, I thought I might join your students to learn what philosophical line you are pursuing nowadays. When we last encountered each other, you were a somewhat introverted student uncomfortably following the precepts of the skeptic Crates.

ZENO: It is true, Epicurus, that I was less sure of myself in those days, and uncomfortable with the antics that Crates had inherited from Diogenes to demonstrate his freedom from the conventions that constrain ordinary folk. I am still of the opinion that those of us who follow Socrates in seeking to live an examined life should put aside the aspirations that motivate most of our fellow men, but there is no need to make a show of our beliefs. I think that we are so far in agreement. Where we differ is in my conviction that we should devote our lives to the pursuit of virtue. Your reported hedonism seems repugnant to me.

EPICURUS: I think, Zeno, that we are closer than you imagine. My hedonism is not at all the mindless pursuit of pleasure advocated by such as Aristippus of Cyrene.

METRODORUS: Alas that my brother Timocrates should shamefully have taken to misrepresenting Epicurus after his expulsion from our group! He hates Epicurus for supposedly alienating my affections from our family. I fear that others have taken up the same slanders to discredit Epicurus's philosophy. Gluttony and lust play no part in our little community at the Garden. In fact, Epicurus eats little beyond barley bread and some occasional cheese. As for sex, he teaches that it is better avoided, but probably does no harm.

ZENO: Is it not true that your community welcomes both women and slaves as full members? For what purpose are women included?

EPICURUS: Women are not included for immoral purposes. Metrodorus' wife Themista, for example, is the intellectual equal of us all. We exclude nobody on the grounds of social status or sex. We understand that ordinary folk will not approve of our lack of respect for their social mores, but we try not to provoke their enmity unnecessarily by staying clear of the social and political life of Athens.

ZENO: I hope, Epicurus, that you will forgive my having listened to common gossip. I see that your style of life is in fact close to the ascetic ideal that I have come to prize. We both teach that what matters is the attitude to life that one can achieve through rational reflection. A true philosopher is immune to the sufferings that trouble our fellow human beings once he has learned that we can only genuinely be injured by what we choose to perceive as an injury. It is not what happens to you, but how you react to it that matters. We must not seek the good in external things, but in ourselves.

EPICURUS: I sometimes say that the wealth required by nature is limited and easy to procure; but the wealth required by vain ideals extends to infinity. I am perhaps not so fierce in my defence of asceticism as you seem to be, but we certainly hold very similar views on how best to live one's life. Where I think we may differ is in the goals to which we believe philosophers should aspire. What, may I ask, is your conception of virtue?

ZENO: There is just one simple Good. Happiness is to be achieved by using one's Reason to conform to the Universal Logos that governs everything. Living a life according to Reason generates a consistency of soul, from which morally Good actions flow. A bad feeling is a disturbance of the mind repugnant to Reason, and against Nature. This is my conception of Virtue.

EPICURUS: I agree, Zeno, that we would do well to live according to the laws of nature that one might perhaps describe as the universal logos. I agree also that we should use our reason to this end as best we can. But what argument leads to the conclusion that there is only one Good that determines the character of Virtue? How do we know what actions Reason will count as Virtuous?

ZENO: I do not follow the Cynics in denying that actions which aid the natural instinct for self-preservation have value, but they do not contribute to happiness, which depends only on moral actions. Even passive mental states or emotions that are not guided by Reason are immoral, and produce immoral actions. The negative emotions are desire, fear, pleasure and sorrow. The positive emotions are will, caution and joy.

EPICURUS: I hope, Zeno, that you will not be offended when I say that your answer evades the question in a manner similar to religious folk when they are asked why they believe in Zeus rather than Mazda like the Persians, or Ra like the Egyptians. One receives in reply the answer to some other question. I agree that happiness is to be found by living in accordance with the laws of nature, but an empiricist like myself believes that we can know the laws of nature that apply to human happiness only through our senses. It seems to me that our senses tell us to seek pleasure and avoid pain.

ZENO: How can you know for certain how best to live if you rely only on your senses? We must use our Reason to perceive the Truth. Even an empiricist like yourself must surely see the folly into which the kind of sensuality you advocate so often leads the young.

EPICURUS: You play with words by choosing to interpret my reliance on the senses as sensuality. It is true that younger folk will often disagree, but the wisdom that comes with age leads me to favor a life of tranquility that emphasises the avoidance of pain. You are correct that empiricists cannot know with certainty that there may not be a better way to live, but empiricists believe that nothing can be known with the certainty that philosophers sometimes claim. However, I would very much like to hear how your conception of Reason leads to the conclusion that to experience pleasure is incompatible with Virtue.

ZENO: I do not think, Epicurus, that it can be explained to somebody who fails to see that we can perceive with the mind as well as with our bodily senses.

EPICURUS: The same answer that Plato would perhaps have given! Here we must agree to disagree. It is a pity that two philosophers who have so much in common in what we believe about the practicalities of living the examined life should differ so much about the reasons why.

ZENO: Our conversation has at least taught me not to believe the slanders that circulate about what goes on in your Garden. I still find it hard to credit that women or slaves might have anything to contribute to a serious philosophical discussion, but here again we must agree to disagree.

So the two parted on good terms but without any genuine meeting of minds. The future was to mirror their fault line. Some Stoics like Marcus Aurelius wrote of Epicureans with respect, but others like Seneca chose to repeat the slanders that Zeno accepts are false in our imaginary dialogue.

Chapter 6
Sextus Empiricus versus Marcus Aurelius

Context

Marcus Aurelius (121–180 AD) was the last of Edward Gibbon's five good emperors of Rome. He left behind a fascinating book called the *Meditations* in the form of notes to himself on how better to conform to the Stoic principles that he espoused. Although he is counted as a philosopher, he had nothing new to offer beyond the thoughts of the great Epictetus, for whom I cannot find a worthy partner. Cicero and Seneca are much quoted as earlier Roman Stoics, but I find Cicero too smug, and Seneca too dishonest for inclusion.

Marcus Aurelius is partnered with Sextus Empiricus, who represents a late flourishing of the Skeptic tradition. He advocated seeking relief from philosophical striving for certainty by suspending belief or disbelief after exploring all arguments for or against a proposition (although it seems to me that identifying the tranquility to be obtained in this way with the Epicurean notion of ataraxia is a bit of a stretch). His argument against those who think they have access to some absolute notion of truth goes like this. Someone who thinks they know the truth must have a criterion for judging what is true. But how do they know that their criterion is to be trusted? Applying the criterion to itself simply initiates an infinite regress. As Pierre Bayle, put it in the heat of the Enlightenment, "The grounds for doubting are themselves doubtful; we must therefore doubt whether we ought to doubt."

Much of the work of Sextus Empiricus survives, providing not just insight into his own ideas but into the ideas of philosophers of the late Hellenic period that he seeks to debunk. We do not know much of his personal circumstances. Both his dates and his choice of a place to live are very uncertain. However, I have taken advantage of the fact that respectable scholars have speculated that Sextus

Empiricus may be the same person as Sextus of Chaeronea in Boeotia, who acted as a kind of tutor to Marcus Aurelius in his maturity. A curious story tells how Marcus Aurelius explained to somebody he met in the street that he was on his way to visit Sextus of Chaeronea to improve his philosophy—to which the response was, "Oh Zeus, the king of the Romans in his old age takes up his tablets and goes to school." My own reaction is not so much surprise that Marcus Aurelius should be willing to humble himself by seeking instruction, but that he could be stopped in the street for a chat.

In a real dialogue, Marcus Aurelius would have been a very soft target for the skepticism of Sextus Empiricus, but I have taken the liberty of allowing him to answer back by challenging the idea that one can manage to get by in life without any beliefs at all. The view he expresses anticipates both the foundations of modern decision theory and the views of the pragmatist Charles Peirce. In classifying religious belief as a form of knowledge-as-commitment, Peirce observes that: "To be deliberately and thoroughly prepared to shape one's conduct into conformity with a proposition is neither more or less than the state of mind called Believing that proposition."

The son mentioned by Marcus Aurelius is Commodus, who turned out to be comparable to Nero or Caligula. He appears as the evil emperor in the movie *Gladiator*, but there is no historical reason to suppose that he murdered his father. In the imaginary dialogue that follows, Marcus Aurelius expresses concern about the possibility of civil unrest following a disorderly succession after his death. His fears were well founded. After the assassination of Commodus, the Praetorian Guard murdered his successor Pertinax after a few months, and then auctioned off the empire to one Didius Julianus, whose reign was equally short. Even when the strong man Septimius Severus seized power, he was obliged to campaign against several rival claimants.

Dialogue

Marcus Aurelius arrives at the residence of Sextus Empiricus in Rome accompanied by several bodyguards. They are served refreshments in an ante-room while Marcus and Sextus sit at their ease in the atrium after dismissing the house slaves, whose excitement at yet another visit from the Emperor is somewhat tiresome.

SEXTUS: Once more, the emperor of the Roman Empire visits my home, with a wax tablet in his hand on which to take notes like a schoolboy. The people of Rome are indeed fortunate that their prince aspires to play the role of a philosopher-king.

MARCUS: I find, Sextus, that to be an emperor who would rule as a philosopher is to be enslaved by a thousand responsibilities, and to be victimized by the importunities of a thousand ambitious courtiers. But Epictetus teaches us that where life is possible, then it is possible to live the right life—life is possible in a palace, so it is possible to live the right life in a palace.

SEXTUS: Your willingness to live according to the principles of Epictetus although Emperor of Rome must be a constant source of amazement to the flattering horde you have no choice but to tolerate.

MARCUS: It is for this reason that I find our meetings so valuable. Your skepticism—your insistence on seeing both sides of any question—are in stark contrast with my courtiers, who always have some personal axe to grind. Even within philosophy, I have learned through your influence to value not just the Stoic tradition in which I was raised, but also the thoughts of Epicurus and his followers. But today, I hope that instead of continuing our study of the poem of Lucretius in which he expounds the Epicurean doctrine, we can turn our attention to your own skeptical notion that there is no necessity to subscribe to one philosophical belief or another—that tranquility is to be found in suspending belief or disbelief so long as no argument guarantees certainty on either side.

SEXTUS: I see from your demeanour that tranquility escapes you today.

MARCUS: I will tell you the reason, since I know that I can count on your discretion. It will be announced tomorrow that my son of sixteen years is to become co-emperor with me. My intention is to facilitate a smooth transition to a new regime after my death, without the civil wars that have troubled Rome so often in the past. My lack of tranquility derives from the grave doubts I entertain about the character of my son.

SEXTUS: You have had to weigh in your mind the risk that your son may prove a tyrant against the prospect of civil war if a dynastic succession is not maintained?

MARCUS: The philosophical question my decision raises is that, in choosing to elevate my son, I am behaving *as though* I believe that this choice minimizes the risk to Rome. But though I am without certainty in my conscious mind that I have made the right choice, does not the fact that I have made this particular choice imply that I actually believe somehow that it is the better choice?

SEXTUS: You propose what might be said to be a theory of revealed belief—if consistent, your actions determine the beliefs that would be necessary to explain them as rational choices. Would you also apply this theory of revealed belief to the habituated behavior that I have argued is how skeptics like myself get by without committing themselves to any particular system of beliefs?

MARCUS: I have always been troubled by the thought that simply following the habits that one inherits from one's past life and the behavior of those around you is inconsistent with the Socratic principle that the unexamined life is not worth living. But I am more concerned with the fact that a ruler has to face problems for which there are often no obvious precedents. Suicide is an example that everybody faces. Does one continue to stay alive simply because that is what one has done in the past? When Nero ordered the philosopher Seneca to commit suicide, on what basis did Seneca decide to comply rather than to flee into exile?

SEXTUS: You might pose the same question of Socrates, who held the soul to be immortal. But for most people I think the reason they continue to live from day to day is indeed a matter of habit. The actual problem they face—even if they follow Epicurus in genuinely believing that there is no life after death—is whether it is better to continue to endure another miserable day or to go to all the trouble of summoning up the courage to do away with oneself.

MARCUS: Your cynicism, Sextus, is a constant delight! However, I want to press you further on the question of suicide. We can only commit suicide once. How can a philosopher make a rational decision in such circumstances without beliefs to guide him?

SEXTUS: I think Epicurus would say that one is choosing between two lives to be evaluated from the point of view of a rational individual looking back over them from the moment of death. Sometimes the shorter life will be preferred. Since you follow Epicurus in denying that we have immortal souls, you can make your decision on a similar basis. I will continue to behave like the generality of ordinary folk.

MARCUS: Should I assume that you reject what you call my theory of revealed belief?

SEXTUS: By no means! In its favor is the possibility that a properly worked out theory of revealed belief—and of revealed preference—might provide a useful tool in predicting the future behavior of human populations. Against is your own unease that your decision in elevating your son to be co-emperor might be mistaken—that the belief that you supposedly reveal in doing so is not what you would really believe if you were able to assess the facts available to you in a fully rational manner. Being a follower of the arch-skeptic Pyrrho, I see no reason to choose between these two conflicting attitudes.

MARCUS: It is such a pleasure to meet with someone who is willing to disagree with me—who offers no flattery—who seeks no reward. I shall return to my duties as emperor with a more positive attitude. My decision to elevate my son may be a mistake—as many of my decisions have been in the past—but decisions must be made. They reveal what my beliefs must be, if only to myself.

SEXTUS: For my part, I am delighted if I have been instrumental in your learning to be skeptical even about the skepticism of skeptics like myself!

Chapter 7
Augustine versus Hypatia

Context

This imaginary dialogue is perhaps the least likely of several unlikely meetings yet to come. St Augustine (354–430 AD) was Bishop of Hippo in North Africa, when it was still part of the Western Roman Empire, although he died while it was under siege by the Vandals, to whom it eventually fell. Rome itself had already been sacked by the Visigoths, which led to Augustine writing his famous *City of God*—with its foul doctrine of original sin—to explain that Rome may fall, but the domain of God is not of this world.

Hypatia (355–415 AD) was the philosophically minded daughter and successor to Theon, head of the Mouseion in Alexandria (which was not the original Mouseion that housed the famous Great Library, but a feeble imitation of no great distinction). Egypt was part of the Eastern Roman Empire, but in former times it would not have been implausible that Augustine should have taken ship from Hippo to Alexandria so as to intervene in the historical power struggle between the Roman Prefect and the followers of Bishop Cyril—later St Cyril—but we will need to suspend disbelief on this count.

Hypatia is celebrated as the first woman to be recognized as a philosopher (although she and her father might be better described as mathematicians). Augustine's condescension in the dialogue is typical of the prejudice she would have faced. However, she was apparently much respected in Alexandria—a city famous for civil unrest—for her peace-making abilities. But her attempt to make peace between Bishop Cyril and the Roman Prefect eventually led to her violent death at the hands of Cyril's fanatical followers; she was torn limb from limb and her remains abandoned in a midden. A movie has been made about her life, somewhat hampered by the fact that she was a very determined virgin. However, she remains a hero of the women's movement to this day.

Although Hypatia was a pagan and Augustine was one of the founding fathers of the Christian Church, they both regarded themselves as neoplatonists—a decadent version of platonism put together by the philosopher Plotinus that emphasized

Plato's attachment to the notion of the Good and the One, but discarded the sharpness of thought that Plato inherited from Socrates. However, they do not discuss what they have in common, but whether it is moral to lie to the common people for their own good—a doctrine endorsed by Plato and, for example, by John Stuart Mill in modern times.

Their debate is prompted by Augustine inquiring whether any works of the heretic Epicurus survive in the famous Great Library of Alexandria so that they could be burned. She informs him that the Library is sadly long gone (although stories of its destruction at the time of her own death, or by later Islamic conquerors remain popular to this day). Actually, the Great Library was apparently lost as much through neglect as violence, although some scrolls must surely have been destroyed in multiple burnings of the neighborhood in various civil wars, notably those between Julius Caesar and Pompey, and later between the Emperor Aurelian and Queen Zenobia of Palmyra. Whatever the truth may be, the loss of the Great Library of Alexandria is one of the low points of human intellectual history.

Dialogue

Augustine has come from Hippo to Alexandria to intervene in a power struggle between Orestes, the Roman prefect, and Cyril, the recently appointed bishop of Alexandria. To his considerable surprise, he finds Orestes in the company of a woman, who turns out to be Hypatia. She is the head of what survives of the famous Mouseion of Alexandria.

Orestes explains that Hypatia is much respected in Alexandria because of her facility in finding compromises between the many rival factions that regularly threaten the city's precarious tranquility, but Augustine refuses to discuss the dispute with Cyril in the presence of a woman. However, he asks Orestes to introduce him to Hypatia after their meeting, so that he can satisfy his curiosity about the nature of a woman with philosophical pretensions.

So Hypatia waits patiently on a terrace until after the meeting between Orestes and Augustine, which unsurprisingly proves to be fruitless.

ORESTES: My dear Hypatia, Bishop Augustine of Hippo and I have concluded our meeting. He would now like to discuss the Mouseion and its famous library with you. If you are willing, I will leave you together. The slaves will serve some refreshments.

HYPATIA: It is a great privilege for me to meet the famous Bishop of Hippo. Perhaps we could sit here together in the shade of the trees of the Prefect's roof garden, with a view of the famous harbor that has been the scene of so many significant events down the ages.

AUGUSTINE: I am astonished to find a woman acting as head of the Mouseion. Orestes tells me that you inherited the position from your father.

HYPATIA: There was no great competition for the post after my father's death. The current Mouseion is a pale shadow of its famous predecessor. The Great Library established by Ptolemy Soter is no more—lost through fire and neglect. I would be ashamed to show you the collection of scrolls that remain.

AUGUSTINE: It is your remaining collection of scrolls about which I wish to inquire. The Church insists that all heretical works be burned.

HYPATIA: The followers of Bishop Cyril have already been active in this regard. Even the few remaining fragments of Epicurus were burned in spite of my protests that he could not be a heretic as he died hundreds of years before the birth of Christ.

AUGUSTINE: We are particularly concerned that all remaining embers of the philosophy of Epicurus be eliminated, once and for all. He denied the immortality of the soul. He doubtless burns in hell for turning his followers away from salvation. The Church must expose him as a pig who revelled in gluttony and lust.

HYPATIA: The idea that he was a pig is an invention of his enemies, taken up by disreputable Stoics like Seneca seeking to discredit what they saw as a rival philosophy. Epicurus had no interest in sex, and lived mostly on barley bread and some occasional cheese.

AUGUSTINE: Orestes told me that you cling obstinately to the pagan beliefs of your ancestors, but not that you are an Epicurean.

HYPATIA: I do not worship pagan gods. Nor am I an Epicurean. I follow the philosopher Plotinus in his reassessment of the ideas of Plato. In particular, I hold to his notion of the One that embodies the Good. Thus far, I thought myself in line with modern thinking in the Church. However, I am troubled by Plato's endorsement of the idea that it can be legitimate to lie to the common people for their own good. When God sits in judgement, will He not judge us on the basis of the sins we would have committed if we had been told the truth?

AUGUSTINE: We have the Word of God in Matthew's Gospel: By their fruits you shall know them. God will judge us on our behavior in the world that He created, and not in some possible world that He chose not to create. Otherwise it would be our duty to put temptation in the way of the righteous lest it be argued that they would have sinned had they been tempted. But the Church takes the opposite view—that it is sinful to tempt the righteous lest their fruit whither on the vine. In particular, whatever the historical truth may be, it is our duty to discredit Epicurus so that his surviving heretical works are thought unworthy of serious attention.

HYPATIA: This talk of possible worlds leads me to mention the Problem of Evil that is commonly attributed to Epicurus, although it must surely have been invented by a much later follower.

AUGUSTINE: You mean the heretical argument that asks why God allows evil in this world. Is He not able to prevent evil? Does He not want to prevent evil? But if He is neither omnipotent nor benevolent, why call Him God? You perhaps mean to comment on the fact that this world is the best of all possible worlds in which Man is gifted with free will?

HYPATIA: I meant rather to propose a *reductio ad adsurdum* that could be offered in response to the heretical argument. It implies that in considering all the possible worlds that He might have created, God actually created a world without evil. But this world contains evil. Therefore he did not create it! But who is going to believe that the world in which we live does not exist?

At this point, Hypatia realizes that her delight in having an intellectual equal with whom to discuss philosophical issues has got the better of her discretion. She seeks to distract Augustine by refreshing his glass of wine, but he is not to be distracted.

AUGUSTINE: I think, on the contrary, that heretics would be only too ready to accept that we exist only as possibilities in a world that exists only in the mind of God—a world that He rejected when choosing which possible world to create. They would say that our sense of our own reality arises only because God would not otherwise have envisaged this evil possible world perfectly.

HYPATIA: Alas that I should have let my thoughts run away with me into such dangerous ground.

AUGUSTINE: When we were introduced, I thought it impossible that a woman might be an adequate philosopher, but your proposal of an entirely original heresy shows that I was mistaken. But I see no need to pursue the issue, for who would listen to a mere woman expounding such an esoteric argument? But Bishop Cyril would certainly not be so tolerant. For your own safety, I urge you to keep such thoughts to yourself.

HYPATIA: I am grateful for your tolerance and will take your advice to heart.

So they parted on reasonably good terms, but it is doubtful whether Hypatia heeded his advice. Augustine had actually departed on his return trip to Hippo when Hypatia was torn to pieces by a band of fanatics led by an acolyte of Cyril for seeking to make peace between him and Orestes. Her philosophical opinions and her sex were doubtless additional incentives for the hatred of a religious mob who cared nothing for the fact that Jesus taught that peacemakers are to be counted among the children of God.

Chapter 8
Anselm versus Abelard

Context

Peter Abelard (1079–1142) is remembered nowadays largely because of his scandalous love affair with his pupil Héloise. (She was not only lovely to look at, but later revealed an intellect arguably a match for his own.) However, her uncle and guardian was outraged at Abelard's betrayal of his trust. He took his revenge by sending a bunch of roughnecks to break into Abelard's lodgings, and castrate him. Abelard survived, but was later brought low by accusations of heresy from the many enemies he had made in a meteoric career, in which he came from nowhere to be regarded as the foremost logician of his times. He was apparently one of those aggressive folk who cannot control their urge to show how much cleverer they are than everybody else.

Abelard belongs in this book as a representative of nomos in the physis versus nomos debate. He was famously a nominalist who dismissed Plato's ideal forms as simply the names of collectives. For example, beauty is not an ideal of which beautiful things in the world are mere shadows, but merely a name that we use to identify what beautiful things have in common.

Anselm—later St Anselm—is a representative of physis. He is famous for the ontological argument for the existence of God, which still engages the attention of modern philosophers (who have lost interest in the various versions of the cosmological argument offered by St Thomas Aquinas). The ontological argument purports to deduce the existence of God simply from the meaning of certain words, without any input from facts about the world.

Anselm (1033–1109) was born an aristocrat in northern Italy, but gave up the advantages of his birth to become a monk. Eventually he rose to be Abbot of the monastery of Bec in Normandy, which perhaps explains why William Rufus—King of England in succession to his Norman father William the Conqueror—made him Archbishop of Canterbury. However, Anselm would not accept royal control of the English church, and so was exiled. After William Rufus was killed in a suspicious hunting accident, Anselm was recalled by King Henry I but exiled again for the same reason. Eventually, some compromise was reached, and he died as reigning Archbishop in Canterbury. Such a history suggests that he would have been no walkover in a debate with the aggressive Peter Abelard, even when Anselm was old and Abelard was a brilliant new star in the theological firmament.

The imaginary dialogue that follows is set in the Benedictine Abbey of Bec, where the ageing Anselm is assumed to be spending some of his time during his second exile. Abelard was French, and a visit from him to the founder of medieval scholasticism before the scandal with Héloise would not have been so extraordinary.

Abelard and Anselm discuss Anselm's ontological argument. In doing so, they anticipate a version of the ontological argument seriously defended by the modern philosophers Malcolm, Hartshorne and Plantinga—as Abelard actually did anticipate Pascal in formulating what we nowadays call Pascal's Wager. (An excellent account of the ongoing debate on the ontological argument appears in the on-line *Stanford Encyclopedia of Philosophy*.)

Dialogue

It is mid-morning on a fresh spring day in 1105 AD. Abelard and Anselm have attended Terce and joined their prayers with the monks of the Abbey of Bec. They now meet by arrangement, and walk together in the cloisters in the classical philosophical style. Except for the absence of an audience, their meeting has something of the character of Plato's *Protagoras,* since Anselm is old and famous while Abelard is young and anxious to show his mettle. After the introductions are over, Anselm seeks to put his young visitor at his ease by commenting on the beauty of the plain chant they listened to at Terce.

ANSELM: The Gregorian chant at Terce is an innovation since my time as Abbot of Bec.

ABELARD: Scholars are doubtful that plain chant originates with the first Pope Gregory.

ANSELM: It is in the nature of scholars to be skeptical, but we must not allow their doubts to cloud our appreciation of beautiful music written to glorify the one true God.

ABELARD: Do you feel the same of the skeptical comments that Gaunilo of Marmoutier makes about the ontological argument for the existence of God in your *Proslogion?*

ANSELM: We already agreed in our correspondence that we would discuss this question. But first I would like to be reassured that there is no misunderstanding of what the argument is.

ABELARD: I have studied your argument so hard that I know it by heart. To simplify its expression, let us define a deity to be something greater than which cannot be thought. Even a fool is compelled to grant that such a deity exists in thought, because he understands what he hears, and whatever is understood exists in thought. And certainly a deity cannot exist only in thought, for if it exists only in thought it could also be thought of as existing in reality as well, which is greater. Therefore something than which greater cannot be thought undoubtedly exists both in thought and in reality.

ANSELM: Gaunilo responds by applying the same argument to islands: You cannot doubt that an island more excellent than all other islands really exists somewhere, since you do not doubt that it is in your mind; and since it is more excellent to exist not only in the mind but in reality as well, this island must necessarily exist.

ABELARD: How do you respond to this criticism?

ANSELM: I believe Gaunilo has identified a flaw in my argument. But I hope you do not think that I am therefore led to question my faith in the existence of God. We have knowledge-as-certainty of this Truth, both through the scriptures, and through God's revealing Himself to us in prayer. Proofs for what you and I already accept through faith are not necessary for us, but God has not gifted us with reason without a purpose. We are like students who, unable to solve a mathematical problem, are given the answer to it, and then discover they can reason out why that answer is correct.

ABELARD: My faith in the existence of God is as solid as yours.

ANSELM: I do not doubt your sincerity in declaring your faith, nor that of Gaunilo. I believe my proof can survive his criticism by restricting it to necessary beings: beings that—if they exist at all—exist in all possible worlds.

ABELARD: I dare say that Gaunilo would respond that such a restriction begs the question. However, it is certainly true that a being no greater than which can be conceived, must exist in all possible worlds because otherwise a being that existed in all possible worlds would be greater. We therefore only need to assume that there is a possible world in which God—as you define Him—can be conceived, to deduce that He exists in the actual world.

ANSELM: Your reputation for logic is well-deserved! It is indeed said that I beg the question in restricting the ontological argument to necessary beings, but I had not thought through the response that you propose.

Abelard is delighted to have succeeded in his immediate aim of impressing Anselm with his cleverness. Anselm feels the need to think over the gloss on the ontological argument that Abelard has proposed. So they agree to part for the moment, and to meet again briefly the same afternoon after Sext, since Abelard will have to start out for Paris very early next morning. When they meet for the second time, Anselm reassures Abelard that he still thinks Abelard's gloss is valid, and so Abelard seizes the opportunity to propose his version of Pascal's Wager.

ABELARD: We share knowledge-as-certainty of the existence of God. But is knowledge-as-commitment adequate, as the Jews maintain? Is it enough that we live as a Christian should live, or does God require that we honor his rules because we sincerely believe in Him?

ANSELM: I suspect that you have an argument for the latter proposition.

ABELARD: Rather as you described your ontological argument this morning as demonstrating a proposition known to us already through revelation, so I regard the argument that I wish to submit for your judgement as demonstrating a proposition that we know in advance—namely that intentions are key to assessing the morality of our actions. For example, one should not be judged adversely for a sinful action committed out of ignorance.

ANSELM: You doubtless have examples.

ABELARD: To take an extreme case, the crucifiers of Christ were ignorant of His divine nature, and so should not be judged as supremely evil. On the contrary, they would have sinned had they thought crucifying Christ was morally imperative, but failed to go through with it. It is the failure to abide by one's conscience that makes an agent blameworthy.

ANSELM: I agree that it is the failure to abide by one's conscience that makes an agent blameworthy, but I strongly advise against using the crucifixion as an example. It will persuade nobody, and you will be accused of heresy.

ABELARD: Your advice is much appreciated. But perhaps we can move on to my argument against those who think that it is enough to honor the precepts of a religion while privately retaining doubts about its truth. A gambler might take this position if he thought a religion unlikely to be true, but the consequences in the afterlife of behaving sinfully if this supposition turns out to be wrong are so large as to outweigh any pleasures to be derived in our life here on earth.

ANSELM: I believe the Jews do indeed take this attitude to observing the Mosaic Law. Like us, they hold only one religion with only one set of precepts to be worthy of their attention.

ABELARD: I agree that it is necessary to assume that only one religion need be considered. The argument would fail if a second religion were thought equally likely that counted as virtue what the first religion counted as vice.

ANSELM: How does your argument continue?

ABELARD: I argue that the gambler is mistaken in not appreciating that virtue is its own reward, and that the joys or sorrows that await us in the afterlife are not necessary to motivate us here on earth. But it is impossible to understand that virtue is its own reward without the faith in God necessary to give priority to the dictates of our conscience.

ANSELM: I believe the argument that you should gamble on the existence of God already appears in an immoral play called the *Bacchae* by Euripedes. I fear that it convinces only those who are already converted. But I thank you for bringing it to my attention. Now, if you will excuse me, I see that I am being summoned for a conference with the Abbot.

Abelard is not very pleased to be so summarily dismissed, but recognizes that he needs to improve his version of Pascal's Wager. However, he takes comfort in having impressed Anselm earlier in the day, and sets off cheerfully for Paris early next morning, unaware that he is fated to be a leading character in the romantic tragedy of Abelard and Héloise that will thrill Europe for centuries to come, and forgetting altogether Anselm's warning that he is liable to be held to account for heresies that he had no intention of committing.

Chapter 9
Thomas Aquinas versus Roger Bacon

Context

Both St Thomas Aquinas and Roger Bacon come with large reputations. Aquinas is thought to epitomize faith. In 1879, Pope Leo XIII declared Aquinas's theology to be the definitive statement of Catholic doctrine. Bacon is placed at the opposite extreme as the philosophical pioneer of experimental science.

Actually, they had a lot in common. Both surfed the intellectual wave that followed the discovery that original works of Aristotle had been preserved in the Muslim world, but with Aquinas focussing on Aristotle's metaphysics, and Bacon on his scientific contributions. Either way, they both got into trouble with the old guard for being innovators.

Aquinas championed natural theology, in which one supposedly suspends one's faith in God while exploring what pure reason has to say about His nature and existence. Bacon's scientific endeavors in optics and elsewhere never led him to doubt either his faith in God, nor the value of metaphysical theorizing. Both are over-valued as philosophers in my unorthodox opinion—Aquinas almost absurdly so, since his natural theology manifestly consists of inventing clever arguments that are acceptable only if they support the dogma of his faith—Bacon because he was by no means unique in speaking up for science during the long run-up to the Enlightenment. However, it is worth including them as opponents in our imaginary dialogues because they are seen as icons of faith on the one hand and science on the other. I hope it will not be disappointing that their imaginary dialogue is confined to a discussion of Aquinas's naive concept of a "just price".

Thomas Aquinas (1225–1274) was born into an aristocratic Italian family that disapproved so much of his intention to become a Dominican friar that two of his brothers were dispatched to kidnap him while he was on his way to join up. They apparently held him for a year, but he remained celibate in spite of their best efforts to the contrary. Eventually he escaped, and embarked on a meteoric career in the Church, featuring two periods as Regent Master of the Dominican Order at the University of Paris, where our imaginary dialogue is set in the year 1257. His books remain very influential within the Catholic Church, but his much admired *Summa Theologica* was never finished. It is said that he abandoned it because of an intense religious experience that led him dismiss all of his theological efforts as so much worthless straw. But perhaps the fact that he died not so long after was also relevant.

Roger Bacon (1219–1292?) is easily confused with the later Francis Bacon, who also promoted experimental science (but was much more modern in how an experiment should to be defined). His contemporaries took umbrage at his advocating the Aristotelian idea that facts should be gathered before scientific truths are proposed, for "thence cometh quiet to the mind". His career in and out of the Franciscan Order is somewhat chaotic, but it is unlikely that he was never in Paris at the same time as Aquinas. However, there were doctrinal differences between the Franciscan and Dominican Orders that would perhaps have prevented their actually discussing philosophical matters in a civilized way. Bacon eventually proved influential in reforming the medieval university curriculum. In particular, he succeeded in making optics—his own scientific subject—into part of the standard syllabus.

Bacon is curiously remembered by those who delight in the occult as Dr Mirabilis— the possessor of a brazen head animated by a demon. He did indeed dabble in both alchemy and astrology, but before he is judged too harshly, it should be remembered that Isaac Newton also took alchemy very seriously, and although astrology seems not to have interested him, he certainly gave a lot of time to numerological studies of the Bible.

It is not very fanciful to suppose that Aquinas and Bacon may have actually encountered each other in Paris in the late 1250s. Aquinas was certainly there and scholars think that Bacon was probably there too, but their difference in status would have been a major obstacle to any serious interchanges between them, even if their respective Orders had not been at loggerheads. Both were also relatively young, and so it is necessary to overlook the fact that it is probably anachronistic for them to be discussing the idea of a just price. Nor is it likely that Bacon would have anticipated arguments against the idea that might have been made by Adam Smith.

Dialogue

Much of the original work of Aristotle was preserved in the Arab world, and had recently filtered back into the west. It will eventually replace the neoplatonism of St Augustine as the philosophical framework of Christian theology. St Thomas Aquinas refers to Aristotle simply as "the philosopher". But in 1257, the Dominican and Franciscan Orders differ on the extent to which the commentaries of the Muslim philosopher Averroes on Aristotle should be retained in the new theology—a matter of personal importance to everybody at a time when accusations of heresy were rife, and even taking account of Aristotle at all was somewhat risky.

The imaginary dialogue that follows is set during a pause for refreshments in a meeting between representatives of the Franciscan and Dominican Orders convened to see if common ground could be found. Both Aquinas and Bacon are young, but their differences in status are large, as Aquinas is Regent Master of the Dominican Order in Paris, and Bacon is a clever nobody attached to the Franciscan delegation as an afterthought. However, Aquinas has recognized Bacon's talent, and approaches him with a view to getting some independent input about his idea of a just price, that he will develop in his later work. Bacon is flattered at getting such attention, but also anxious to show his intellectual mettle. The other delegates look on with interest at such an unexpected pairing.

AQUINAS: I do not think we have been introduced.

BACON: You are the renowned Thomas Aquinas. I am Roger Bacon—a Franciscan monk who has yet to receive any recognition for his efforts in logic. However, I believe we both share an enthusiasm for Aristotle, of which some delegates on both sides disapprove.

AQUINAS: It is true that those of us from both orders who delight in the recently available works of Aristotle would do well to make common cause, but the Franciscan enthusiasm for the infidel Averroes is an obstacle.

BACON: Is there not a case for some toleration in both our orders? It looks to me that we are currently in danger of provoking accusations of heresy from both sides. I once witnessed a recalcitrant heretic tortured to death, and I still sometimes suffer from nightmares as a consequence.

AQUINAS: We must harden our hearts in seeking to implement God's Will here on earth. But your plea for tolerance, and your training in logic make me wonder whether you might be willing to offer criticism of a thought that came to me yesterday on the notion of a just price. It is totally unrelated to the controversy to which we shall have to return when this interval for refreshments is over.

BACON: I am immensely flattered that you should think me worthy.

AQUINAS: My thought is that it is immoral for one person to take advantage of another by selling him an item of which he is in great need for more than it is worth. The Church should therefore use its authority to ensure that nothing is sold at an unjust price. In particular, nobody should be allowed to make a profit from selling on goods to whose value he has made no contribution.

BACON: Your thought is that the price at which goods are currently exchanged is determined by supply and demand. When a good is in short supply and great demand, the price is high, and so the buyer suffers. Equally, when the the market conditions reverse, the price is low, and it is the seller who suffers. One might say that the price determined by the market reflects only the exchange-value of a good. You, on the other hand, advocate fixing the price of a good at its use-value.

AQUINAS: I am gratified that you should see my point immediately.

BACON: How would the use-value of a good be determined? I see difficulties, for example, in determining the use-value of water as compared with that of diamonds. Water is freely available here in France, and so its current price is usually zero, although it is essential to human life. Diamonds on the other hand have no intrinsic value, but are priced high because of their rarity.

AQUINAS: I do not envisage the Church making a wholesale revaluation of all goods that takes account of how they are used, and the amount of labor necessary to produce them. It seems to be that the price at which goods are traded under normal circumstances can be counted as just. It is only under abnormal circumstances—like a famine or some other disaster—that the Church would need to intervene to prevent profiteering.

BACON: I see another problem. If you are willing to be patient with me, I will explain it using a kind of parable in which two dairymaids from neighboring villages seek to trade the ingredients for making cheese according to differing traditional recipes. Anne has twenty buckets of milk, but no rennet to reduce them to curds and whey. Beatrice has thirty spoonfuls of rennet but no milk. Anne's recipe requires one spoonful of rennet for each bucket of milk to make one round of cheese. Beatrice's recipe requires two spoonfuls of rennet for each bucket of milk to make one round of cheese. They will throw away as useless any ingredients left over. It seems to me that they would then do best to exchange ten buckets of Anne's milk for ten spoonfuls of Beatrice's rennet. Both would then make ten rounds of cheese. Any other trade would leave one or the other worse off.

AQUINAS: I am surprised that a logician should be so well-informed about the making of cheese. But what has this to do with just pricing?

BACON: If Anne and Beatrice were to sell each other their respective ingredients, the price of a bucket of cheese and a spoonful of rennet would need to be equal if neither were to gain or lose any money from the transaction. One might say that this is the price determined by the demand and supply conditions in their little market. But suppose the local priest were to assess the use-value of a bucket of milk at half the use-value of a spoonful of rennet? Unless somebody ended up with less money in her purse after the transaction, only a total of fifteen rounds of cheese would be possible instead of twenty.

AQUINAS: All this in your head? You must be a fine logician! But your point is well-taken. There will generally be a loss of efficiency in divorcing prices from questions of supply and demand. But reforms often involve robbing Peter to pay Paul. On the other side, there would be the elimination of usury, in which the lender extracts money from the needy without contributing anything of value to what is traded.

BACON: I suppose a critic would argue that the borrower pays to persuade the lender to take on the risk that the loan may never be repaid. However, I share your distaste for the foul practice of usury. Doubtless the Jews would take over the business of lending money if it were forbidden to Christians.

AQUINAS: The Jews will have to look to the fate of their own souls. But I see that we are being called to renew our negotiations. It has been a pleasure to engage with such a sharp intellect. My advice to you personally is to leave Paris if you can, before the affair we are here to discuss blows up into something more serious.

BACON: You are very gracious, and I shall take your advice. It was, in any case, my plan to see more of the world before settling down.

Afterword

Aquinas was right that the dispute over Averroes eventually blew up into something more serious. After his term as Regent Master was over, he was called back for second term to deal with it. As for his notion of a just price, it was eventually partially implemented, to the general impoverishment of all. In our final dialogue, John Rawls and Derek Parfit are still discussing eight hundred years later whether fair division should take priority over the Pareto principle (that one outcome should be preferred to another if nobody is worse off in the second outcome and some are better off).

Chapter 10
William of Ockham versus Duns Scotus

Context

The imaginary dialogue between Anselm and Abelard is set at the beginning of the scholastic period, which is nowadays often dismissed as an era in which rival medieval theologians disputed how many angels can dance on the end of a pin. The current imaginary dialogue comes at the end of the scholastic period.

The work of both William of Ockham and Duns Scotus is certainly full of fine distinctions that modern scholars find uninteresting, but they deserve to be remembered because they kept the flag of logical reasoning flying at a time when it could be dangerous to follow arguments wherever they may lead. They appear here because William of Ockham was a determined nominalist, whereas Duns Scotus was an equally determined realist .

John Duns Scotus (1265–1308 AD?) was one of three philosophers regarded as preeminent in the scholastic period, the others being St Thomas Aquinas and William of Ockham. It is a pity that Aquinas could not be included in their dialogue, but he had been dead for thirty years at the time of the imaginary meeting between the other two. As his name indicates, Duns Scotus was a Scot, born in the town of Duns. He became a Franciscan friar, who established a reputation for philosophical subtlety in Oxford. He was then dispatched to Paris, where he was popular as a teacher. But all was not sweetness and light, since he was temporarily expelled from Paris for siding with the Pope against the King of France on a taxation issue. But he was back in Paris at the time of the invented visit of William of Ockham. The dialogue is imagined to end dramatically with the arrival of a message from the Franciscan Minister General ordering Duns Scotus to leave precipitately for Cologne.

The reason is unknown. Was he in trouble with the King again? However, he seems to have lived peacefully in Cologne until his death a few years later.

William of Ockham (1287–1347 AD) was born in the village of Ockham not very far to the south of London. He was educated by the Franciscans in London, where it is assumed that he established such a brilliant reputation as a young scholar that he was allowed to travel to Paris to consult with Duns Scotus. His later life was quite exciting. While teaching in England, he was accused of heresy, and dispatched to Avignon—the current seat of the Pope—to defend his views to a special commission of theologians. The commission fell short of finding him guilty, but he later fell foul of Pope John XXII when he sided with his Franciscan confreres in a dispute over whether Jesus and the Apostles owned property. Ockham accused the Pope of heresy, and was duly excommunicated. He fled by night, ending up eventually in Munich under the protection of the Holy Roman Emperor, who was at loggerheads with the Pope. He died there at age sixty.

Ockham's Razor says that simpler models should be preferred to complicated models—that explanatory entities should not be multiplied unnecessarily. Disregarding historical chronology, Duns Scotus uses this principle against Ockham when Ockham challenges his version of the First-Cause Argument for the existence of God in the imaginary dialogue that follows. The First-Cause Argument has a long history, going back at least as far as Aristotle, and extending at least as far as Leibniz in modern times. For Ockham and Duns Scotus, it would have been the version offered by St Thomas Aquinas that inspired their interest. The later version of Duns Scotus is much more carefully crafted, but seldom gets a mention nowadays.

In our imaginary dialogue, Ockham and Scotus dispute whether an infinite regress can actually be realized. Their arguments mirror a mathematical dispute of the nineteenth century about whether the infinite can be regarded as a realized mathematical object, or whether to speak of the infinite is merely to deny that finite sets can have certain properties. The work of Georg Cantor settled this issue for most mathematicians in favor of infinity as a real object—or rather, as an infinity of infinities represented by Cantor's theory of transfinite numbers. But there remains a small school of mathematical constructionists who obstinately insist on applying Ockham's Razor to the question.

Dialogue

It is October in the year 1307 AD in Paris, but the sun is shining intermittently. After his teaching obligations are over, Duns Scotus therefore decides to stroll in the Pre-aux-Clercs, which was an open space in Paris where teachers and students at the University of Paris would sometimes meet to discuss controversial issues in an informal way. He is approached by a bunch of students who have an awkward youth in their midst. The students explain that the youth—who is William of Ockham looking a lot younger than his twenty years—has been sent from the Greyfriars Convent in London to consult with Duns Scotus, but has been too shy to make an approach. William of Ockham introduces himself in Latin, but Duns Scotus puts him at his ease by responding in the English dialect he had learned in Oxford after finding his native Scots was seldom understood.

SCOTUS: It must have been an adventure for you to come from London to Paris, where things are so different. It reminds me of my own experiences when I was sent from Scotland to study in England. For what reason were you sent to consult me?

OCKHAM: Your argument for the existence of God is one of the great contributions to natural theology. It seems to me a substantial improvement on the argument of Aquinas that there must have been a First Cause. The argument of Aquinas is itself an improvement on the thoughts of Aristotle on the same subject. With such predecessors, I am apprehensive that you will feel me to be disrespectful in voicing my doubts about your claim that an infinite regress of causes that cause other causes is impossible.

SCOTUS: You are not the first to express such doubts. Why is an infinite regress impossible? I follow Aquinas in arguing that the infinite is a negative concept referring to whatever cannot be confined within bounds. But a realized infinite regress in the hypothesized absence of God, would make infinity into a positive concept. Infinity would then become a thing to be discussed in the same way as tables or chairs.

OCKHAM: Is this not inconsistent with the realism you profess in other contexts? I had thought that you had been seeking to persuaded theologians to reconsider the nominalism of Aristotle in the light of the realism of Plato.

SCOTUS: I do not think the work of Aristotle can be labelled in any simple way. But I suspect from your manner that you yourself are a nominalist.

OCKHAM: I am certainly drawn to the nominalist position—that Plato's ideal forms are not really real, but just the names of what some real things have in common. However, your position on the impossibility of an infinite regress leaves me conflicted. It seems to me that the integers 1, 2 and 3 are all real. But one cannot bound the integers, because whatever integer is said to be largest is smaller than the integer obtained by adding one. So the set of all integers is unbounded, and therefore infinite in the negative sense of Aquinas. But the set of all integers also seems to be a real object, and should therefore be regarded as infinite in the positive sense of Plato.

SCOTUS: So your putative nominalism is threatened by your feeling that the set of all integers is a real object—so to say that there are an infinite number of integers means more than simply saying that there is no largest integer. At the same time, you feel that my putative realism is threatened by my denial of the real existence of an infinite regress. It is a delight to me when I find a student who questions the teachings of his masters. Without such questioning, the search for a convincing natural theology to buttress our faith in God could never succeed.

OCKHAM: I am also delighted to find a master who does not talk of heresy when questioned. But may I persist in asking how you resolve the issue?

SCOTUS: You are not so shy as you first appeared! What if I were to say that it would be an imperfection in God to multiply the entities He creates without necessity? That to make the number of all integers into a real entity that one might call omega (after the Greek letter ω) would be to challenge the perfection of His creation?

OCKHAM: But to take this line would be to make your argument circular. Do you not hold that natural theology must not rely on revelation?

SCOTUS: Excellent! But a better argument occurs to me. If one could say that the number of integers were ω, then one would also have to say that the number of even integers was ω as well, because one could count the even integers by assigning 1 to 2, 2 to 4, 3 to 6, and so on. But there are twice as many integers as even integers, and so the concept of ω implies a contradiction.

Ockham is taken aback at such an ingenious answer, but is saved from having to reply by the arrival of a messenger from the Franciscan Minister General with an urgent letter for Duns Scotus. It instructs him to go immediately to Cologne without pausing to gather his personal possessions. Duns Scotus mumbles his apologies, and hurriedly rushes away. The students, who have been listening avidly as Ockham succeeds in holding the attention of their master, burst into speculation about what the letter contains.

So Ockham's moment of glory is occluded, but his contacts with the students he met in Paris were to serve him well in his later eventful life. But he was never to forget the off-the-cuff argument that Duns Scotus gave against multiplying entities unnecessarily, which we now know as Ockham's Razor. On the other hand, he would never understand how the number of even integers could be the same as the number of all integers. He would have profited from listening to the imaginary dialogue between Georg Cantor and Bertrand Russell coming up later.

Chapter 11
Thomas Hobbes versus René Descartes

Context

Descartes and Hobbes are said actually to have met face-to-face in 1647 or 1648. It must have been a bad-tempered occasion if Descartes' written replies to Hobbes' objections to his famous *Meditations* are any guide. Hobbes is seriously rude and Descartes responds with contempt. Descartes says somewhere else that Hobbes is "aiming to make his reputation at his expense, and by devious means".

The *Meditations* contains Descartes' famous attempt to doubt everything, except *cogito ergo sum*—I think, therefore I am. Hobbes is the first of many who think that the enterprise may be worthy, but its execution falls flat on its face. But in their actual exchanges, they talk past each other on this subject. Descartes also replies to Hobbes' objections to his revival of St Anselm's ontological argument for the existence of God. They engage better on this subject, and so I have made it the topic for their imaginary dialogue, since it also provides some continuity with the preceding scholastic dialogues. However, as in my imaginary *Protagoras*, I have rewritten both sides of the debate.

Descartes (1596–1650) was first and foremost a mathematician and scientist. Even if he had not been crucial in reviving philosophy in modern times, he would still be a significant figure in human intellectual history. He was born in the French town of La Haye, which has been renamed Descartes in his honor, but he is better commemorated by the Cartesian axes of analytical geometry. His family wanted him to be a lawyer, but he chose instead to become a gentleman soldier. The story goes that he had three dreams while on campaign in Bavaria that left him with the belief that he had a mission to reform all knowledge. He is not the only person to dream that he had a mission, but perhaps the only person ever to come up with the goods.

Eventually he settled in the Dutch Netherlands, where he found the intellectual climate less oppressive than in France. He felt sufficiently threatened for thinking his own thoughts that he changed his address frequently, commenting that he "who lives well hidden, lives well". He died in Sweden complaining of the bitter cold, after accepting an invitation from Queen Christina of Sweden to teach her philosophy, which turned out to require his rising absurdly early in the morning.

Thomas Hobbes (1588–1679) was the clever son of an English clergyman. After an Oxford education, he became tutor to the aristocratic Cavendish family, who remained his patrons throughout his life. His support for the royalist cause in the English Civil War led to a long exile abroad during which he acted as mathematics tutor to the future King Charles II.

His *Leviathan* famously argues that the natural state of the human race is a "war of all against all" in which life is "solitary, poor, nasty, brutish, and short". He contends that we can only escape this miserable state of nature by surrendering our freedom to a central authority or king. The materialist sentiments he expresses along the way are remarkable for the times, and it is not surprising that the English parliament suspected him of atheism, but he was rescued by the restored Charles II on condition that he wrote no more provocative works. His stubborn character is captured by his refusal to accept that the mathematicians who rejected his various attempts to square the circle knew what they were talking about.

I have been creative in setting the 1648 meeting between Descartes and Hobbes in the Place Royale monastery in Paris. Scientific meetings were occasionally held there under the auspices of the monk Marin Mersenne, who had previously put together the book *Objections and Replies,* in which Descartes' replies to objections from Hobbes and others are published.

Mersenne (1588–1648) was a scholar of considerable interest himself. He will be remembered forever because of his discovery of the class of prime numbers that bear his name. (The largest known Mersenne prime is $2^{282,589,933} - 1$, discovered in 2018.) However, he was more important as a facilitator of seventeenth century scientific endeavor, known affectionately as the "postbox of Europe" because of his enormous scientific correspondence. It was Mersenne who brought the work of both Descartes and Galileo to the attention of the intellectual world.

Descartes was in Paris briefly in 1648, and would probably have visited his old friend Mersenne. Although Mersenne died later that year, and would have been ill at the time of the imaginary dialogue between Descartes and Hobbes, it is consistent with his sense of mischief that he might have organized their meeting in the hope of watching the sparks fly as the most unyielding of all philosophical hedgehogs pit his wits against a philosophical fox of the first order.

Dialogue

It is hot summer's day in 1648 when Mersenne welcomes Descartes and Hobbes to the Place Royale monastery in Paris, but they do not step outside because Mersenne is physically frail, although his mind is as sharp as ever. They speak in French—although Hobbes is not very eloquent except in his native tongue—because the English way of pronouncing Latin is hard to follow. Nor is Hobbes very comfortable in the small stuffy room into which they have been ushered. Descartes is similarly gloomy when he recalls that—in accordance with the minimal life-style of the branch of the Franciscan order to which Mersenne belongs—they can hope for no more in the way of refreshments than watered wine and perhaps some bread and cheese. However, they soon forget their personal discomforts when Mersenne reverts to type by opening the proceedings with a scarcely concealed attempt to sow a little discord.

MERSENNE: It is a pleasure to entertain two famous scholars with such different attitudes to the mind-body problem. You embody the clash between rationalism and empiricism!

HOBBES: I am certainly an empiricist. Now that your old friend Pierre Gassendi has shown that history has unjustly maligned the ancient philosopher Epicurus, I can say that I follow in his empirical tradition. As for rationalism, I suppose that M Descartes must be the rationalist in your dramatization of our meeting. But I am no less rational than he!

MERSENNE: A rationalist is a philosopher who believes that it is possible to discover things about the world simply by thinking hard about them. An empiricist believes that it is necessary to consult the evidence of one's senses for this purpose. The distinction expands the Greek debate between physis and nomos, or the scholastic debate between realism and nominalism, where the differences in terminology reflect historical changes in focus that have followed the debate down the ages.

HOBBES: These new definitions seem bound to lead to confusion! As for the mind-body problem, the differences between M Descartes and myself have already been thrashed out in the *Objections and Replies* that you assembled after his *Meditations* became notorious for the claim that one can deduce much of the nature of the world—including the existence of God—from the dictum *cogito ergo sum*. I do not see that there is more to say.

MERSENNE: My dear Mr Hobbes, I had hoped that M Descartes would comment on your idea that our minds are part of our bodies—that a thought is perhaps akin to the flow of water in a pipe, or the vibration of a violin string. You might similarly want to challenge his speculation that it is through the pineal gland that our spirits animate our bodies. What of the "I" in "I think, therefore I am"? Is it merely our name for the thoughts that circulate in our brains? Or is it a window into a noumenal universe that houses our immortal souls?

DESCARTES: I agree with Mr Hobbes that there is no point in our continuing to pursue such questions. However, I would welcome the opportunity to explore further his comments on my ontological argument for the existence of God—which I insist is not an attempt to improve on St Anselm's argument of which I did not know at the time the *Meditations* was written, although I was aware that St Thomas Aquinas held that existence is part of the essence of God.

MERSENNE: Excuse me gentlemen while I locate the Fifth Meditation in my copy of M Descartes' book. Here is the passage I want to read. It follows an expression of his very simple argument in formal terms. "Whatever method of proof I use, I am always brought back to the fact that it is only what I clearly and distinctly perceive that completely convinces me. Some of the things I clearly and distinctly perceive are obvious to everyone, while others are discovered only by those who look more closely and investigate more carefully; but once they have been discovered, the latter are judged to be just as certain as the former. In the case of a right-angled triangle, for example, the fact that the square on the hypotenuse is equal to the square on the other two sides is not so readily apparent as the fact that the hypotenuse subtends the largest angle; but once one has seen it, one believes it just as strongly. But as regards God, if I were not overwhelmed by philosophical prejudices, and if the images of things perceived by the senses did not besiege my thought on every side, I would certainly acknowledge him sooner and more easily than anything else. For what is more manifest than the fact that the supreme being exists, or that God, to whose essence alone existence belongs, exists?"

HOBBES: Your choice, M Mersenne, of a passage to read is very apt. I agree—and I think perhaps that M Descartes will also agree—that his ontological argument is offered not so much as a formal proof, but as a self-evident axiom to be grasped intuitively by a mind free of philosophical prejudice.

DESCARTES: I do so agree. Do you, Mr Hobbes, have anything to add to your objection that your mind is inadequate to grasp the concept of a being whose essence includes its own existence?

HOBBES: Not only my mind, but that of St Thomas Aquinas also! It is for good reason that he says that we cannot fully grasp the essence of God. But I would go further. Not only is it not self-evident that a supreme being exists, it is not even self-evident that the angles of a triangle sum to two right angles, as your geometric analogy takes for granted. Euclid's proof depends on the Parallel Postulate that geometers have long found suspect, but failed to deduce from his other axioms. We believe that the Parallel Postulate is true for empirical reasons—because it accords with our experience here on earth, and not because our minds somehow have access to an ideal world of geometric shapes.

DESCARTES: I declare, M Mersenne, that it is insufferable that René Descartes—an accomplished geometer in his own right—should be lectured to on geometry by someone whose attempts to square the circle have been met only with derision from established mathematicians.

Mersenne's attempts to pacify a flushed and angry Hobbes after this outburst were unsuccessful, and the meeting broke up in disarray. Descartes left Paris a few days later on hearing that the aristocratic rebellion known as the Fronde was getting perilously close. His old friend Mersenne died not long after. Hobbes had a long wait before Charles II was restored to the English throne, but he then enjoyed the royal favor until he got into trouble again.

Afterword

In the dialogue, Mersenne anticipates some modern terminology so that his contributions can be kept reasonably compact. Hobbes is credited with some skepticism about the physical reality of Euclidean geometry. In fact, Einstein's theory of special relativity implies that space is non-Euclidean even far from gravitating bodies, with the angles of a triangle summing to a bit less that two right angles. On the other hand, Hobbes' attempts to square the circle were fated to fail, as π was later proved to be a transcendental number—and so cannot be the solution of the equations that the analytical geometry invented by Descartes shows would be necessary if the circle could be squared.

Chapter 12

Blaise Pascal versus Pierre de Fermat

Context

Pascal and Fermat are credited with being the fathers of probability theory as a consequence of a sequence of letters they exchanged about how to solve a famous gambling problem raised by the Chevalier de Méré. Their method consists of counting the number of equally likely ways that something can happen. Méré's problem is much more complicated, but their approach is no different from Fermat's earlier proof that Méré will win more often at rolling a six in four throws of a dice than at rolling a double-six in twenty-four throws of two dice. We would nowadays say that the probability of winning is greater in the first case, but the concept of probability had not been invented in 1654.

Many other concepts were waiting to be reinvented after having been discovered in ancient times and then forgotten, but probability seems to have been a genuinely new idea. Modern schoolchildren are taught probability in school as though it were blindingly obvious, but it was not an obvious notion to Pascal and Fermat—whose reputations as creative mathematicians will live forever. How come the idea was so difficult for them and their contemporaries? How come that philosophers are still hung up on the various ways that probability can be interpreted once one moves away from the notion of long-run frequency that is adequate in gambling applications and most of physics? This imaginary dialogue explores the first of these two questions. The second question is left for a later dialogue.

Blaise Pascal (1623–1662) was an enigma in many ways—a subject of great interest to both Freud and Nietzsche. His letters to Fermat are supremely practical. So was his founding of the first bus service in Paris in 1662. He invented an early mechanical computer. He was active in the scientific development of the barometer, demonstrating that the mercury falls further when the barometer is taken up a mountain. He proved a wonderful theorem in projective geometry at the age of 16. In philosophy, he challenged the rationalism of Descartes, but denied that empiricism was adequate on its own for discovering how the world works. There is Pascal's Triangle in combinatorics; the Pascal as a unit for measuring gas pressure; Pascal's Theorem in geometry; and Pascal's Wager in theology. Not only was he gifted as a mathematician and scientist, but he wrote about his insights in a style that is still widely admired as an exemplar of the best in French prose.

Pascal's Wager—whose inadequacy was pointed out to Peter Abelard by St Anselm in their imaginary dialogue—marks an abrupt switch by Pascal from a brilliant career as a French intellectual to a dogmatic defender of Jansenism, which was a controversial French theological movement that emphasized the notion of original sin. He famously experienced a revelatory religious experience, on which he wrote notes that begin, "FIRE. god of Abraham, god of Isaac, god of Jacob, not of the philosophers and of the learned. Certitude. Certitude. Feeling. Joy. Peace."

Whence comes the certitude in such experiences? As Pascal says himself, "The heart has its reasons, which reason does not know." Pascal's own experience certainly did not drive him mad, as his practical letters to Fermat on counting how many times various events can occur in Méré's problem continue as though nothing had happened. But he took to wearing a spiked girdle to chastise a body that had already suffered from recurring illnesses and chronic pain since childhood. Perhaps such revelatory experiences are not just epileptic seizures, but are indeed sent from God. However, the fact that his experience should lead him to use his cleverness to invent rationalizations of the threadbare Jansenist doctrine is a warning to clever folk everywhere. Cleverness just digs you deeper if you are not skeptical about what your unconscious insists on treating as axiomatic.

Pierre de Fermat (1601–1665) was a successful lawyer and public administrator in Bordeaux and Toulouse. His mathematical efforts were therefore merely an entertainment to occupy his spare time—but amateurs everywhere should take heart! He is famous because his pioneering work in number theory led to his formulating "Fermat's last theorem"—proved only in 1994 by Andrew Wiles. But he was influential much more widely. His method for working out the slopes of tangents to curves inspired Isaac Newton's invention of the calculus, as Newton himself acknowledged. He invented coordinate geometry independently of Descartes, with whom he maintained a debate on their differences on a variety of topics through their mutual friend Marin Mersenne. In thinking about refraction, his insight that light travels between two given points along the path of shortest time has led to his being honored by physicists as the key figure in the development of the Principle of Least Action. On top of all this, he shares with Pascal the distinction of being regarded as the founder of probability theory.

This is not the first imaginary dialogue that focusses on the difficulties that the idea of probability created for pioneers of the theory. The actual letters between Pascal and Fermat are seriously technical, and so the Hungarian mathematician Alfred Rényi invented a new set of philosophical letters from Pascal to Fermat on the assumption that Fermat's equally fictional replies had been lost. Rényi's *Letters on Probability* cannot be bettered, but I have done my best to compress his ideas into a smaller compass. Rényi's *Dialogues on Mathematics* are also a good read.

Fermat and Pascal apparently never met. Both were in poor health at the time in 1660 that Pascal wrote to Fermat that he proposed to travel by river to the town of Saumur to stay until Christmas with M le Duc de Roannes, governor of Poitou. Pascal's health was particularly bad, and so Saumur was as close to Toulouse as he was ever likely to come, having long relocated from Clemont-Ferrand to Paris. It was still doubtless too far for the frail Fermat, but I have invented what would have been a very tiring journey for him from Toulouse to Saumur, so that he and Pascal can meet in the governor's house.

Dialogue

The Duke of Roannes is delighted to be entertaining two savants for the price of one, but discreetly leaves an afternoon for them to talk together privately. So after appropriate compliments have been paid, they settle down in comfortable leather chairs. There is some fuss with servants who take too much to heart the duke's stern instructions that Pascal and Fermat are to be treated like philosopher-kings, but eventually they are left alone to talk philosophy.

PASCAL: At last the servants leave us in peace! The feast that they have left behind will be of no interest to two invalids like ourselves, but the large fire is very welcome.

FERMAT: It is such a pleasure, M Pascal, to meet you in person. There is so much to discuss! How goes your discovery that Aristotle was wrong—that Nature does not abhor a vacuum after all? The young Socrates should not have allowed Parmenides to persuade him so easily to the contrary!

PASCAL: Alas, M de Fermat, my education did not include Plato's dialogues. And it is M Torricelli who actually invented the barometer! Nor are all the theologians persuaded. It is argued that some ethereal vapor occupies the space above the mercury.

FERMAT: Your modesty is quite charming. Does it also extend to Pascal's Triangle?

PASCAL: What is Pascal's Triangle?

FERMAT: I must confess to having called it that in a letter to Mersenne, in which case I might as well have trumpeted it from a mountain top! I have a copy of the letter here in my bag. You might wish to see the rest of my correspondence with Mersenne later. If you recall, solving the kind of problems raised by the Chevalier de Méré required working out things like how many ways 5 different hands can be dealt from a deck of 11 cards. I was doing this from scratch each time such a problem arose, but you showed that it is easy to solve all such problems at once by constructing a triangular array of numbers in which one simply adds up two adjacent entries in a row to get the entry beneath them in the next row down.

PASCAL: This triangle was certainly useful in simplifying our calculations when we worked together on Méré's problem. But I hope we will move on from such technical questions today.

FERMAT: You doubtless feel—as do I—that we need to formulate a more general way of thinking about chance than simply counting up the number of ways that different but equally likely events can occur.

PASCAL: I have in mind that we might join in writing a book called *The Mathematics of Chance*.

FERMAT: What would go into such a book?

PASCAL: The first essential would be to deny that we know nothing unless we know something for certain. We can quantify the degree of uncertainty—as when throwing a fair dice. Will we roll a *two*? The answer is that each humber on the dice has an equal chance of being rolled, and so a *two* will be rolled $\frac{1}{6}$ of the time. I suggest we say that a *two* has a probability of $\frac{1}{6}$ of being rolled.

FERMAT: I like your suggested use of the word probability. It would merely provide a way of strengthening the way people already vaguely speak of events being more or less probable. Impossible events would get probability 0. Certain events would get probability 1. To find the probability that one or the other of two events will occur, we would simply need to add their separate probabilities—provided that both cannot occur at once. So the probability that either a *two* or a *three* will be rolled will simply be $\frac{1}{6} + \frac{1}{6}$.

PASCAL: Multiplying probabilities will also make sense. If we roll two dice one after the other, the probability that a *two* will be rolled and then a *three* will be $\frac{1}{6} \times \frac{1}{6}$, because there are 36 equally likely ways that two dice can be rolled.

FERMAT: The probability that a diamond is drawn at random from a deck of cards will be $\frac{1}{4}$ because there are four equally likely suits. If another card is now drawn without replacing the first card, what is the probability that a second diamond will be drawn? it seems to me that we will have to introduce *conditional* probabilities to deal with such situations.

PASCAL: The probability that a second diamond will be drawn is $\frac{12}{51}$ because there are 12 diamonds left out of 51 cards. But we still retain the multiplication rule because the probability of drawing two diamonds without replacement is $\frac{1}{4} \times \frac{12}{51}$.

FERMAT: The general definition of the conditional probability that an event E will occur given that an event F has already occurred should simply be the probability of both E and F happening together divided by the probability of F—which accords with your calculation. If the two events are independent, then the conditional probability of E given F will just be the same as the unconditioned probability of E, so we do indeed return to your original multiplication rule.

PASCAL: For our theory, we can therefore simply define two events to be independent if the probability of their occurring jointly is obtained by multiplying their separate probabilities.

FERMAT: It would be better if we could give an operational definition of independence, but I agree that we cannot hope to solve all problems at once. Let me therefore raise another problem. Suppose that we were rolling a weighted dice? We could then no longer rely on each face being equally likely. How could we then work out the probability of rolling a *two?*

PASCAL: I have been entertaining myself with some experimental work devoted to this very question! In a Roman dicing game, four knucklebones from sheep or goats were thrown. Each knucklebone could end up showing one of four distinct faces. The best throw was the Venus, when each bone showed a different face. I acquired a knucklebone and threw it a thousand times. The four faces appeared 408, 396, 91 and 105 times. I think we might deduce that their probabilities are about $\frac{4}{10}$, $\frac{4}{10}$, $\frac{1}{10}$ and $\frac{1}{10}$. Assuming each knucklebone falls independently, the rules for manipulating probabilities we have invented then imply that the probability of throwing a Venus is roughly $\frac{24}{625}$, so that it will be thrown about once in every twenty-five throws.

FERMAT: Such an empirical approach depends on our assuming that some Law of Large Numbers applies—that the average number of times a particular face of a knucklebone is thrown will converge on a limit that we identify as its probability. But it is possible that the same face might be thrown all the time!

PASCAL: We can only hope that the average would converge on the probability with high probability. But now we are in danger of inventing a circular definition!

FERMAT: We are in worse trouble than that if we cannot resolve this problem! We would not even be able to justify our calculations for the Chevalier de Méré, in which we took for granted that each face on a fair dice is equally likely to be rolled. But what do we do if someone challenges the fairness of the dice? We roll the dice many times to see what happens. We would then have an indefinitely long sequence of the digits 1 thru 6. If we idealized by treating this sequence as infinite, it would serve as our label for the dice—our summary of all available data about how the dice rolls.

PASCAL: Your point is that we would need to be able to deduce the probabilities of the six faces from this data, although we could only hope to be able to do so with high probability. We would also need a criterion which assures us that the sequence of data is random, and hence compatible with being generated by trials that are independent of each other.

FERMAT: I have no idea how to handle the randomness question, but I think I see how one might tackle the problem of deducing probabilities from data. For our approach to be consistent, we need a theorem about the average number of times an event occurs when generated by a sequence of independent identical trials. For example, to justify your probability estimate for the Venus throw at knucklebones, we would first need to decide how close we want the average to approximate $\frac{24}{625}$. We would then need to be able to make the probability that this standard of approximation is achieved as high as we like by throwing the bones sufficiently often. If we could prove this for all standards of approximation, we would have what one might call a Law of Large Numbers to which to appeal when defending $\frac{24}{625}$ as the probability of the Venus throw.

PASCAL: The proof of such a Law of Large Numbers sounds daunting. But I like the idea that it implies that long-run frequencies that do not reflect the probability of whatever produced them—as when the same face of a dice is always thrown—would have an arbitrarily small probability of occurring. Critics will enjoy making fun of the fact that events with zero probability need not be impossible!

FERMAT: I would like to leave further discussion of the Law of Large Numbers until I have had time to consider possible proofs in the quietude of my study. Right now, I want to raise a further philosophical question. All our examples so far have been of repeated situations. But what if a probability cannot be reduced to a long-run frequency? Horse races cannot be run repeatedly under identical circumstances, but people nevertheless bet on horses. Is our theory of probability also to be held relevant to horse racing?

PASCAL: What indeed of uncertain questions in general? Is it meaningful to speak of the probability that the Emperor of China is wearing a red gown today? Or the probability that there is an undiscovered planet? Or the probability that the theorem you just proposed on the Law of Large Numbers is true?

FERMAT: I am not surprised that you find such possible metaphysical applications attractive. How else to explain Pascal's famous Wager? I prefer to stick with more down-to-earth possibilities. One might, for example, consider all possible winners in a horse race and insist that the Chevalier de Méré say how he would bet for or against each horse as the odds vary over all possibilities. If his choices are consistent, my guess is that he will choose as though he is able to attach a probability to each horse.

PASCAL: We then have at least three ways of interpreting probability. First in an objective sense as a long-run frequency. Here I think we are on safer ground than the subjective sense in which probabilities are deduced from a person's betting behavior. Lastly, we have what you call the metaphysical sense, but I would prefer to call the logical or epistemic sense, in which probabilities are interpreted as extended truth values that measure how much the available evidence supports a proposition.

FERMAT: I am not sure to what extent I would wish to defend all our ideas for subjective probabilities. I am doubtful that they make any sense at all for logical probabilities. I am certainly not in favor of taking the ideas we have been developing for objective probabilities, and applying them to a subjective or logical context without reconsidering their foundations.

PASCAL: Perhaps this difference about possible future development of the probability concept marks the spot at which we should think about consolidating what we have so far. We are both tired, and I suggest that we rest until dinner—at which I fear we shall have to do our best at pretending to represent the Parisian intellectual elite in all its up-to-the-minute glory.

Fermat is pleased to fall in with Pascal's suggestion that they rest until dinner—but not with Pascal's mistaken suggestion that they would need to sing for their supper. The two meet again on successive days but are unable to prove the theorem on the Law of Large Numbers that Fermat proposed, which is not surprising since the theory of mathematical convergence had yet to be developed. A stronger version of the theorem is actually true—that the probability the average fails to converge on $\frac{24}{625}$ is zero. Their failure discourages them, and so the writing of books on probability is left to their many followers.

Afterword

The remarks with which Fermat motivates his stab at a Law of Large Numbers remained largely unexplored until Richard von Mises wrote *Probability, Statistics, and Truth* in 1928. Fermat's doubts about applying the rules developed for manipulating objective probabilities to logical probabilities without reconsidering the foundations of the subject remain largely neglected—an attitude that dates all the way back to the very early *Philosophical Essay on Probabilities* of Pierre-Simon de Laplace. It is interesting that John Stuart Mill argued for restricting the use of the probability concept to long-run frequencies until persuaded otherwise by William Herschel—the astronomer who discovered the planet Uranus. Mill then reversed his position entirely by endorsing the logical probability interpretation of Laplace.

The first few rows of Pascal's Triangle are shown below. The first 10 in the bottom row, for example, is the number of ways a hand of two cards can be dealt from a deck of five cards. It is obtained simply by adding the 4 and 6 above it in the preceding row. The triangle can be continued forever in the same way.

$$
\begin{array}{ccccccccccc}
 & & & & & 1 & & & & & \\
 & & & & 1 & & 1 & & & & \\
 & & & 1 & & 2 & & 1 & & & \\
 & & 1 & & 3 & & 3 & & 1 & & \\
 & 1 & & 4 & & 6 & & 4 & & 1 & \\
1 & & 5 & & 10 & & 10 & & 5 & & 1 \\
\end{array}
$$

Chapter 13
John Locke versus Thomas Hobbes

Context

John Locke is sometimes said to be the founding father of empiricism. He is certainly one of three philosophers who make up the traditional British school of empiricists, of whom the other two are Bishop Berkeley and David Hume. (I do not know why Hobbes is omitted from this list, nor why he is similarly omitted from the list of Locke, Rousseau and Kant, who are always mentioned as the primary social contract theorists.) However, the ancient philosophers, Democritus and Epicurus, were much more thorough-going empiricists than Locke.

Locke certainly thought that the mind is a blank slate on which experience can write anything—but he excluded God, Morality and Mathematics, about which he apparently thought that one could know things without the need for any experience at all. Personally, I would make skepticism about the existence of God the touchstone in a list of empiricist philosophers, so excluding Berkeley and including Hobbes. Locke would appear on the list, but certainly not at its head. However, his theory of mind was a notable advance, and nobody can doubt the originality of his liberal contributions to social and political philosophy. His arguments for tolerance and against authoritarianism remain relevant today.

To appreciate the eventual influence of Locke, it is necessary to appreciate something of the history of his times. The English Civil War had concluded with the victory of the parliamentary side with Oliver Cromwell at its head. After the disorder that followed his death, the easygoing Charles II was restored to the throne to be succeeded after his death by his more reactionary and Catholic brother, James II. His supporters became known as Tories, and the opposition as Whigs. The Whigs eventually invited the Protestant William of Orange to come over from the

Netherlands to replace James as William III. He was a grandson of Charles I married to Mary, a daughter of James II, who had been brought up as a Protestant. His succession to the throne was followed by a liberal reform of the constitution known as the Glorious Revolution of 1688, after which no question remained about whether Parliament or King was paramount. But it was only when all the excitement was over that John Locke's *Two Treatises on Government* became accepted as the philosophical justification of the Whig ascendancy that followed.

John Locke was born in humble circumstances to Puritan parents. His father fought on the side of Parliament in the Civil War. Locke was fortunate that his father's commanding officer paid for an expensive education that ended up at Oxford, where Locke was lucky enough to become part of a group of proto-scientists, including Robert Boyle, that became the nucleus of the Royal Society. In later life, he became close to Isaac Newton—insofar as anyone could.

While at Oxford, Locke fell into the orbit of the future Earl of Shaftesbury, who was influential in the Country Party that evolved into the Whigs. As Shaftesbury's secretary, physician and friend, Locke was in the thick of political developments, both in good times and bad. Some of the times were very bad indeed for Shaftesbury, who was forced into exile in 1682, and died the next year. Locke followed him into exile, where he wrote a good deal of the work that made him famous. He returned to enjoy the freedoms of the Glorious Revolution of 1688, living in semi-retirement until his death in 1704.

In spite of his liberal credentials, it is as well to note that Locke was no saint. He is famous for observing that each man owns the property rights to his own body, but nevertheless invested money in the slave-trade. He also commented in a letter that children in the workhouse could usefully be employed turning a treadmill from the age of three.

Some creativity is necessary to invent circumstances in which Locke (1632–1704) might have met Hobbes (1588–1679). I have chosen the year 1667, when Locke was 35 years old and Hobbes was 83. Hobbes had retired from public life after accusations of atheism, and devoted himself to translating the *Odyssey* and the *Iliad*. In spite of his age, Hobbes would still have been mentally active. In fact, the story goes that he eventually died at the age of 92 after contracting a chill as a consequence of stuffing a chicken with snow to prove to skeptical companions on a coach trip that food could be preserved by freezing. At their imaginary meeting, Locke is assumed already to be thinking about the liberal social contract theory with which he eventually justified the new commercial morality that had began to replace such medieval notions of the past as the idea of a just price.

Dialogue

In 1667, Thomas Hobbes is in retirement at Hardwick Hall in Derbyshire, the splendid ancestral home of the aristocratic Cavendish family, who served loyally as his patrons through many years. John Locke has recently joined the household of the future Earl of Shaftesbury as a physician. He accompanies Shaftesbury to consult with the Earl of Derby—who is a fellow grandee of the Country Party—at the equally splendid Knowsley Hall, during which time Locke takes the opportunity to make a side-trip to visit Hobbes. He is shown into Hobbes' bedroom, which is warmed by a blazing fire. Hobbes is in bed, recovering from a chest infection.

Hobbes has heard that Locke organized an operation that relieved Shaftesbury of pain by inserting a silver tube into a tumour in his liver to drain the build-up of fluid. He therefore welcomes the opportunity to consult Locke about his own health problems. But eventually he accepts the necessity of listening to Locke's ideas of a liberal social contract that he greets with a typically irascible stream of criticism.

HOBBES: You have come a long way to visit me, Mr Locke. The time has now come for you to explain why.

LOCKE: It would be sufficient reason, Mr Hobbes, to meet the author of *Leviathan* in person, but it is true that I would like to hear your opinion of an alternative social contract theory that I am turning over in my mind. I expect some fierce criticism, since its adoption would stand your own reasoning on its head.

HOBBES: The founders of social contract theory are usually said to be Grotius and Pufendorf. They seem to have wanted to offer a simplified historical explanation of how modern societies might have evolved over time. My own efforts were more political. I knew the conclusion that I wanted to reach—that the King should rule supreme. I therefore shaped my assumptions to this end. I envisaged the human state of nature to be a war of all against all, to which the only alternative to be considered was for everybody to surrender their autonomy to a central authority that I called Leviathan after the monster in the Bible. My approach was no more honest than the medieval scholastics like Thomas Aquinas, who would have rejected any argument that failed to lead to the conclusions pre-determined by their faith. My own faith was in the traditional virtues of the monarchy.

LOCKE: You are very frank. May I ask how you came to have such faith in the monarchy that you not only shaped your philosophical work to this end, but endured the privations of exile rather than trim your sails to live under Cromwell?

HOBBES: An interesting question! Why do some people adopt one faith and others another? Why was Thomas Aquinas a Christian? Why was he so sure of the truth of Christian doctrine? It was not because he derived knowledge-as-certainty from his metaphysical reasoning—any more than I attained knowledge-as-certainty of the optimality of the monarchy through my philosophical musings. Our upbringing fixed certain axioms in our minds about the nature of truth to which we remained committed through the rest of our lives. Our knowledge of these truths has the status of knowledge-as-commitment.

LOCKE: You suggest that St Thomas Aquinas would have been a Muslim if he had been raised in Damascus! That you, yourself, would have been a Roundhead rather than a Cavalier if you had been born to Puritan parents like myself! That philosophers in general invent clever arguments merely to rationalize their prejudices.

HOBBES: Nothing so clear-cut! We must remember that many families were split during the late Civil War, with one brother a Cavalier, and another a Roundhead.

Aquinas himself diverged from the doctrine that was orthodox in his day to replace its background neoplatonism by the newly recovered ideas of Aristotle.

LOCKE: It would nevertheless have been of great interest to ask Aquinas whether he thought he would have been as convinced a Christian if he had been raised in Syria rather than Italy. I doubt that he would have answered as honestly as you have answered. Your bleak vision of human nature stares back at you from the mirror.

HOBBES: Your vision of human nature is less bleak? Whence comes your knowledge? Is it not merely knowledge-as-commitment you derived from your Puritan parents?

LOCKE: I have put Puritanism behind me. I am officially an Anglican, as indeed are you. But my intention is to transcend such questions. I hope to return to the aspirations of Grotius and Pufendorf in seeking a social contract theory based on empirical data learned from studying the savages of the New World, who are as near being in a state of nature as we can hope to find on this earth. I certainly disclaim knowledge-as-certainty of these matters, but I also hope not to fall victim to knowledge-as-commitment. My aim is to found a theory on rational belief derived from empirical facts—albeit summarized by some highly simplified principles.

HOBBES: I doubt that human beings are capable of viewing the world so objectively, but I would be interested to hear how you plan to proceed. How would you use empirical data to explain, for example, the origins of private property?

LOCKE: We have natural rights not only to property, but to our lives, our liberty, and our health. All people have these rights equally in the state of nature that precedes civil government. It is a law of nature that nobody ought to harm another in his life, health, liberty, or possessions.

HOBBES: What is the origin of these natural rights?

LOCKE: They originate with God, and are confirmed by human reason. The state of nature that I envisage therefore differs from the state of nature described in your *Leviathan*, in which men ignore the dictates of reason to fight a miserable war of all against all.

HOBBES: Leaving aside our differences for the moment, how does it come about that some people are rich and others poor? Is this not a violation of what you see as their natural rights?

LOCKE: In the equality that reigns in the state of nature, each man may appropriate what he will of nature's bounty, provided he leaves enough and as good for others. Its value as property is derived from his mixing his labor with nature's raw materials. A man has a natural right to defend his property against the encroachments of others, but as scarcity develops, a civil society established by mutual consent is necessary to resolve conflicts in a civilized way. With the appearance of money, mutually profitable trade will inevitably lead to inequalities.

HOBBES: I do not see that the liberal natural rights on which your reasoning is based have an empirical basis. My knowledge of the savages discovered in the

New World is admittedly based largely on Montaigne's essay *Cannibals,* in which he describes their inflicting the most terrible tortures on their prisoners before eating their dead bodies. But perhaps you are better informed?

LOCKE: My analysis applies to what happens within a society. Its relationship with rival societies is another matter. We have a right to defend our liberties when they are threatened from outside—as the Dutch Republic is currently defending its liberal social contract against the efforts of Louis XIV of France to reduce it to slavery.

HOBBES: Here we have the nub! It seems to me that if your nascent social contract theory ever sees the light of day, it will be no more empirically based than mine. You would like to see England adopt a liberal constitution similar to that of the Dutch Republic, although doubtless with fewer rough edges. You therefore invent a state of nature and a system of natural rights that lead to this conclusion. The claim that your axioms are founded in reason will convince only those who are already committed to the conclusions at which your arguments are directed.

LOCKE: Your cynicism shocks me. But I thank you for listening so patiently to my ideas, which I see need to be thought out much more carefully if they are to influence traditionalists like yourself. Please forgive me for intruding on your convalescence.

HOBBES: There is no need to apologies. I enjoyed our disagreement immensely!

Afterword

A later imaginary dialogue pits Robert Nozick against David Lewis. Nozick became famous by offering a libertarian alternative to John Rawls' *Theory of Justice,* founded on Locke's natural laws. Locke would have been astounded to find himself recruited as a founding father in such a right-wing cause!

Chapter 14
Gottfried Leibniz versus Baruch de Spinoza

Context

Matthew Stewart's *The Courtier and the Heretic* already offers speculations about what went on when Leibniz and Spinoza actually met over a three-day period in 1676. My imaginary dialogue is less ready to condemn Leibniz. His urge to excel admittedly makes him a less attractive character than Spinoza, but his willingness to follow arguments wherever they may go is surely worthy of our respect.

Spinoza (1632–1677) was a member of a community of Jews expelled from Portugal who found sanctuary in the Dutch Republic. His fellows proved no more tolerant of his perceived atheism than if they had been Christian. As a result of their hostility, he lost both his social niche in the very tight Jewish community in Amsterdam, and his livelihood in the family business. A condition of his being allowed to return to the Synagogue was that he lie at full length at the threshold so the congregation could walk over his prostrate body. He chose instead to live what must have been a lonely ascetic life, making a living by grinding and polishing lenses for scientific instruments, and writing his books by candlelight in the evenings. He seems to have made no display of his enforced isolation, unless calling himself Benedictus rather than Baruch counts as such a display.

Spinoza might reasonably be compared with Epicurus or Epictetus in seeking to live according to the philosophy he espoused. He is widely admired, not just for having the courage of his convictions, but for the liberal character of the ethical and political positions he chose to defend. His arguments are written in the style of geometric proofs, but no mathematician would find them even remotely acceptable. However, they ring with integrity. Nothing is going to prevent his writing down for all to see what he believes to be true. I am with him all the way with his denial

© The Editor(s) (if applicable) and The Author(s), under exclusive license to Springer Nature Switzerland AG 2021
K. Binmore, *Imaginary Philosophical Dialogues*,
https://doi.org/10.1007/978-3-030-65387-3_14

of free will as a personal unmoved mover within our heads, and for this reason I have made free will the subject of his imaginary dialogue with Leibniz. On the other hand, Spinoza's notion that God can usefully be identified with Nature seems to me just the usual metaphysical juggling with words. It is easy to understand why he was treated as an atheist—albeit an exotic atheist of the jewish persuasion.

Both Spinoza and Leibniz count as rationalists in the philosophical sense, since neither thought that it was necessary to examine any empirical evidence before forming an opinion. However, in both cases, some qualification is required. Spinoza thought he had knowledge-as-certainty of his axioms. When challenged, he quoted Descartes, saying his knowledge was no different from knowing that the angles of a triangle sum to two right angles. But he has to be respected for distilling his own wisdom from the air, rather than allowing himself to be conditioned by whatever views it was conventional to hold at the time.

On the other hand, I suspect Leibniz thought that all knowledge is knowledge-as-commitment—but was too intelligent to commit himself to any particular set of axioms. So he explored the implications of many possibilities. His never-to-be-sated need for public recognition then led him to publish only those philosophical explorations that he thought would be likely to be well received. The idea commonly touted that he was committed to a private philosophy that he kept secret from the world seems much too harsh a judgement. He was certainly capable of a good deal of dishonesty, but I doubt whether he was genuinely committed to any philosophical beliefs at all.

Leibniz (1646–1716) was a polymath who could not help but enlighten any subject to which he gave his attention. His childhood as the son of a professor of moral philosophy in Leipzig favored his innate talent, but he wanted more than an academic career. His ambition was to shine in polite society. He found a position with the Elector of Mainz, who sent him on a diplomatic mission to France, where he luxuriated in the company of the Parisian intellectual elite, notably Christiaan Huygens. He was particularly influenced by Pascal, whom he credited with inspiring his invention of the calculus. I do not understand why so much fuss is made about whether Leibniz or Newton deserves the primary credit for the invention of the calculus. Surely there is enough credit to go around that even Fermat might be mentioned for his pioneering contributions to the differential calculus, and Eudoxus for his to the integral calculus. In any case, after Leibniz lost his position in Mainz after the death of his employer, he obtained another position as librarian to the Duke of Hanover. He must have been deeply distressed when his ill-tempered dispute with Isaac Newton was cited as the reason that he was left behind in Hanover when the Duke succeeded to the English throne as George I.

Leibniz made major contributions, not only to mathematics, but to logic as well. He invented a major improvement of Pascal's calculating machine, and toyed with the idea that one day philosophical disputes would be resolved simply by turning the handle on a suitably designed machine of this kind—which reflects his playing with the idea that everything we know about the world really just consists of logical deductions from how things are defined. His exposition of the various arguments for the existence of God are thought to have never been bettered. His metaphysical system is less widely admired. It mimics the atomic theory that was becoming popular among physicists of his time, but replaces atoms by "windowless" monads that nevertheless "mirror" the universe in some transcendental manner that I do not understand.

Two comments from Bertrand Russell will perhaps serve to capture the range of Leibniz's contributions to scholarship—from the sublime to the arguably ridiculous. Of his notes on mathematical logic, Russell says that had they been published, they would have advanced the subject by a century and a half. Of his *Monadology*, Russell says that it is just a fantastic fairy tale. Voltaire is even more scathing of Leibniz's promoting the notion that God created the best of all possible worlds. His *Candide* famously casts Leibniz as Dr Pangloss, who never fails to look on the bright side as disaster after disaster brings the world down around his ears. But in contemplating this public relations disaster, we must remember that it was Leibniz who first had the idea of identifying necessity as truth in all possible worlds.

I follow Matthew Stewart in setting the 1676 meeting between Spinoza and Leibniz in Spinoza's bedroom-cum-workshop, which he rented from a congenial family with whom he also socialized occasionally. Although Spinoza was only in his forties, he was to die a few months later. However, he had all the maturity of a much older man. Leibniz was just entering his thirties, but arguably never reached maturity at all. Leibniz's own notes of the meeting have them discussing ethics, physics, and the ontological argument for the existence of God, but in the imaginary dialogue that follows, they discuss the idea of free will that Spinoza famously thought an illusion. They do not ask why the ancients never discussed free will at all. They probably would have had no better idea than scholars today.

In the dialogue, both Leibniz and Spinoza's remarks are abbreviated by allowing them to speak of *models*, although this is a modern term. In earlier dialogues, there is similarly occasional mention of *possible worlds*, although the introduction of this useful term is usually attributed to Leibniz.

Dialogue

Leibniz has arranged through an intermediary to meet Spinoza in his lodgings. He feels brave to risk his reputation in associating with a notorious atheist, and he was to keep their meeting quiet in later life. However, he decides that he cannot pass up the opportunity of trying out his ideas on the up-to-the-minute philosopher currently regarded as the bearer of the torch of the enlightenment lit by Descartes. He had been told that Spinoza lived a very austere life, and so had dressed down for the occasion, but the children of the family with whom Spinoza lodges still stare wide-eyed at his fancy wig. One can only guess what they would have made of the magnificent wig that he famously wore for grand occasions. He is shown into Spinoza's workshop, where Spinoza leaves off polishing a lens, and greets him with grave respect. After the necessary exchange of compliments, and some discussion of the traditional arguments for the existence of God in which Spinoza shows little interest, Leibniz raises the question of free will.

LEIBNIZ: May we turn to the question of free will? Do you still deny that our wills are free—that we suppose otherwise only because we observe our thoughts or actions, but not how our minds come to think those thoughts or perform those actions?

SPINOZA: We must distinguish between positive and negative freedom. I certainly do not deny the negative notion according to which it makes sense to model people as being free to act or think as they choose provided that nothing external to them constrains their choice. It is in this sense that I argue that he alone is free who lives with free consent under the entire guidance of reason. But I deny the positive notion that postulates the existence of an unmoved mover within our heads. I hold that this idea is not so much wrong as incoherent.

LEIBNIZ: You are regarded by the world as Descartes' torchbearer, but you would seem not to share his dualism between the world of the spirit and the world of the body.

SPINOZA: It is true that I am an admirer of Descartes, but one cannot be led by Descartes without being willing to do all one's thinking for oneself rather than simply following whatever the intellectual fashion may be. I cannot follow him in separating the mind from the body. His speculation that we have a soul that somehow controls our body through the pineal gland in our brains is not even remotely convincing. I think he is right in arguing that animals are automata, but they are not *mere* automata, because we are automata too.

LEIBNIZ: This view follows from your contention that the universe is determinate? That time is an illusion—that everything just is how it is—that even God did not exercise free will in creating the universe?

SPINOZA: In my philosophy, God *is* the Universe. We are certainly free to model Him as creating the world in which we live because there is nothing outside the Universe to constrain Him. But it is not a useful way to channel our thoughts, because there is no point in saying that the Universe created itself. The Universe simply *is*.

LEIBNIZ: But your work on an enlightened system of ethics is celebrated! How can it make sense to write on ethics if our behavior is already determined?

SPINOZA: One might similarly ask why Pascal proved his celebrated theorem in the tradition of the great Euclid when the outcome of his researches was already preordained! Pascal's theorem is now part of our knowledge base because Pascal proved it. It is part of the way the Universe is put together that we cannot know Pascal's theorem without its having been proved.

LEIBNIZ: This observation moves me to try out my own attempt to resolve the mind-body problem created by Descartes. I agree that his attempt to implicate the pineal gland lacks conviction. But one cannot deny his contention that we only have direct knowledge of what passes in our minds. Only the world of the mind is therefore real to us. The material world is just a model that we use in attempting to make sense of our thoughts. How do we explain how our thoughts control our interventions into this material world? I contend that we need no such explanation. We model events in the material world so that they run parallel to the thoughts in

Leibniz versus Spinoza 73

our minds. Similarly, two pendulums may swing in unison although neither causes the motion of the other.

SPINOZA: I contend that only one world exists. Your argument concedes existence only to a world of the spirit, which view you defend on empirical grounds. I think we have no need to appeal to the illusions of the senses when the propositions from which we reason are as self-evident as the fact that the angles in a triangle sum to two right angles. But I am curious. Does your belief make you a solipsist, conceding existence only to your own spirit?

LEIBNIZ: I am a young man who has yet to commit himself to any particular philosophical system. I find that my mind explores the implications of different assumptions whether I like it or not. It is for this reason that I take delight in being in the company of someone who is fearless in expressing the conclusions to which his reason leads him.

SPINOZA: Perhaps I would be less fearless if I were not a citizen of the tolerant Dutch Republic, in which bookshops abound that sell works promoting all kinds of opinion. Perhaps indeed this is why you are here yourself. May I ask what varieties of opinion you are currently turning over in your mind?

LEIBNIZ: Let me begin with one thought that is perhaps closest to your own position. I have been fascinated by the logic of Aristotle ever since my youth, and I hope I will eventually be recognized as having improved on his system. In studying syllogisms, it is inevitable that one ask the metaphysical question: Are all true propositions really analytic—is the predicate already contained in the subject when the subject is defined in full detail? It seems to be a contingent fact that Socrates happened to debate with Protagoras, but perhaps the definition of Socrates should include all the events of his life, including the fact that he debated with Protagoras. A true model of the world would then just consist of a static list of the definitions of the entities it contains and whatever can be deduced from them by logic.

SPINOZA: One would have to ensure that the definitions were consistent with each other.

LEIBNIZ: Absolutely! Indeed, one might perhaps hope to put together a system based only on a logical Principle of No Contradiction and a metaphysical Principle of Sufficient Reason—that nothing exists without a reason.

SPINOZA: Would not your Principle of Sufficient Reason follow from your Principle of No Contradiction? If there were a truth that had no reason, there would be a proposition whose subject did not contain a predicate to which it was attached.

LEIBNIZ: Just so! However, I see little prospect of gaining acceptance of such a bleak view of the world.

SPINOZA: This is what is said of my system, but I see no reason why it should be said to be bleak when it simply says that things are the way they are. But what other views are you considering that you feel are more likely to gain acceptance?

LEIBNIZ: I have hopes of my solution to the Problem of Evil. Why did God create a world in which evil flourishes? Since God is both omnipotent and infinitely benevolent, logic demands that He created the best of all possible worlds. He could have created a world without evil, but such a world would not be optimal because, without the freedom to choose evil, we would be lesser beings. I have not forgotten that you hold that free will is an illusion, but people in general regard the freedom of their will as the most solid fact of their experience.

SPINOZA: And what of the suffering caused by famines, plagues, and other natural disasters? A skeptic might even make an argument that we live in the worst of all possible worlds!

LEIBNIZ: It is a poor answer I know, but all that can be said is that we poor mortals cannot hope to fathom the mind of God.

SPINOZA: How do you reconcile the various philosophical systems that you seem unwilling to choose between? Are you not troubled by their leading to inconsistent conclusions?

LEIBNIZ: Contradictions are anathema in logic, but logic has no role to play in choosing what assumptions we should treat as axiomatic. We do not need to treat philosophical systems as dogma. They can simply be regarded as different models of the world that may be useful in different contexts. For example, we nowadays think that matter consists of atoms flying around in a void, but it does not follow that we should abandon the idea that tables are solid. Similarly, free will may be an illusion, but predicting people's behavior on the assumption that free will is real works out well in practice.

SPINOZA: You now sound as though you are as extreme an empiricist as Epicurus! Such a Protean attitude is alien to me. How would you know how to live your own life if you had no solid principles on which to rely?

LEIBNIZ: I confess that I do not know how best to live my own life. I imagine that all philosophers agree with Socrates that the unexamined life is not worth living, but when I examine myself I do not find the certitude with which you are gifted.

SPINOZA: Am I gifted with certitude, or do I merely maintain my ascetic life-style from habit? But it grows late, and perhaps we should postpone further discussion until tomorrow now that we have started to question our own place in the universe.

So they break off to continue their dialogue the next day, although they never paint their views with such a broad brush again. When they finally part, Leibniz has learned a lot of philosophy, but not why Spinoza is held in such deep affection by those who know him well. Leibniz is fated only ever to have acquaintances and never friends. Perhaps he recognizes that people do not like being used as means rather then ends, but finds himself unable to do anything about his own need to get ahead.

Afterword

Why is there something, and not nothing? Leibniz was perhaps the first to formulate this most basic of philosophical questions explicitly. It is not mentioned in his dialogue with Spinoza. but it is addressed later in an imaginary dialogue between Popper and Wittgenstein. What a pity that they fail to come up with an answer!

The fact that logic allows anything whatever to be deduced from a contradiction is mentioned several times more in the coming dialogues. The trivial proof goes like this. Assume both *X* and *not X*. From *X* follows *X or Y*, where *Y* can be anything. But *X or Y* and *not X* implies *Y*.

Chapter 15
David Hume versus Jean-Jacques Rousseau

Context

Hume and Rousseau most certainly met. In fact, their meeting became a sensation in philosophical circles after Rousseau accused Hume of black treachery, and Hume—who was guilty at worst of participating in some horseplay involving a spoof letter from Frederick the Great—responded in an undignified way. However, their imaginary dialogue occurs some time before all this unpleasantness. It takes place in a cabin on a cross-channel ferry that Hume and Rousseau shared after Hume undertook to look after Rousseau in England, where Rousseau had eventually decided to live after being exiled from France.

Hume (1711–1776) is the leading light of empiricism. In searching his own mind for an ego, he found only a fleeting nest of perceptions. Where, he asked, is the "I" that Descartes took so confidently for granted? His skepticism about causality and the principle of scientific induction were less shocking, but still very hard for traditionalists to swallow. Even the empiricism of Locke was a target. How could experience write on the blank slate of the mind, if there were nothing already there with which to write?

Hume was born the younger son of a decayed family of minor Scottish gentlefolk, and so had to make his own way in the world. He did so by living in penury while developing his philosophical ideas, which he naively thought would bring him wealth and fame when eventually published as the *Treatise on Human Nature*. But the book famously fell "dead-born from the press". He rescued himself financially by writing a history of England that proved very popular. But he was eventually vindicated, becoming a philosophical hero of the Scottish Enlightenment. While working at the British embassy in Paris, he was lauded by the French intellectual elite, which must have been good for his self-esteem. But he was never offered a Chair in Scotland because of his suspected atheism.

Rousseau (1712–1778) is one of the most influential philosophical writers ever, although Bertrand Russell asks whether he can be considered a philosopher at all. Rousseau not only wrote his *Inequality of Man* and *Social Contract* that led to his being exiled in the long run-up to the French Revolution; his novel *The New Héloise* was a huge success, and his play *Pygmalion* was widely admired. His opera is now largely forgotten, but it seemed pretty good to me when I heard a recording. In fact, the initiative he gave to the Romantic movement that brought the Enlightenment to an end is sometimes said to be more important than his propaganda for a new social contract famously characterized by the slogan, "Man is born free, but he is everywhere in chains".

Rousseau's eventual falling out with Hume was only one of a whole series of enmities he provoked with other intellectuals of his time. Voltaire responded with pure venom. Rousseau's behavior led Diderot and the other Encyclopedists to sever relations with him. His *Confessions* are hard to believe—can he really have abandoned his five new-born babies one-by-one to almost certain death on the steps of an orphanage? He was clearly the victim of a mental health problem, but to me it sounds less like the paranoid schizophrenia with which he is usually diagnosed than some kind of bipolar disorder.

To keep the debate between Hume and Rousseau within reasonable bounds, I have restricted their discussion to an analysis of Rousseau's fable of a stag hunt that raises the question of how and why people trust each other. Rousseau is impatient with what he sees as Hume's pettifogging criticism of his logic. Nor does he care for Hume's attempts to rescue his analysis, which he does not see requires any rescuing at all.

The real Hume would not have expressed his ideas in terms of a social contract, which he interpreted as implying that we have an obligation to honor an agreement reached in some ancient conclave. Nor would he have spoken of an equilibrium—a word he never uses in his own writings, although his examples show that he understood the concept perfectly well. Rousseau similarly left formulating the categorical imperative to Immanuel Kant.

Dialogue

It is an unusually fine day for the English channel, but when the wind blows up a little, Hume and Rousseau retire below to their cabin to talk philosophy. They have already discussed how Hume can help Rousseau be reasonably comfortable in his exile from France. Rousseau has refused Hume's selfless offer to lodge him in his own house in Edinburgh, preferring to take rooms in London, although he will eventually opt to live in the country. Hume will find suitable lodgings for Rousseau, and seek a pension from the king to support him financially. At this time, they are on the best of terms, although Rousseau is later to claim that he heard Hume gleefully exclaim on the voyage that now he had Rousseau in his power! Hume should have listened to the warning he received from the Baron d'Holbach the night before they set sail that he was warming a viper in his bosom.

HUME: In your great *Social Contract,* you begin by saying that you plan to "unite what right sanctions with what is prescribed by interest, in order that justice and utility may in no case be divided". I share your aspirations in this regard, but have difficulties in seeing my way through particular cases. The fable of a stag hunt from your *Inequality of Man* provides a stereotypical case study of how people need to trust each other if they are to reap the rewards of cooperation. I hope you are not too tired to discuss the logic of this example.

ROUSSEAU: I am always tired, but one must keep going nevertheless. As I recall, my story of a stag hunt envisages a number of men who promise each other to cooperate in an uncertain attempt to hunt a stag. They separate to put their plan into action, but each may be tempted to abandon the joint enterprise if he happens to see a hare that he can hunt alone. If he yields to temptation, the stag hunt is even more likely to fail without his participation.

HUME: We are to assume no doubt that the individual reward a defector anticipates from pursuing a hare exceeds his expectation from continuing with the hunt—whatever strategies may be pursued by his companions.

ROUSSEAU: Certainly! Otherwise the issue of trusting others to honor their promises would not arise.

HUME: Are justice and utility not then divided? Justice demands that you honor your promise to your companions, but your expected utility is increased by abandoning the stag hunt if you spot a hare. It is certainly immoral to let your companions down, but is it irrational?

ROUSSEAU: It is rational to bend your individual will to the General Will—which is not at all the same thing as the Will of All, but is known only to those of sublime wisdom.

HUME: To submit to the rule of a philosopher-king?

ROUSSEAU: But not a philosopher-king as described in Plato's *Republic.* With the flowering of the Enlightenment, we can hope to design a society on firmer foundations. The keeping of promises will naturally be one of its foundational principles.

HUME: Here you could quote Spinoza as an authority: "What if a man could save himself from the present danger of death by treachery? If reason should recommend that it would recommend it to all men."

ROUSSEAU: Spinoza is too cold a fish for a hot-blooded advocate of revolution like myself! But he is right about what Reason recommends.

HUME: But what of people who do not share your vision of the nature of Reason?

ROUSSEAU: It is only through the corruption of man that we need to ask such questions. In the utopian society I envisage, children will be raised to be as free of evil as a noble savage in the original state of nature.

HUME: I have a suggestion that might help to bridge the gap between the utopian society at which you aim and our current corrupt society, in which people so often lie and cheat without scruple. If we restrict the class of social contracts we consider to those that are in equilibrium, no conflict between justice and utility will arise. It is true that even the best equilibria will not be utopian, but they can be improvements on what we endure at present.

ROUSSEAU: What do you mean by an equilibrium?

HUME: In an equilibrium, no person can improve their individual utility by unilaterally deviating from whatever conventions the current social contract prescribes.

ROUSSEAU: But this is a recipe for pure selfishness! In the fable of the stag hunt, everybody can improve their utility by breaking their promise if they see a hare.

HUME: The idea is to use the selfishness of uneducated folk to sustain a social contract—much as a masonry arch is held aloft by the weight of the stones pressing against each other as they each seek individually to fall to the ground. To quote myself: Two men, who pull the oars of a boat, do it by an agreement or convention, though they have never given promises to each other. Each is then doing the best he can for himself, given the behavior of the other.

ROUSSEAU: But then it will not be in equilibrium for people to keep their promises.

HUME: It is true that the idea of an equilibrium is of no help in your fable of the stag hunt, as it takes no account of the future, but if the hunters are to interact in the future, each will need to take account of their reputation for honest dealing. Who will believe someone promising to cooperate in a joint enterprise who has betrayed his partners in the past? You can perhaps gain more utility today by cheating your companions, but you will thereby lose all the utility you would have acquired in the future from being able to participate in cooperative enterprises.

ROUSSEAU: Your argument is reminiscent of Hobbes. Do you also see the world as a war of all against all?

HUME: I am not a Tory! I am only said to be so because I once remarked that it is possible to shed a tear for the beheaded King Charles I. As for Hobbes, I think his parable of how civil societies originated is implausible. Nor do I accept that there is only an authoritarian alternative to whatever the true state of nature may have been. There are many equilibria that would be improvements on our current social contract. We do not need to be bound by chains to get along together better than we do. Nor do we need to change ourselves into saints. But you and I agree that we need the help of enlightened philosophers to teach us how to coordinate on equilibria that will improve all our lives.

ROUSSEAU: Your lack of ambition is very British! In France, we look for greater things. Rationality is not just a matter of grubbing after your personal welfare. It is irrational to pursue a course of action that would bring down society if everybody were to act that way. We need philosophers of sublime wisdom not just to help us decide whether one money-grubbing scheme is less bad than another, but to teach us how to reason properly.

Hume sees that further discussion is likely to become heated, and so proposes that they prepare for bed. He certainly thinks it wise to keep to himself that his own fable that philosophers call the farmer's dilemma anticipates the point Rousseau is making with his story of a stag hunt by some years. Rousseau is only too pleased to agree to retire, since the motion of the boat is making him feel uneasy. But he is less pleased that Hume should have proved not to be an altogether admiring disciple—perhaps the first sign of a breach that will eventually widen into a public slanging match.

Afterword

Nowadays, the differences between Hume and Rousseau revealed in the dialogue would be expressed in terms of game theory. Rousseau would be said to be claiming that it is rational to cooperate in the one-shot Prisoners' Dilemma—discussed later in the dialogue between Nozick and Lewis—and Hume would respond that such behavior is not a Nash equilibrium. To locate an equilibrium in which people cooperate efficiently, it is necessary to move to the indefinitely repeated Prisoners' Dilemma.

Modern philosophers may dislike my implicit identification of Rousseau's story with the Prisoners' Dilemma because the philosopher David Lewis identified it with what is nowadays called the Stag Hunt Game. As explained in Brian Skyrms' *The Stag Hunt and the Evolution of Social Structure,* Lewis's simple game has two pure Nash equilibria, a good one and a bad one. Rousseau can then be treated as though advocating that we move from the bad equilibrium to the good one—which is really Hume's story, shorn of the necessity to consider the repeated case. But Hume only had Rousseau's original story to consider, which is shown to be equivalent to the Prisoner's Dilemma in a numerical example used in my own *Game Theory and the Social Contract I* (page 122).

Chapter 16
Immanuel Kant versus Adam Smith

Context

Immanuel Kant is commonly said to be the greatest philosopher ever, having supposedly rescued rationalism from an empiricist assault reaching its peak in the work of David Hume. Kant was certainly inspired by Hume, whom he credited with waking him from his "dogmatic slumber", but it stretches the imagination too far to suppose that an elderly and ailing Hume would have somehow found his way to the Prussian city of Königsberg long before Kant's philosophical ideas had been acclaimed as the culmination of the Enlightenment. However, as a fellow Scot, Hume acted as mentor to Adam Smith, both in economics and in philosophy. It is still a very considerable stretch to get Adam Smith to Königsberg (modern Kaliningrad), but perhaps not such a stretch as getting St Augustine to Alexandria while the western Roman Empire was collapsing around his ears.

Kant (1724–1804) was apparently seriously obsessive. People are said to have set their watches by the time he passed their houses in his daily walk through Königsberg, whose environs he never left. The one time he planned a trip of any consequence, he supposedly stopped the departing coach on the outskirts of the city, and went home. However, he is said to have been congenial company, and he was certainly imbued with the kind of enlightenment values that we continue to prize today. Even if he were not a great philosopher, he would be remembered with Laplace for originating the Nebula Hypothesis—that planets, stars, and galaxies are formed by gravitational accretion from clouds of gas and dust.

Kant is essential in this collection of imaginary dialogues because he made the idea of what he called a *synthetic a priori* respectable to erstwhile empiricists. This is a contingent proposition—one that might be false—which we nevertheless know to be true without needing any evidence. His leading example is Euclidean geometry, which we now know to be false of real space. However, in their imaginary dialogue, Smith and Kant continue the discussion of the earlier dialogue between Hume and Rousseau. Smith explores Kant's use of his categorical imperative to defend Rousseau's analysis of his fable of the stag hunt. Kant responds with an abbreviation of the justification of the categorical imperative given in his *Groundwork of the Metaphysic of Morals*. If you think I have abbreviated the sense out of the argument, I recommend reading the original, which is only a few pages long in Paton's excellent English translation.

Adam Smith (1723?–1790) is famous as the father of modern economics, but his book *Wealth of Nations* is more than a narrow text on economic theory, and not at all incompatible with his earlier book on how morality works—in spite of his having been made into a libertarian icon by people who seem never to have read his work. David Hume urged him not to acknowledge their close association lest he too be denied a Scottish Chair on suspicion of atheism, but Smith was fulsome in his praise after Hume's death.

It is no fiction that Smith abandoned his Chair in Glasgow to accompany the young Duke of Buccleuch on a grand tour of Europe that included a visit to Voltaire in Geneva. But I have imagined a (very long) side-trip to Königsberg that Buccleuch proposes after listening to Voltaire read an invented passage from one of the letters actually written to him by Frederick the Great of Prussia—who fancied himself a pillar of the Enlightenment as well as a military genius.

It is necessary to apologize in advance for having Kant speak of a stimulus-response machine and Smith of a robot, but the alternative circumlocutions would have been too lengthy.

Dialogue

Voltaire has mixed feelings about the young aristocrats and their tutors who nowadays seem to regard his receiving room in Geneva as one of the sights in their Grand Tour of Europe. He would be unhappy to be forgotten, but their foppery can be very tiresome. However, the Duke of Buccleuch is a serious young man, and his tutor Adam Smith is a regular philosopher, so Voltaire reads them some passages from his correspondence with Frederick the Great, of which he is very proud. One passage refers to an obscure Prussian philosopher called Immanuel Kant, whom Frederick has had to ask to suppress further publications, as his enlightened views cause inconvenient rumblings in conservative circles.

Buccleuch is fired up with the idea of visiting the court of this modern philosopher-king, and then continuing from Berlin to Königsberg to meet Kant. Adam Smith had no idea of the enormity of this project, or he would perhaps have wriggled out somehow. But they eventually find themselves being entertained to tea in Kant's parlor, although Buccleuch is somewhat subdued, having been treated with minimal courtesy in Berlin, and not being accustomed to the quiet domesticity of Kant's bachelor household. They speak in French—the lingua franca of the day. However, I pretend that Kant is considerably less obscure in French than in his native German.

KANT: I hope you will excuse the clumsiness of my servant, who is not used to aristocratic company. For my part, I am overwhelmed to be visited by two such distinguished philosophers of the Scottish Enlightenment, especially since I am proud of my Scottish descent through Hans Kant, who was my father's father.

BUCCLEUCH: We were recommended to you in Geneva by François-Marie Arouet—who calls himself Voltaire. He reports that you have been greatly influenced by David Hume, who mentored my tutor in his younger days.

KANT: I am surprised that the celebrated Voltaire should know of my existence. However, it is correct that Hume awakened me from my philosophical slumbers, in which I saw no further than tradition permitted. However, you may not approve of the way in which I am going about reconciling what can be rescued of rationalism from the wreck of the empiricist storm whipped up by the British empiricists.

BUCCLEUCH: We were told in Berlin that your written works have been suppressed.

KANT: An exaggeration! King Frederick—rightfully called the Great—has asked me to censor myself for a while. The wounds left by the Teutonic Crusades against the pagan Lithuanian tribes are still raw in places. It is therefore not always politic to offer criticism of what is sometimes naively regarded as Catholic orthodoxy.

BUCCLEUCH: In Scotland, it is the Calvinist orthodoxy that hampers the advance of science. Our mentor, David Hume, is denied a University Chair because his enlightened views are thought to be tainted with atheism.

KANT: Alas that toleration should be so rare! However, I am no atheist, although I deny the validity of the arguments for the existence of God given by St Thomas Aquinas and others. If the goal of humanity is to achieve perfect happiness, an afterlife must exist. Without God, this would not be possible.

SMITH: Perhaps we could discuss your general approach to both philosophy and theology as you have leisure in the coming week. While on our way from Berlin to Königsberg, his Grace and I have been discussing Jean-Jacques Rousseau's fable of the stag hunt from his *Discourse on Inequality*. In the hour or so that remains of daylight, perhaps we could hear your view of Hume's criticism of Rousseau's analysis.

KANT: It will be a great pleasure to comment on Rousseau, whom I regard as the Isaac Newton of the moral world. It seems to me that my notion of the categorical imperative bears directly on the issue—categorical in the sense that it must be obeyed whatever a person's preferences or beliefs may be in the circumstances in which they find themselves.

SMITH: So Voltaire was correct in reporting that you are a determined deontologist—that you have broken free of the utilitarian notion that the morality of an action is to be judged by its consequences. Do you really hold that I cannot count an action as moral if I want to do it? Even if I want to do it to promote the public good?

KANT: I do indeed! But I am anxious to return to Rousseau's stag hunt problem. Can you remind me of how it goes?

BUCCLEUCH: Some men are engaged in a cooperative hunt for a stag that is likely to fail even if pursued wholeheartedly by all. If one man sees the opportunity to abandon the stag hunt in favor of a more profitable hunt for a hare, is it rational for him to do so?

KANT: A parable for the cohesion of societies! My categorical imperative prescribes optimal social behavior for such social situations unconditionally: Act only on the maxim that you would will to be a universal law. In Rousseau's case, the issue is whether to keep your promise to cooperate in hunting the stag. But if the maxim of breaking your promises were made into a universal law, it would destroy the institution of making promises. The same goes for lying.

SMITH: Hume says to the contrary: Surely I am not bound to keep my word because I have given my word to keep it. Would he be persuaded by your argument? I think his innate skepticism would lead him to question both the basis on which you advance your categorical imperative, and the maxim you use to challenge the rationality of breaking promises or telling lies. But perhaps I am wrong in assuming that you defend your categorical imperative as a principle of rationality rather than morality?

KANT: You are not wrong. Rationality implies the categorical imperative from which moral principles are deduced. The categorical imperative explains Rousseau's General Will, which he explains is not the Will of All, but is known only to those of sublime wisdom.

BUCCLEUCH: We Scots like to keep our feet on the ground! The negation of always keeping your promises is not *always* breaking your promises, which would certainly make the institution of making promises impossible. We need to consider the maxim of *sometimes* breaking a promise—breaking promises or telling lies when it suits you. But this is what happens now, and the institution of making promises survives. We do not need sublime wisdom to see our way through this logic!

KANT: But the only *categorical* alternative to always keeping your promises is indeed never keeping your promises.

Buccleuch obviously thinks this answer is ridiculous, and is about to persist with his objection, but Smith intervenes. Having suffered so much in coming so far, Smith is anxious that the meeting not now break up in an unproductive squabble. So he seeks to pour oil on the troubled waters, although it means breaching his usual respectful behavior towards his employer.

SMITH: Let us leave these very general considerations for another time. It seems to me that if Herr Kant's categorical imperative were valid, it would indeed solve situations like the fable of the stag hunt in which there are strategies that would profit each person individually, but would be bad for everybody if everybody were to follow them. Perhaps Herr Kant would be kind enough to explain the reasoning that leads to his categorical imperative.

KANT: Why has Nature equipped us with reason in the first place? It cannot be to promote our happiness, because this aim would have been better achieved by making us into stimulus-response machines programmed with an optimal response for each possible stimulus.

SMITH: Nature here is synonymous with God? If so, I suppose the complexity of the task of constructing such an optimal stimulus-response machine would count as nothing in the face of His almighty power. But would such a robot have a soul?

KANT: The true function of our reason must therefore be to produce a will which is good, not as a means to some end, but in itself.

SMITH: It seems to me that to make something good is in fact to operate towards some end: the end of being good. But proceed—we can clarify my difficulties later.

KANT: A good will entails a duty to act out of reverence for the laws a person makes for himself.

SMITH: So God endows us with the power of reason so that we can both choose for ourselves the personal laws we live by, and commit ourselves to honor those laws?

KANT: Precisely. No ingenuity is then necessary to deduce what rationality now prescribes. In choosing what strategy to follow, rational beings need only ask themselves if it would be a good idea if everybody else were to follow it too. If not, throw it out.

SMITH: My own ingenuity is inadequate to make this last step at the moment. Perhaps we might break off now, and resume tomorrow afternoon if you are free. In the interim, I will ponder the issues you have raised, and perhaps resolve the doubts with which I am currently plagued. I hope you will forgive the skepticism with which his Grace and I have been imbued by David Hume. Even in his old age, he would certainly not forgive me if I were to return to Scotland without having a thorough command of your principles.

KANT: Gentlemen, I can be at your disposal from an hour after noon. It is such a pleasure to have enlightened company, that I shall dispense with my afternoon walk through the town that the burghers joke is so regular that a person can set his watch by the time I turn each corner.

After leaving for their lodgings, Smith is at some pains to pacify Buccleuch, who is still hot under the collar at his logical difference with Kant being talked over. However, he is unable to persuade Buccleuch to return for more discussion the next day, when Kant will explain why his categorical imperative implies the existence of Free Will to an Adam Smith who remains quietly polite but profoundly skeptical.

Buccleuch finds his way instead to the harbor, where he meets an English merchant Joseph Green, to whom he has been recommended by Kant before their philosophical discussion began. Green shows him Königsberg's famous seven bridges, and they consider together possible solutions to the famous problem of whether they can all be crossed without ever retracing your steps.

Green helps Buccleuch book a passage for Smith and himself to Copenhagen a few days hence. Once on the boat carrying them away from Königsberg, they agree that Joseph Green talked more sense than Immanuel Kant, utterly unaware that

Kant was shortly to become—not only the philosophical hero of the Enlightenment—but the most admired philosopher of all time.

Afterword

Two rivers join in Königsberg with an island at their confluence. The seven bridges linked the various pieces of dry land separated by the rivers. The mathematician Leonhard Euler proved that the Königsberg bridge problem has no solution—there is no way to cross all seven bridges without retracing your steps. This result is celebrated as the origin of the mathematical discipline of graph theory.

Chapter 17
Edmund Burke versus Thomas Paine

Context

The American War of Independence and the subsequent French Revolution form the background to an imaginary dialogue between Tom Paine and Edmund Burke. They exchanged inflammatory books and pamphlets that were lapped up by the general public of three nations, but it seems that they never met. Some creativity is therefore necessary to get them together, but the story that locates them both at a dinner hosted by William Godwin in 1791 is more plausible than the stories invented to justify several of the earlier dialogues.

Edmund Burke (1729–1797) was born in Dublin to a prosperous middle-class family. Although raised as a Protestant, he was gifted with the classical silver tongue of the Irish. His eloquence made him hugely influential after being elected to the English parliament, where he became a leading light of the Whig party, which was founded to maintain what was seen as the Lockean social contract established by the Glorious Revolution of 1688. As for his intellect, it is worth quoting Adam Smith: "Mr Burke is the only man I ever knew who thinks on economic subjects exactly as I do, without any previous communication having passed between us."

Burke's 1774 speech to the electors of Bristol continues to be quoted today in opposition to the modern enthusiasm for referenda and the like. It argues that members of parliament should be regarded as representatives, who make their own minds up about how to vote on specific issues, rather than as delegates, who do no more than vote according to the prejudices of those who elected them. One might see his differences with Paine as centering around this very issue. What constitution is to be preferred: direct or representative democracy? Or to step back for a longer view, Burke might be said to embody the *nomos* philosophical tradition. He would probably have been happy to be regarded as an empiricist, following in the footsteps of Locke. Paine can then be identified with the *physis* tradition as a consequence of the rationalism implicit in the standard revolutionary view that the right way forward is self-evident.

Burke argued unsuccessfully for the demands of the American colonists that they should not be taxed without representation, but he was implacably hostile to the philosophy championed by Rousseau that motivated the movers and shakers behind the French Revolution. His 1790 *Reflections on the Revolution in France* argues that it is absurdly naive to suppose that conventions established by many years of political evolution can be junked in favor of a newly invented "rational" constitution without risking war and military dictatorship. Nowadays, Burke is often said to be the father of modern conservatism for his view that the rational way forward lies in incremental reform of the traditions of the past rather than some leap in the dark to a wholly new type of social organization.

Thomas Paine (1737–1809) was born of humble parents in England. He was not very successful in pursuing various ways of making a living, but certainly got around a good deal. He knew Benjamin Franklin for example, who suggested that he move to Philadelphia to make a new start after the early death of his young wife. The magazine he started in Philadelphia did well enough that he was encouraged to write pamphlets supporting the cause of American independence, of which *Common Sense* became particularly influential—not only in the thirteen colonies, but also among revolutionary thinkers in England and France. He spent the rest of his very eventful life exploiting the hero status he enjoyed as a consequence of being regarded as one of the founders of the American Republic.

After his visit to London in 1791, he moved on to Paris where he was elected to the French National Convention in spite of speaking little French. But when the Jacobins came to power, he was imprisoned for more than a year, and narrowly escaped execution. The story goes that the chalk mark on the cell door of someone to be guillotined on a particular day was mistakenly marked on the inside of his door, which happened to be open while he received official visitors. So he survived until the death of Robespierre a few days later, after which his life was safe until his release was secured by James Monroe, the future US president.

He remained in France until personally requested by President Jefferson to return to the USA. He could not return to England, where he had been convicted of treason in his absence. He was certainly guilty of treason! He even published plans to invade England that he had drawn up with Napoleon Bonaparte when the latter was a revolutionary general. However, the particular offence of which he was convicted was the publication of his *Rights of Man*, which provides the occasion for our imaginary dialogue.

Paine eventually retired to a farm in New Jersey which had been gifted to him by the American government as a reward for his role in generating enthusiasm for American independence. He died lonely and neglected as a result of his public ridicule of orthodox Christianity after being converted from his native Puritanism to some kind of deism.

Burke and Paine were certainly both in London in 1791. The British government had yet to convict Paine of treason, and so he was safe from arrest. It is therefore plausible that he would have accepted a dinner invitation from William Godwin, who is still remembered as a utilitarian anarchist. It is much less plausible that Burke would have accepted an invitation from Godwin. Burke had been a leading light of the Whig party, which he was now in the process of splitting over the very issue that Godwin wanted him to discuss with Paine. So it is necessary to suspend disbelief in imagining Burke and Paine dining together at Godwin's not entirely respectable table. However, we have no reason to suppose that either would have lost their cool if confronted with each other.

William Godwin is of some interest himself as an early utilitarian. He is remembered best for asking who you should save from a burning room if only one person can be saved, when the choice is between the enlightened Archbishop Fénelon, and a common chambermaid—if the chambermaid happens to be your mother. He succeeded in reconciling his utilitarian aspirations with his anarchic instincts by arguing that nothing more than rational persuasion was needed to achieve a utilitarian utopia. He therefore shared Paine's goals, but not his commitment to violent revolution. His view of the means by which a utopian society was to be achieved was much closer to Burke's concept of incremental reform. Godwin might therefore have been regarded at the time as a reasonably neutral chairman of a debate between Burke and Paine.

Godwin actually met Paine at a dinner in 1791 to celebrate the publication of Paine's *Rights of Man,* which was an incendiary reply to Edmund Burke's *Reflections on the Revolution in France.* The early feminist Mary Wollstonecraft was among other radical celebrities of the day who were invited to meet the author. Godwin observed later that he had heard too little of Paine, and too much of Wollstonecraft on that occasion. She was in fact the first to reply in print to Burke's condemnation of the French Revolution with her *Vindication of the Rights of Men* (to be followed by her *Vindication of the Rights of Women*). However, Godwin and Wollstonecraft later got together in a scandalous relationship, which became more scandalous when they married some years later to legitimize their daughter Mary—who was herself to marry the poet Shelley, and achieve immortal fame as the author of *Frankenstein.* Before their marriage, it had not been known that Wollstonecraft had been living in sin with her previous lover. However, in 1791, this scandal lay in the future.

Dialogue

After meeting Tom Paine at a dinner to celebrate the publication of his *Rights of Man,* Godwin has invited both Paine and Burke to dinner at his own house later in the week. Burke was very busy in 1791, and so must have been very curious about his adversary to accept such an invitation, since Godwin was notorious for his ramshackle household. The dinner was predictably very poor, but when bottles of port were put on the table, the mood improved and a serious conversation between the principal guests began when Godwin tapped his glass for attention.

GODWIN: Gentlemen! It is our custom at this table to attempt a little serious debate after dinner. Might I call on our distinguished guest, Thomas Paine, to open the proceedings.

PAINE: Thank you, Mr Godwin. With your permission, I shall address my remarks directly to Mr Burke. I am dismayed, Mr Burke, by your *Reflections on the Revolution in France*—as you will perhaps be dismayed by my *Rights of Man*, published this very week. After you brought your eloquence to bear in support of an accommodation with the American colonists before the late War of Independence, I thought you could be counted on to support the overthrow of the French ancien régime, whose behavior was far worse than anything the English governing classes ever inflicted on either their colonists or their native population.

BURKE: Revolutionaries like yourself believe that history does not matter—that we can throw away the lessons of the past, and create a new social contract from self-evident first principles. You believe you are justified in crushing any opposition from traditionalists who do not share your confidence that you know the best way forward. Whigs like myself look back at the failure of the revolutionary extremists who came out on top in the English Civil War to create any lasting settlement. The military dictatorship of Oliver Cromwell that followed is a dreadful warning of the fate that awaits the revolution in France. The Glorious Revolution of 1688 is imperfect in many ways, but it represents a compromise between the stability to be hoped for in maintaining the traditions of the past, and the need for reform to accommodate the fact that the world in which we live never stands still.

PAINE: But the American revolution did not lead to a military dictatorship.

BURKE: The founders of the American republic did not throw away the lessons of the past. Their new social contract is an egalitarian version of the mixed system of representative democracy so painfully learned over many years in Britain. What a pity that the Tories in power in Britain at the time were unwilling to grant the thirteen colonies the same freedoms guaranteed to the British by the Glorious Revolution! Nor does it seem likely that the lessons learned from the American revolution are to be applied in my own country of Ireland.

PAINE: I do not think you appreciate the enormous resentment felt by those who do not enjoy the privileges enjoyed by the aristocracy in Britain—but they count as nothing compared with the plight of the French peasantry trampled underfoot by the ancien régime. Can you blame them for rising up against their oppressors?

BURKE: The ancien régime was a disaster waiting to happen, but how much better it would have been if the revolutionaries had been willing to accept that a new social contract could have been put together bit by bit without risking the stability of the whole French nation.

PAINE: When the dam bursts, the water runs where it will. Nobody wants to listen to philosophers making up theories about social contracts—unless their conclusions accord with the prejudices they already hold. The French listen to Rousseau for this reason. The Whigs in Britain prefer to listen to Locke because he can be interpreted as supporting the compromises built into the so-called Glorious Revolution.

BURKE: You will forgive my not having yet had time to look over your new book, which I am told not only seeks to refute my criticisms of the French Revolution, but also proposes a radical program of egalitarian reform in Britain. Do you also deny the social contract theory on which Whigs like myself rely?

PAINE: I follow David Hume in denying social contract theories which postulate that we are somehow morally obligated to honor ways of organizing ourselves supposedly made by our ancestors in the past. So I am unpersuaded by your eloquence when you argue to the contrary. You say in your *Reflections* that a social contract is a partnership not only between those who are living, but between those who are living, those who are dead, and those who are yet to be born—that men are born into a community, endowed with the benefits that accord with the social state of their parents, but also loaded with the duties of their situation. But I see no reason why the peasants of France should accept their being taxed to the hilt to support the fopperies of aristocrats who pay no taxes at all simply because this is what has happened in the past.

BURKE: We can agree that the ancien régime was desperately in need of reform. I also agree that we need not treat Locke's approach to social contract issues as beyond criticism. There is indeed a case for retreating to Hume's view that social conventions are simply devices that have evolved to coordinate our behavior on equilibria in what one may call the game of life. But he directs our attention to equilibria because some measure of stability is essential to a viable society. What point is there in promoting equality if nobody can settle down to enjoy its fruits in a stable society? Why should we suppose that a government drawn from the uneducated ranks of the lower classes will be better able to maintain stability than an aristocratic regime? It seems to me that the emergence of a military dictatorship like that of Oliver Cromwell is inevitable.

PAINE: I see no need for such a gloomy prognosis, but even a military dictatorship would be better than the ancien régime.

BURKE: What of my point that we should elect representatives from the educated classes to govern us? I guess you would argue for a form of direct democracy in which the views of the Voltaires of this world count no more than those of an ignorant peasant.

PAINE: It turns out that the commoners who founded the American republic were better at the job than their aristocratic predecessors.

BURKE: But they were educated folk. A better comparison would be with the direct democracy of ancient Athens in the throes of the Peloponnesian War. Disaster after disaster followed once Athens dispensed with the services of aristocrats like Pericles in favor of a series of demagogues whose only talent was for pandering to the prejudices of the common man.

PAINE: Your contempt for the common man does you no credit. It is true that we need to make education more widely available, but we cannot wait forever while aristocrats delay their own demise by standing in the way of the schools that need to be made available for the young—to say nothing of the provision that needs to be made available for the old who are no longer able to work.

GODWIN: Perhaps this is the time to open the debate to everyone at the table. Who else thinks that further reform in our own country is long overdue?

Burke unsurprisingly found himself in a minority of one at Godwin's table, but he was accustomed to defending the middle ground he espoused from attacks from both the revolutionaries of the left and the traditionalists of the right. However, he listened patiently while Paine was praised for his enthusiasm until taking his leave after the last bottle of port had been emptied.

Chapter 18
Jeremy Bentham versus John Stuart Mill

Context

Jeremy Bentham and John Stuart Mill were thorough-going empiricists. They are jointly credited with inventing utilitarianism, although Bentham gives priority to the Swiss philosopher Helvétius. It is usually said that Mill provides the intellectual underpinnings for utilitarianism that Bentham neglects, and it is true that Bentham was brutally honest in identifying points in his theory where crucial assumptions are made without adequate foundations. What is utility? Why maximize your utility? How is your utility to be compared with mine? Why should society not maximize some other function of everybody's utilities rather than their sum? The world had to wait for John Harsanyi for coherent answers to these questions. Mills' contribution was rather to round off the rough edges of Bentham's exposition to make his theory acceptable to the intellectual elite of his time. However, orthodox opinion nevertheless credits him with being the leading exponent of naturalist philosophy in the nineteenth century.

Mill acted as Bentham's secretary on occasion, and so they met many times, but I doubt whether they ever had a discussion like the following imaginary dialogue in which Bentham challenges some of the grace notes with which Mill will eventually embellish Bentham's theory. They were certainly not on the best of terms if the sour obituary that Mill wrote for Bentham is any guide. My guess is that Mill never forgave Bentham for being a close associate of his philosophical father, who stole his childhood by turning him into a hothouse scholar from the age of three.

Bentham (1748?–1832) was a political radical active in modernizing the Victorian practice of law. He famously thought talk of inalienable or imprescriptible Natural Rights in documents like the 1789 French Declaration of the Rights of Man is "nonsense upon stilts", but he worked hard to extend the actual legal rights of English citizens of his time. He was against censorship, slavery, and capital punishment. He was for the separation of church and state, equal rights for women, and the civilized nurturing of children.

As a person, Bentham was seriously exotic—a full-blown English eccentric. His will specified that his corpse be stuffed and mounted, so that he could always chair meetings of the governors at my old college in London. Nowadays, his corpse is kept on display in a glass cabinet. I sat next to it once as a guest at a dinner of the Jeremy Bentham Society. In spite of his eccentricity, he was taken seriously by the movers and shakers of his time. James Madison refused his 1811 offer to rewrite the American Constitution, but Simon Bolivar actually had him write a constitution for the mega-state he hoped to create in South America.

John Stuart Mill (1806–1873) gets both his forenames to distinguish him from his utilitarian father James Mill. He is widely quoted for saying that people should be free to do what they want, provided they do not thereby infringe the freedom of others. But people prefer to forget that he thought it acceptable for governments to lie to their citizens for their own good. I find him eminently worthy, but appallingly dull. Economics is famously the dismal science, but never so dismal as in his book on the subject! His attempts to contribute to logic and the foundations of mathematics are not much better. However, he was on the side of the angels as an early campaigner for women's rights, egged on by his intellectual wife Harriet with whom he carried on a scandalous—albeit platonic—affair before she was widowed. Like many other philosophers, he seems to be judged by whether one likes his conclusions rather than the arguments he uses in their defense.

Bentham was proud of being regarded as one of the founders of what is now University College London, famously described by Thomas Arnold as "that godless institution in Gower Street" because it practised religious toleration. However, Bentham was only its spiritual father, in spite of the mural under UCL's landmark rotunda showing him receiving UCL's charter. It is under this rotunda in the late 1820s that our imaginary dialogue between Bentham and Mill is set after they have toured the newly built premises. Bentham would then have been eighty or so, and Mill in his early twenties. However, Mill is assumed already to be thinking through the ideas that he publishes only much later.

Dialogue

John Stuart Mill has been taking notes at a meeting of the governors of the original University of London (now UCL) on behalf of Jeremy Bentham. After touring the new buildings, they return to the committee room for a cup of strong coffee and Bentham's favorite hot spiced ginger nuts. Mill then takes the opportunity to challenge what he sees as Bentham's bleak view of human nature.

MILL: Is this a good occasion for me to express some doubts about the style of utilitarianism that my father taught me in my cradle?

BENTHAM: Any time would have been a good time, but you find me now in a good mood, with a cup of coffee in my hand after touring the magnificent premises of the newly built University of London, for which I agitated so long and hard.

MILL: Thank you for indulging me. I have no doubt that only natural philosophy makes sense, and I remain a convinced hedonist. But I am unhappy with the idea that human beings are motivated only by narrow self-interest—that utility is only to be measured in tangibles, such as whether people get enough to eat, or are adequately clothed. You summarized my disquiet yourself when you wrote that poetry is no better than the tavern game of push-pin as a source of pleasure. What of the higher pleasures? Are we really to ignore the ancients when they tell us that the unexamined life is not worth living? Is it not better to be a dissatisfied human being than a pig satisfied; better to be Socrates dissatisfied than a fool satisfied?

BENTHAM: I would say that it is not better to be Socrates dissatisfied than a fool satisfied. Epicurus hit the nail on the head here. The reason that one examines one's life is to seek to attain satisfaction, which for Epicurus and the Stoics included putting an end to vain striving after goals that bring no genuine contentment. A fool may think himself satisfied with such vain strivings, but we could make him better satisfied if we could cure him of his folly.

MILL: Here you come closer than I would have predicted to the thoughts that have been troubling me. People who are taught to appreciate the refinements that appeal to our higher faculties almost universally agree that they are better off as a consequence. We should therefore value poetry well above push-pin and the like, and promote the kind of education that focusses on the virtues of such civilized pleasures.

BENTHAM: I have a whole list of things to say in reply. The first is that the kind of utilitarianism I support requires that everybody should count for one, and nobody to count for more. Queen Victoria doubtless prefers a glass of the best wine to a pint of beer, but Jeremy Bentham prefers the beer. Why should her preference prevail over mine? Only because such preferences are not fundamental, but are shaped by the human urge to get ahead in society—to conform to whatever is currently the fashionable norm. Your choice of poetry as an example of a refined taste is a case in point. We all sneer today at the efforts of Alexander Pope and other poets who followed in the footsteps of the Enlightenment because romantic poets like Coleridge and Wordsworth are now all the rage. We look back at Samuel Johnson, so admired by his biographer James Boswell for being the literary arbiter of his age, but find Boswell's own writing to be infinitely superior. We need to ground our notion of utility in something more solid than the passing fashions of the upper classes.

MILL: What of music? What of philosophy? What of the beauty of a sunset?

BENTHAM: I appreciate all these things myself, as indeed I prefer the poetry of Lucretius or Catullus to push-pin or cricket. But it is not for us to impose our own preferences on others. We need to go deeper into the human psyche to find a level beneath the superficial at which we can genuinely compare the felicity that different people find in different activities. Epicurus thought that the only fundamentals are pleasure and pain. He would have advocated asking civilized folk *why* they like some particular thing—and to continue questioning whatever they answer in the same way. He thought that they would eventually be reduced to saying that it is because it gives pleasure or avoids pain at some basic level.

MILL: Are you then in favor of following Epicurus in identifying happiness merely with experiencing pleasure and avoiding pain?

BENTHAM: I do not think as utilitarians that we need to be so specific, but it is important that we count only intrinsic preferences when assessing a person's utility—preferences for which no explanation can be given for why they are held. I would count the preferences you wish to include as *instrumental,* in the sense that they are desired because they allow access to our *intrinsic* motivations. One of my great regrets is that when seeking a more scientific word for happiness, I fell in with the consensus on *utility* rather than my own preference for *felicity,* which would have avoided the implication that people like only what is useful. On the contrary, we should estimate a person's basic utility in terms only of what people desire for its own sake alone—which I believe is much the same for both a duchess and her footman.

MILL: Are we then not to value the English love of liberty, for which so many have given their lives down the ages?

BENTHAM: Liberty is a good example of what I am talking about. Of course it is valuable! I have spent a good deal of my life promoting liberal reforms in the legal world. But it is valuable for instrumental reasons. We do not know what choices await us in the future—what the feasible sets will be from which we will seek to make an optimal choice. It is therefore in our interests that these feasible sets not be artificially constrained more than necessary to maintain public order. But such a concern for liberty—although of great importance—is instrumental rather than intrinsic. We need not write liberty directly into what we count as utility because people seeking to maximize what we do count as utility will automatically favor their future feasible sets being free of unnecessary constraints. The same instrumental reason speaks for a universal education, after which everybody would know enough about art and literature to make an informed choice between poetry or push-pin.

MILL: I feel a deep need to persuade others that everybody should be free to do whatever they please provided they do not infringe the rights of others to do the same. I feel a similar urge to promote the cause of equal rights for women. But how can we persuade the world to abandon its authoritarian traditions if we are shackled by too rigid an adherence to the metaphysical foundations to which you insist that utilitarians must subscribe?

BENTHAM: I do not insist on anything. I would like to see a world in which people who have been educated scientifically make their own minds up about everything. Our aim should be to put forward a platform that rational folk will adopt because they see it is in their best interests—and not because they have been coerced into agreement.

MILL: I share your aspirations for the future, but there is so much that needs immediate reform. Are we not entitled to do whatever is necessary to eliminate suffering right now—even if it means lying to people for their own good.

BENTHAM: I cannot agree. We must hold fast to the truth as best we can. One day everybody will be utilitarian, and the world will be a much happier place. By muddling our doctrine in the hope of making it more immediately acceptable, you delay its eventual triumph. We need, on the contrary, a purer utilitarianism whose basic assumptions are better founded. I had hoped that the younger generation that you represent would tackle the questions that my generation left unanswered, but I see that you are in too much of a hurry.

MILL: I recall, for example, that you say somewhere that to compare the utility of two different people is like adding so many apples to so many pears. A genuine scientific utilitarian theory would indeed not leave such issues hanging in the air, but we cannot fiddle while Rome burns. For me, utilitarianism will always be a way of arguing for political reform rather than a scientific theory.

BENTHAM: It is a sad fact that philosophers have always been judged on whether the society in which they live likes their conclusions or not, rather than whether their reasoning is sound. I guess history will find in your favor rather than mine. But history can go hang. For the moment, I care only that these ginger nuts remain very palatable, albeit no longer hot.

Afterword

Mill is not very pleased to have his aspirations trivialized in the same manner he had suffered for many years from his father. However, Victorian society did indeed judge in his favor as Bentham ironically predicted. Modern philosophers have yet to revise this opinion, as John Harsanyi's answers to the utilitarian questions left open by Bentham were written in a mathematical jargon that is outside the scope of most moral philosophers.

Chapter 19
Friedrich Engels versus Karl Marx

Context

There is no problem in finding an occasion for Marx and Engels to meet in 1846. Although their first meeting in 1842 did not go well, they eventually became close collaborators, meeting many times when both were living in Brussels between 1845 and 1848. Marx was then editing a radical newspaper, in which he published an essay by Engels on the current state of what was then called Political Economy. The essay apparently persuaded Marx to adapt his ideas on economics to the approach advocated by a new wave of British economists led by Adam Smith (1723?–1790) and David Ricardo (1772–1823). This decision to use models in which people supposedly act in their own enlightened self-interest was highly significant for Marxian theory, but what Engels and Marx talk about mostly in their imaginary dialogue is the labor theory of value that Engels thinks they should borrow from David Ricardo.

Friedrich Engels (1820–1895) was born to a wealthy family of German industrialists near the modern town of Wuppertal. They owned cotton mills, one of which was conveniently located in Manchester, England. Engel's father did not approve of his son's involvement with a variety of radical organizations while a student. He approved even less of his active participation in a series of failed revolutions that shook Europe to its roots in the year 1848. However, father and son eventually came to some compromise that allowed Engels to continue his revolutionary activities while managing the family's Manchester cotton mill. He was therefore able to supplement Marx's meager income from journalism when Marx had nowhere left to flee but London after being banished from everywhere else. Without this help, it would have been impossible for Marx to have labored for many years writing *Das Kaptial* in the reading room of the British Museum.

Engels provided more than financial help to Marx. His contributions to socialist theory have now largely been assimilated to Marx himself, but he still gets credited for his rhetorical efforts. The Marxian aphorism that says history repeats itself, first as tragedy and then as farce, is actually Engel's comment on the fact that the 1851 coup of the slightly absurd Louis Napoleon took place on the 18th Brumaire—the same date on which Napoleon Bonaparte had seized power 56 years earlier in revolutionary France. More seriously Engels was a coauthor with Marx of the *Communist Manifesto*, which famously tells the working classes of the world that they have nothing to lose but their chains in rebelling against their capitalist masters.

More on Marx (1818–1883) appears in a later dialogue with Darwin, which is imagined to take place after the publication of the first volume of *Das Kapital*. At the time of his imaginary dialogue with Engels, Marx was just one more revolutionary agitator among many. His subversive journalism had worn out the patience, not just of the reactionary governments of Prussia and France, but also of the numerous revolutionary enthusiasts with whom he had associated along the way. At the time of his dialogue with Engels in Brussels, he is at risk of wearing out the patience of both the Belgian government and the revolutionary Communist League, with which he and Engels were currently associated. Their stirring *Communist Manifesto* of 1848 rescued them from the latter fate, but only served to bring forward the time when both would need to seek sanctuary in England.

The imaginary dialogue coming up begins with Marx and Engels achieving an unlikely clarity in an area where clarity has yet to be achieved in philosophy even today. How can cooperation be possible if people act in their own self-interest? Why act to promote the welfare of others rather than your own? Tradition holds that we have a duty to do so, but Edmund Burke is not alone in observing that the reasons remain "dark and inscrutable". In the dialogue, Marx accepts Engel's overly modern exposition of David Hume's answer—that cooperation can be consistent with enlightened self-interest for the simple reason that people who reveal that they cannot be trusted will be excluded from the benefits that derive from sharing the extra profits that flow from pooling our efforts.

For reasons better addressed in later dialogues, Hume argues that a social contract is no more than a bunch of social conventions, whose observation results in the citizens of a society coordinating on a Nash equilibrium of their game of life. It matters that the outcome be such an equilibrium because nobody can profit from deviating from a Nash equilibrium, and so we do not need to invent dark and inscrutable reasons why they can be trusted not to do so. All that Hume then needed to add is that games like the human game of life that extend into the indefinite future have equilibria in which all the fruits of cooperation are available.

It is a pity that the modern language that makes this conclusion seem trivial took so long to develop. Hume, for example, never speaks of an equilibrium, although he gives many examples. Nor would he have identified an equilibrium of our repeated game of life with a social contract. For Hume, the traditional concept of a social contract necessarily required postulating dark and inscrutable reasons why it should be honored.

Dialogue

Marx has published Engels' *Critique of Political Economy* in the Neue Rheinische Zeitung, which he edits for the Communist League in Brussels. (The original Rheinische Zeitung was suppressed by the Prussian government.) They now meet by arrangement in a Brussels café in 1846 to discuss what their joint attitude should be to the theories of economics that Engels reviewed in this essay. Marx is reluctant to take on board the insights of Adam Smith's *Wealth of Nations,* but Engels argues that it is not the mere apology for capitalism that Marx imagines, but a major scientific advance.

The waiter who take their orders is used to the eloquence of their circle, and sighs at the thought that they will still be going hammer-and-tongs at closing time. He nevertheless uncomplainingly brings two glasses of absinthe with sugar cubes on slotted spoons. Engels takes pleasure in pouring water over the sugar cube into his absinthe. As the water acquires a decadent green tinge, he opens the dialogue by seeking to persuade Marx that a scientific socialist theory should attribute some measure of enlightened self-interest to the workers rather than a selfless enthusiasm for the welfare of the working class as a whole.

MARX: You asked for this meeting so that we could discuss what our joint attitude to the new British economists is going to be. What is your agenda?

ENGELS: We certainly do not want to adopt any of the policies put forward by the British school of economists, but we might usefully adopt their foundational assumptions. If you agree, we would need first to decide whether we should be methodological individualists like Adam Smith and David Ricardo, or utilitarians like Jeremy Bentham and William Godwin.

MARX: I like the term methodological individualism. It has a satisfying weighty sound, like dialectical materialism. But all these economists argue that utility should be maximized, so do they not all count as utilitarians?

ENGELS: They differ in whose utility a person should seek to maximize, your own or the sum of everybody's utility.

MARX: Since we are socialists, we should presumably opt for the utilitarian option.

ENGELS: It would certainly ease our task to follow the utilitarians, but is their position consistent with our desire to create a scientific theory? The utilitarians have no answer when asked why an individual person will do what is best for the community as a whole rather than what is best for himself.

MARX: But the alternative is to follow Adam Smith in championing the invisible hand that supposedly guides his market to an efficient outcome. However, markets work by setting each man against his brother in a selfish scramble for the trinkets that the bourgeois prize so much. Where is the fairness in that?

ENGELS: Nothing in methodological individualism says that property needs to be private, or that goods should be distributed using markets. Adam Smith would agree that it can also be applied when property is held in common, and goods are distributed according to the principle that each should contribute according to his ability, and receive according to his need. To see how this would work, we have only to adapt what David Hume—who was Adam Smith's mentor—says in his essay arguing against protectionism in international trade. I think you would like the essay, because he denounces the protectionists for treating foreigners as competitors in a race, rather than as partners across the sea with whom we should cooperate to create a source of wealth that would otherwise be unavailable.

MARX: How does Hume explain why traders trust each other when there is no international government to enforce the promises they make to each other?

ENGELS: He explains in his *Treatise of Human Nature* that it is rational to honor your promises when the result of cheating a partner is that the future profits from a continuation of the partnership will be lost.

MARX: Is this all that enlightened self-interest requires to sustain cooperation? How simple! We could therefore adopt methodological individualism without needing to attribute much rationality to the workers of the future when they unite to throw off their chains.

ENGELS: Throwing off their chains! We must include that phrase in the manifesto for the Communist League we are planning to write. So you are willing to consider Methodological Individualism as a basis for a socialist economic theory?

MARX: Let us proceed on that basis for the purpose of this discussion—although I certainly do not want to discourage utopians who think self-interest and socialism are incompatible.

ENGELS: I want next to draw your attention to the relevance of Adam Smith's story of a pin factory to your notion of the alienation of workers from the production process. When each worker is restricted to a particular part of the process—like sharpening the pins or attaching their heads—their joint productivity is enormously increased. But where is the satisfaction in doing nothing but sharpen pins all day?

MARX: More than this! The skill required to sharpen a pin can be learned in a moment. So workers who agitate for higher wages can easily be replaced by unskilled workers from the reserve army of the unemployed. As long as such a reserve army exists, workers in a modern factory will therefore be reduced to subsistence wages. They will be paid the minimum necessary to keep their families alive.

ENGELS: Spoken like Adam Smith himself! We have no disagreement with each other on this subject. You have seen my notes on the misery of the working classes in the cotton mills of England, which I plan to work up into a book.

MARX: But let us stay on the subject of what we can learn from the British school of economic theory. I am particularly interested in what you have to say about the ideas of David Ricardo in the article you wrote for my Neue Rheinische Zeitung.

So Engels embarks on an impassioned exposition of Ricardo's economic theory. He is explaining Ricardo's definition of economic rent as "that portion of the produce of the earth which is paid to the landlord for the use of the original and indestructible powers of the soil" when he realizes that Marx has lost interest in all this technical stuff. So he cuts short his attempt to explain why Ricardo advocated a socialist solution to the ills of the world (that still retained a small following among British intellectuals in 1846). He turns instead to Ricardo's labor theory of value.

ENGELS: The Ricardian socialists of whom I have been speaking have developed a theory of capitalist exploitation from Ricardo's idea that labor is the true source of all wealth. They trace the idea as far back as Aquinas's concept of the just price, but the philosopher they admire most is John Locke. They argue that private ownership of the means of production should be supplanted by cooperatives owned by associations of workers.

MARX: I am suspicious of such bourgeois intellectuals. A revolution is inevitable. There will be much suffering until it ends in the triumph of socialism. By delaying its onset, these utopian socialists will merely make the necessary suffering worse.

ENGELS: It is nevertheless worth listening to their labor theory of value. In arguing that only the value of the labor that goes into the production process should count towards the total value of the product, they implicitly deny the dogma of their hero Locke that people in the state of nature are entitled to appropriate the bounty of the earth, provided as much and as good is left for others. Nor do they accept that there is a natural law that justifies the inequalities that will necessarily result when the property rights created by such appropriations are traded as time goes by.

MARX: I recall that Adam Smith distinguishes between use-value and exchange-value, but it sounds like Ricardo's labor theory of value comes under neither of these headings. However, I take it that Ricardo anticipated Proudhon in regarding all property as theft. In the classical division of the factors of production into capital, land and labor, only labor is therefore to be counted as private property. Everything else is the property of the community to be used as society sees fit. A labor theory of value then seems inevitable in the ideal society that will eventually succeed the dictatorship of the proletariat. But private property has yet to be eliminated. Does Ricardo claim that his labor theory of value predicts workers' wages right now?

ENGELS: If so, he would confuse what ought to happen in an ideal world with what actually happens in the world as it is. However, he does not make this mistake. In fact, Ricardo reports a difference of at least 7% between the predictions of the pure labor theory of value and wages actually paid in practice.

MARX: He sounds unusually honest for a banker who made himself immensely rich by being quick to exploit the news that Britain was on the winning side at the battle of Waterloo! You convince me that a labor theory of value should lie at the heart of the socialist theory we are developing together, but it will be necessary to replace Ricardo's version with something that is less easily refuted by the facts on the ground.

Engels is untroubled that Marx remains unconvinced by his exposition of Ricardian socialism. He reflects that Marx's great book—when finally written—need no more be built on solid foundations than such iconic works as Plato's *Republic* or Aquinas's *Summa Theologica*. All one needs to offer to those already converted is a book that they are sure would prove them right if only they devoted enough time and effort to its study. A few contradictions are even to be welcomed. Even within the tiny Communist League, there are endless disputes on what should count as the true faith. But all sides of any argument can be justified by the same book if it contains a contradiction or two.

Afterword

Purists may think it a shame that Marx is only willing to go along with Engels to a limited extent. In the world that might have been if Marx had been won over altogether, socialism would have had firmer theoretical foundations, but Marx was doubtless right that you are more likely to recruit revolutionaries by rationalizing their prejudices than by challenging them.

Chapter 20
Charles Darwin versus Gregor Mendel

Context

Darwin's *Origin of Species by Natural Selection* was a revolutionary step forward in an environment in which even the open-minded David Hume had taken for granted that animal species are immutable. Darwin's argument has three strands. The first is that his researches aboard the Beagle had shown that species must have evolved—as was obvious in the case of Galapagos finches. The second is that Malthus had claimed that populations will increase exponentially unless checked somehow, and so there will necessarily be competition for resources. As Henry Spencer put it, only the fittest will then survive. The third is that animal traits are inherited somehow—as in the case of selective breeding by farmers. Darwin's Achilles heel lay in the fact that the mechanism by means of which traits are passed from parents to their offspring was unknown. The double helix of Crick and Watson was a long way in the future.

Darwin's own speculations about the mechanism incorporated ideas of pangenesis that date back at least as far as Aristotle, but his thoughts are often identified with Lamarckism these days. Lamarck suggested, for example, that stretching to reach the leaves high up in a tree lengthened a giraffe's neck, which became a useful trait that got passed on to future generations. However, the work of Gregor Mendel demonstrated that the actual mechanism does not involve the transmission of acquired characteristics at all. But Mendel labored alone and unrecognized, and it was not until the middle of the next century that statistical tools were brought to bear to combine the rediscovered laws of Mendelian genetics with Darwin's theory of evolution to create what is nowadays known as the neo-Darwinian synthesis.

Our imaginary dialogue between Darwin and Mendel asks *what if* Darwin had heard of Mendel's work? Would Darwin have then created the neo-Darwinian synthesis himself? But we cannot allow our imaginary dialogues to change the course of history, and so I have used Mendel's unscientific way with statistical outliers to allow Darwin's cousin Francis Galton to persuade him to reject Mendel's conclusions.

Charles Darwin (1809–1882) was born to a well-off family with intellectual interests. He flirted with becoming first a medical doctor and then a parson, but his scientific propensities eventually triumphed. He began training as a geologist, but his future was finally determined by his decision to join the five-year voyage of the Beagle around the world. He worked tirelessly over many years to gather evidence in support of the theory of evolution that he developed on the voyage. Publication of his ideas was finally precipitated by the news that Alfred Lord Wallace had come up with the idea of natural selection independently while gathering biological specimens in Indonesia. Both men behaved unusually well about sharing the credit that eventually accrued. Their theory was, of course, greeted with outrage by religious folk—anticipation of which doubtless contributed to Darwin's long delay in publication—but Darwin had reason to be pleased at the surprising extent to which Victorian society accepted his revolutionary ideas. As for his own religious sentiments, they seem gradually to have faded from the Unitarianism of his mother to the unaggressive atheism of his old age.

The much-told story of his decision to marry says something about his mild character and self-consciously rational outlook. The paper on which he listed the pros and cons for marrying his cousin Emma Wedgewood still survives. In spite of her strongly held religious convictions, the marriage was a success. On his deathbed in 1882, he told Emma, "I am not the least afraid of death—remember what a good wife you have been to me—tell all my children to remember how good they have been to me."

Gregor Mendel (1822–1884) was born into a humble German-speaking family in what is now the Czech Republic. He seems to have become a friar to avoid the "perpetual anxiety about a means of livelihood". He repeatedly failed the oral part of the examination to become a certified high-school teacher, which suggests that he was seriously introverted. If he had been visited by Darwin in real life, he would likely have been rendered dumb-struck to have been sought out by such a celebrity. However, he explains his discovery of dominant and recessive genes reasonably adequately in the coming imaginary dialogue with Darwin, although it is unlikely that he spoke any English at all. At the time of their fictional meeting in 1867, he has just been appointed abbot of St Thomas's Abbey, which was an Augustinian monastery in Brno, where he seems to have devoted much of the rest of his life to disputing its taxes with the Austria-Hungarian government.

In his later years, Darwin was troubled by a series of distressing symptoms that are thought perhaps to be the consequence of chronic Chagas disease, contracted by being bitten by the "kissing bug" in Argentina while traveling with the Beagle. He would therefore certainly not have traveled alone to Brno. The story offered is that he is accompanied there by his cousin Francis Galton—their differences over Galton's claim to have refuted Darwin's theory of pangenesis being two years in the future in 1867.

Francis Galton (1822–1911) spent much of his life exploring the statistical implications for human populations of Darwin's ideas. In the process he made numerous scientific discoveries that have stood the test of time, but all his work is overshadowed nowadays by his inventing the word *eugenics*. He was certainly racist, but so were the vast majority of his Victorian contemporaries (although Darwin himself was a life-long opponent of slavery, and judged the native intelligence of even the wretched inhabitants of Tierra del Fuego to be comparable to that of Europeans). It is sad that we seem unable to separate the wheat from the chaff in looking over the work of dead white males like Galton. Who knows what prejudices the future will condemn in our own unconsidered beliefs?

In real life, a major controversy resulted in 1900 when Mendel's principles were rediscovered. The followers of Galton's Law of Ancestral Heredity were very reluctant to admit that their views could be reconciled with Mendel's proposals, and it is likely that Galton himself would have been equally reluctant. But in the fiction to be offered next, Galton approaches Darwin with the rumor that an obscure Austrian monk may have solved the mystery of how traits are transmitted between generations. Other possible sources of data lacked Mendel's supposedly meticulous record of the transmission of traits in the edible pea, uniquely supported by statistically significant sample sizes. Darwin sees the potential significance of Mendel's study, but is reluctant to travel so far because of his continuing ill-health, but is finally persuaded when Galton explains that they can go most of the way by rail.

Dialogue

Darwin was totally exhausted when he and Galton finally arrived in Brno. So Galton visited Mendel alone on the appointed day. He found Mendel lacking in the social graces, and very anxious not to be patronized. So they did not get on too well, but Mendel was willing both to lend Galton the notebooks in which he had recorded his experiments in growing peas, and to make a second appointment a few days later, at which Darwin would be present. This meeting went a lot better, as Darwin was naturally much less brash than his cousin.

In the interim, Galton studied Mendel's data with growing excitement. Could this data really be correct? Could traits really be determined as though by pairs of colored beads strung together side-by-side on two parallel wires? Surely things must be more complicated? If not, his own Law of Ancestral Heredity was in question. Why then was it supported by his own data? He decided not to give expression to his doubts until Darwin had the opportunity to make an independent assessment of Mendel's competence.

On arrival at St Thomas's Abbey for the second meeting, Darwin spends some time in charming Mendel to the best of his ability. Mendel thaws somewhat in response, and gives them both a tour of the walled garden in which he had carried out what had clearly been very extensive experiments in growing the edible pea. Darwin privately thought that Mendel's obsessive nature was just what was needed to make a success of such an enterprise. They then return to Mendel's office, where some minimal refreshments are served. Darwin explains that Galton has filled him in on the essentials of Mendel's discoveries, but would like Mendel himself to outline his own explanatory theory in simple terms. Mendel becomes less awkward as he explains his ideas about dominant and recessive genes.

MENDEL: Dr Galton has encouraged me to propose a model of what is passed from one generation to the next as pairs of colored beads strung together side-by-side on two parallel wires. One of the beads in each pair is derived from the mother, and the other from the father. The locus at which the pair of beads sits on the pair of wires determines or modifies some physiological or behavioral trait of the animal or plant under study. In my own research on edible peas, perhaps the clearest case of the seven traits I considered is the height of the plant: Is it tall or short?

GALTON: In the human case, eye-color might possibly be a trait determined by the beads—or perhaps we might say genes—at just one locus. But most traits will presumably be determined by the genes at many loci.

DARWIN: Let us use the word *gene,* although I cannot see it catching on. What if a child gets a blue gene from its mother, and a brown gene from its father?

MENDEL: I prefer not to speculate about human biology, but to stick with the only case for which I have data. However, I also studied the case of color in the edible pea, where the relevant question becomes whether a child becomes yellow or green if it gets a yellow gene from its mother and a green gene from its father. The answer in this case is green. For this reason, I say that the green gene is dominant, and the yellow gene recessive.

DARWIN: In the case of eye-color in humans, the brown gene would be dominant. I am delighted that your theory breaks away from the standard assumption that traits from the parents will necessarily be *blended* in the child. Indeed, your theory allows a mother and father who both have brown eyes to give birth to a child with blue eyes—which certainly sometimes happens in practice. But how often a child gets a blue gene that is present but unexpressed in both parents will depend on the mechanism that determines which of a parent's two genes at a particular locus are transmitted to the child.

MENDEL: My data suggests that nature makes the choice at random—each gene is equally likely to be transmitted. But it is a long step to argue that what is true for the edible pea also applies to human beings. Some of the friars for whom I am responsible would regard the suggestion as heretical.

DARWIN: One would not need to argue that the choice is genuinely random—only that God's reasons for making the choice are beyond our understanding.

GALTON: Let me encourage you, my dear Dr Mendel, to tell Mr Darwin the data that supports your theory of the random transmission of genes.

MENDEL: I am not a doctor!

DARWIN: No more am I, but those of us who care about what is true in the world need not concern ourselves with such worldly matters. What data is this of which my cousin speaks? Why is it not published?

Darwin versus Mendel   111

MENDEL: The data is in fact published in the proceedings of the Natural History Society of Brno. Let me find some offprints for you to study at your leisure. The part relevant to our discussion argues that if the basic model is true, then the probability a child of two parents who both have a dominant and a recessive gene at a particular locus will have two recessive genes at that locus is one fourth. To test this proposition in the case of color, I first located two populations of true-breeding peas—one whose offspring were always green, and one whose offspring were always yellow. I then created a new population by cross-breeding these two populations. The peas in this new population should all be hybrids, with one green gene and one yellow gene. Offspring of this hybrid population should then have both their genes yellow with probability one fourth. We ought therefore to expect one fourth of the total population of the grandchildren of the original two populations to be colored yellow.

GALTON: This is indeed what Mendel's data shows—and with population sizes so large that there is no problem about the statistical significance of the results.

MENDEL: The results on dominant and recessive genes are merely the most striking conclusions of generalizations of my data that I call the Laws of Segregation and Independent Assortment.

DARWIN: If you can spare the time to meet with us again, perhaps we could discuss these laws tomorrow. Right now I am excited by the prospect of having a possible explanation of the cause of the variation in traits necessary for a theory of evolution to work. Where do the new genes come from that are necessary if natural selection is to have alternatives amongst which to select? Your theory would allow the explanation that they are due to copying errors in whatever biological mechanism transmits genes from a parent to a child.

GALTON: If Mendel's theory is true, there must indeed be a copying mechanism, but any errors—which one might call mutations—must surely be very rare.

DARWIN: The discoveries of Lyall and others that the geological history of our time must extend millions of years into the past implies that the mutations can indeed be rare.

MENDEL: You now broach upon issues that test my religious faith. I prefer to confine my claims to the inheritance properties of the edible pea.

The three continue their discussions the next day by looking over Mendel's laws, but they have already covered the essentials of the theory. Galton studies Mendel's data very closely on the long journey home. The English channel is unusually calm when they finally make it that far. He puts his conclusions to Darwin while they relax in deckchairs enjoying the intermittent sunshine.

GALTON: You will be aware that I had grave doubts about Mendel's work. I was up late last night finishing my analysis of his data, with the result that I am now even more skeptical.

DARWIN: I thought perhaps his results were too good to be true. He must surely have doubts himself. Otherwise he would have attempted to published somewhere less obscure.

GALTON: My first problem is with the almost absurdly simple model of beads strung on a wire. How could this evolve? What possible replication mechanism could copy such a string of beads from a parent to a child? How would a physiological trait be created from the information encoded in such a string of beads?

DARWIN: If Mendel were willing to make any claims beyond the inheritance properties of the edible pea, he might respond that no theory at this stage can possibly hope to resolve all mysteries.

GALTON: My second problem is that his results seem incompatible with the data that supports my own Law of Ancestral Heredity.

DARWIN: A possible explanation lies in the fact that Mendel studies much simpler traits than you. His traits are discrete: either on or off. It is implausible that the continuous traits on which you focus could similarly be determined by a single gene.

GALTON: Admittedly so. However, the final nail in Mendel's coffin is that his data is not to be trusted. It is too exact. If one of a parent's pair of genes at a locus were passed on at random to a child, his data would necessarily be considerably more random—there would be more outliers. It is on this issue that I have been working so hard on the long rail journey home.

DARWIN: You think his data is faked?

GALTON: I think it unlikely that it has been invented altogether. Perhaps he deleted inconvenient outliers that he thought must have resulted from some experimental error because they failed to conform to the theory to which he had already become attached.

DARWIN: He was certainly shifty in his manner. I guess I was naive in thinking that the problem of where mutations come from could be so easily solved.

Afterword

I wonder how often the work of outsiders like Mendel is similarly disregarded because their behavior does not accord with the expectations of the nomenclatura. The fact that Mendel's data is too exact, was actually discovered by the statistician Fisher much later—the same Fisher who was a major player in putting together the neo-Darwinian synthesis that Darwin and Galton are imagined to have missed their chance at creating in their dialogue.

Did Mendel actually cheat? If so, he would not be the only one! The economist Milton Friedman systematically deleted what he called outliers from the data that he claimed supported his now discredited theory of monetarism. After his death, the notebooks of the physicist Millikan revealed that he had similarly deleted outliers from the data he used to estimate the mass of the electron. Both were nevertheless awarded Nobel prizes, even though Friedman was quite open about his manipulation of the data.

It seems out of character for Mendel to have deliberately cheated like Millikan. The explanation offered that seems most likely to me is that when the data deviated from his predictions too much, he increased his sample size until the new data fitted the prediction better. Such ignorance of statistics is quite common even today, but in Victorian times only a statistical pioneer like Galton would have been aware of the necessity of being careful about such matters.

Chapter 21

Karl Marx versus Charles Darwin

Context

Charles Darwin spent his final years at Down House, a country residence only sixteen miles south of central London. Down House is maintained today as a museum in Darwin's honor. One of its trustees told me of finding a volume of Marx's *Das Kapital* on his bookshelves, but with its pages still uncut. A Marxian scholar later explained that it was sent to Darwin by Marx himself in 1873. Darwin responded by writing, "I thank you for the honour you have done me in sending me your great work of Capital; and heartily wish that I was more worthy to receive it, by understanding more of the deep and important subject of political economy."

Other sources also suggest that Marx would have welcomed more approval from Darwin of what he thought of as his evolutionary ideas, but the ill-health of both men makes the idea that Marx would have invited himself to Down House seeking Darwin's endorsement very unlikely. Darwin, in any case, would probably have found Marx's reasoning impenetrable, and his occasional personal rudeness unacceptable. However, the dialogue that follows is helped along by imagining that Darwin knows something of Hegel, who was in fashion at the time. Marx is assumed to be on his best behavior, reverting to the bourgeois manners of his childhood.

Karl Marx (1818–1883) was perhaps the most influential philosopher of all time but—as with Jean-Jacques Rousseau—it is possible to wonder whether he should be counted as a philosopher at all. He certainly became the intellectual source of authority for revolutionary socialists across the globe, but does his reasoning hold together, or is he simply telling revolutionaries what they want to hear? Perhaps the contradictions that scholars find in Marx's work are necessary for the latter function, so that the Lenins and Trotskys of this world can deduce whatever they find convenient from his writings. If so, he would not be the only philosopher in this book who is more valued for his conclusions than his arguments.

Marx was born into a bourgeois family in Trier, Germany. Some commentators make more of the conversion of his family from Judaism to Christianity than it deserves, since religion seems never to have been of any importance to Marx. He was one of those university students who neglect their studies in favor of student politics. He was particularly active in a group called the Young Hegelians, with whom he was later to quarrel—as he was to quarrel with many of his later associates. Hegel was the fashionable philosopher of the day, and Marx's dialectical or historical materialism is an attempt at a practical version of Hegel's notion that the human spirit advances through an inevitable process in which contradictions inherent in various historical ways of thinking about the world are surmounted by new syntheses that are eventually fated to generate an intellectual utopia. The teleological nature of this grandiose system does not prevent its being called evolutionary by some scholars. Marx would therefore have regarded his own version of Hegel's system as evolutionary too.

An earlier dialogue introduces Friedrich Engels, who was an exception to Marx's propensity to disagree with his associates. Engels was the son of a rich German entrepreneur, who managed a factory in England for his father. His *Condition of the Working Class in England* was a major influence on Marx. When Marx's journalistic activities finally resulted in his being banished to England to live in poverty in London with his wife and children, subsidies from Engels kept the family from starving altogether. Marx and Engels wrote the hugely influential *Communist Manifesto* together. Engels was also responsible for getting the second and third volumes of *Das Kapital* into print after Marx's death. He also wrote a number of reviews of the first volume under various names, expressing a variety of opinions, in the hope that their publication would drum up interest in Germany and elsewhere.

The first volume of *Das Kapital* is mentioned in the imaginary dialogue. Marx sent Darwin a copy in 1873, but could not reasonably have hoped that Darwin would read it, since the world would have to wait until 1887 for an English translation. In spite of his polite letter to Marx, Darwin would probably have counted him as just one more of the sellers of intellectual snake-oil who tried to cling to his coat-tails after the unexpected success of his *Origin of Species*. Einstein must have felt much the same about his theory of relativity being quoted as though relativity in physics was somehow relevant to relativism in the social sphere.

The so-called Social Darwinists led by Herbert Spencer would have been particularly offensive for someone with Darwin's liberal outlook. It is therefore not easy to imagine a reason why Darwin would have replied positively to a letter from another potential crank inviting himself to Down House. The expedient I propose is that he accepts Marx's proposal of a visit for the sake of his wife, whose grandfather Josiah Wedgewood is credited with being the founder of the utopian socialist movement in England. Only when it is too late to retract his acceptance does he learn that, not only is Marx a vocal opponent of utopian socialism—which he sees as diluting support for wholesale revolution—but an atheist to boot. So he finds himself stuck with the necessity of entertaining his exotic visitor single-handed.

This story is somewhat implausible, but it provides an opportunity for drawing attention to the considerable support for socialism in bourgeois England during Victorian times. Josiah Wedgewood was particularly influential. His pottery business made him immensely rich—Wedgewood pottery continues to be prized today—but he never abandoned the liberal aspirations of his youth. He was a partner with Robert Owen in organizing worker communities based on socialist principles that were forerunners of the kibbutzim which still survive in attenuated form in modern Israel. Wedgewood was also a friend of Erasmus Darwin—evolutionary pioneer and grandfather not only to both Charles Darwin and Frances Galton, but also to Emma Wedgewood, to whom Darwin was blissfully married in 1873.

Emma Darwin would have been brought up to share her grandfather's liberal ideas—notably his utopian socialism and his determined opposition to slavery. Emma had known her cousin Charles since childhood, and so their marriage was somewhat cold-blooded, but like many arranged marriages, it was very successful. Her very firm attachment to the Unitarianism of her family was not allowed to become an obstacle as Darwin himself became increasingly skeptical—arguing, for example, that no good God would have created the parasitic wasps that inject their eggs into the paralyzed bodies of living caterpillars. Emma had ten children, the last at the age of 48. Three died in childhood, which was common in Victorian times. Darwin was particularly upset at the death of his beloved daughter Annie, who made it to age ten. Karl Marx had seven children by his long-suffering wife, Jenny von Westphalen, of whom four died in childhood—two more committing suicide later. The deaths of his young children are usually attributed to the family's poor living conditions in London, but Darwin's dead children would have had the best life that money could buy.

Dialogue

Marx's arrival at Down House after lunch on a fine day in May 1873 creates something of a domestic upheaval in the Darwin household. Marx's bristling beard and Bohemian manners quite upset the servants' bourgeois expectations. Nor are they used to their mistress scurrying upstairs lest she be offended by a visitor's irreligious attitudes. However, they serve tea for their larger-than-life guest in Darwin's study, and await developments. Darwin himself settles down to make the best of what he feels likely to be an unproductive afternoon. After a minimal exchange of courtesies, Marx gets right down to business.

MARX: I see the copy of my *Das Kapital* that I sent you on your table, but you probably speak no more German than most English intellectuals. So I have come in person to seek your endorsement of my attempt to make political economy into an evolutionary science.

DARWIN: I am told that you apply the methods of the philosopher Hegel to political economy. There is perhaps something to Hegel's claim that human understanding advances through surmounting the contradictions that arise through the use of inadequate models of ourselves and the world around us. One might even think of such contradictions in terms of what I believe Hegel calls a dialectic, in which a synthesis is created by the tension that arises when a thesis is opposed by its antithesis. However, I do not see that it follows that such a process will necessarily carry us to some ideal model that cannot be bettered—still less that human intellectual history has already reached this ideal in Hegel's work. It seems to me that Hegel's dialectical method is profoundly unscientific, since it allows a philosopher enough freedom to justify any prejudice whatever. Nor do I care for the theory of evolution I defend in my *Origin of Species* to be thought supportive of Hegel's metaphysics merely because some authors speak of the dialectic process he describes as evolutionary. In English, the word *table* is used both of a piece of furniture and of a list of numbers, but it does not follow that a list of numbers is a piece of furniture. Hegel's teleology makes his kind of evolutionary process utterly incompatible with mine.

MARX: We share the same views on Hegel! I was an enthusiastic Hegelian in my youth until I realized that philosophers may interpret the world in whatever way suits their prejudices—but the point is to change it. For this purpose, we need to replace Hegel's dialectic by something scientific. I call my replacement dialectical materialism, or sometimes historical materialism. It is an approach to human history that takes account only of material issues that can be measured scientifically. Instead of some metaphysical concept of the human spirit, it studies the evolution of the economic means of production.

DARWIN: I presume your calling yourself a materialist includes a denial of religion.

MARX: I do deny religion, which I call the opium of the masses in one of my books. It serves in modern times as an instrument of control that the bourgeoisie uses to keep the proletariat in check.

DARWIN: I guess that capitalism is one of the material phenomena that replaces Hegel's metaphysical theses. You presumably argue that it will eventually founder on its own contradictions.

MARX: I model human social and economic history as a war between social classes—freeman against slave, patrician against plebeian, lord against serf, guildmaster against journeyman—in a series of battles ending either in the revolutionary reconstitution of society at large, or the common ruin of the contending classes.

DARWIN: So you see capitalism arising from the ruins of a feudalism brought low by its internal contradictions. Presumably socialism will similarly arise like a phoenix from the flames when capitalism in turn falls prey to its own set of contradictions. Here we have some common ground, since the intellectual circle in which I move sees that the current misery of the English working classes as unsustainable. Those with the power to influence things therefore seek to build a better life for everyone by designing workers' cooperatives. You will know, for example, of the efforts of Robert Owen and my wife's grandfather, Josiah Wedgewood.

MARX: I am sorry to disappoint you, but I agitate against the proponents of such utopian socialism, whose well-meaning benevolence merely delays the inevitable revolution that will eventually sweep away the sick capitalist society that currently exploits the working classes. They need to heed the message of the *Communist Manifesto* I wrote with Engels: Workers of the world unite! You have nothing to lose but your chains.

DARWIN: It seems to me that the workers of the world risk a great deal in a revolution—and their wives and children even more. However, let us put rhetoric aside, and focus on the scientific basis of your modeling approach. You presumably believe that the utopian aspirations of Robert Owen and the like are doomed to fail because they are unrealistic about the ability of human beings to put their selfish urges to one side in favor of working towards the common good. Utilitarians face the same problem. Why work for the welfare of the whole community rather than your own?

MARX: Your own Thomas Hobbes remarks that bees and ants live sociably together, so why can mankind not do the same? His answer is that the common and the private good of an ant or a bee are the same.

DARWIN: The social insects are one of many problems that the theory of evolution has yet to solve. I guess such problems will remain unresolved until we understand the mechanism by means of which traits are passed from one generation to the next. It is a great pity that my recent long journey to Brno in search of an answer should have proved to be fruitless.

MARX: But we cannot wait for ever for scientists to solve every problem! Action is needed to relieve the suffering of workers who earn only just enough to keep their families alive—with many more who would take their job if they could rather than starve.

DARWIN: It is true that attempts at reform are often stabs in the dark. However, we will make a bad mistake if we treat humans as though they were ants or bees. My guess at the explanation for the close cooperation between social insects is that their family relationships bind them together much more closely than in our own species. But Hobbes is surely right that we need a different explanation for why humans and the other great apes are sometimes able to put their differences aside to cooperate in joint enterprises. You criticize utopian socialism for proceeding as though apes can be treated like social insects, but the same might be said for your treating capitalists and workers as monolithic blocs with a common aim.

MARX: It is still shocking to hear of a human being described as an ape!

DARWIN: I have written somewhere that someone who understands baboon would contribute more to understanding human social contracts than John Locke himself! If I might be allowed to speculate again, I think we have to listen to what David Hume says about reciprocity to appreciate that human cooperation works no differently to cooperation among the great apes. One baboon scratches the back of another because he expects to get his own back scratched in return.

MARX: You do not shock me with your reduction of human cooperation to enlightened self-interest. Engels and I have committed ourselves to the British School of economics, which argues similarly. We are whole-hearted admirers of both Adam

Smith and David Ricardo. An adaptation of Ricardo's labor theory of value is one of the foundation stones of our approach. We hope that a biologist like yourself will be pleased that we style ourselves fellow-travelers in the scientific enterprise.

DARWIN: I am certainly sympathetic with your socialist aspirations, but my instinct is to follow Edmund Burke in his great debate with Tom Paine—to seek reform by measured steps, as in last year's legalization of trade unions. Otherwise we risk the series of catastrophes that followed the French Revolution. But perhaps I might be persuaded otherwise if I understood your system better.

MARX: Perhaps you could explain where your reservations lie.

DARWIN: My understanding is that you seek to demystify Hegel by replacing his attempt to describe the development of human consciousness with a model of actual human history that is continued into the future to an inevitable conclusion.

MARX: Capitalism will indeed collapse under the weight of its own contradictions. It will be replaced in the first instance by a dictatorship of the proletariat, but the trappings of government will gradually be eroded as the new social contract becomes established. The detailed structure of the final state will depend on matters that cannot be predicted, but it will inevitably be both fair and free.

DARWIN: Hegel's teleological story is therefore replaced by the historical inevitability of the general shape of successive social contracts—which certainly makes your model a candidate for scientific respectability if its empirical claims could be verified. But it is not reasonable to hope that skeptics like myself can be convinced of your predictions for the future unless your account of the past is based on a systematic study of the actual facts of economic and social history. I spent more than twenty years researching the details of the science on which my theory of evolution is based. My *Origin of Species* summarizes a very large data set gathered not only by myself, but by many other researchers in biology and geology. I was indeed hurried into publication before I felt that the grounding of the theory in data put the theory beyond doubt. I therefore feel entitled to ask where I might find the exhaustive analysis of historical data that entitles you to the certainty that you clearly feel for your account of history.

MARX: The biology of beetles and snails is no more common knowledge than the anatomy of finches in the far-off Galapagos Islands. But to learn the facts of the bourgeois exploitation of the proletariat, one need only open a newspaper.

DARWIN: It is one thing to appreciate that our society is inefficient and unfair, but quite another to make sweeping claims about the inevitability of a model of history. What data we have from the French Revolution would even seem to refute the claim that the trappings of a dictatorship of the proletariat will necessarily be eroded away by time. But perhaps you will accept that such a claim is made only for rhetorical purposes.

MARX: I accept nothing of the sort! I should have known better than to expect anything but bourgeois prejudice in such a household as this.

So Marx leaves in a rage. The servants, who have been listening at the study door, now gather at the upstairs windows to watch him go. Such excitement has never been known at Down House before! But the boy who cleans the boots is thoughtful. Can it really be that God did not make us high or lowly, and order our estate?

Chapter 22
Georg Cantor versus Bertrand Russell

Context

Bertrand Russell's (1872–1970) famous *Principia Mathematica* written jointly with Alfred Lord Whitehead was published in 1910, the year before the dialogue between Russell and Cantor is imagined to take place. Whitehead went on to become a famous philosopher in his own right—the author of the much quoted claim that philosophy consists of nothing more than footnotes to Plato. Their joint book is generally acknowledged to have completed the work pioneered by Gottlob Frege in reducing mathematics to a sufficiently widely interpreted version of logic.

Georg Cantor (1845–1918) was born in St Petersburg, the oldest of six children, but the family moved from Russia to Germany in search of milder winters. After being awarded a doctorate by the University of Berlin, he finally succeeded in getting a position at the University of Halle, from which he was never able to move on because the work for which he eventually became famous caused such an uproar in parts of the German mathematical establishment. Among the less offensive epithets publicly directed at him were "scientific charlatan" and "corrupter of youth".

The reason for such disapproval was his treating infinity as a definite object rather than as a manner of speaking about sequences of operations that can be continued indefinitely but never completed. Worse still, he distinguished an infinity of infinities of ever increasing size. What madness is this! He did not help things along by believing that his ideas not only came from God, but provided insights into His infinite Nature. Even so, it is hard nowadays to understand the fury that his claims provoked, and the persecution to which he was subjected by defenders of various sects of philosophical mathematicians, who would have been the first to condemn any persecution of religious heretics.

Cantor did not cope well with the storm that he provoked. He suffered severe bouts of depression, eventually suffering hospitalization in 1884. The sudden death of his youngest son Rudolph was a further blow, and Cantor was hospitalized again in 1903, and on and off again throughout the rest of his life. But there were intervals in which he was able to lecture and receive the plaudits of those who were able to appreciate his achievements. He retired in 1913, to live in penury during the First World War. In 1917, he was hospitalized for the last time, continually writing to his wife asking to be allowed to go home. He died there from heart failure in 1918.

In one of the brighter episodes in his unhappy life, Cantor was invited as one of the great and good to the 500th anniversary of the founding of the University of St Andrews. He is said to have attended in the hope of meeting Bertrand Russell. If so, he was disappointed—but not in the imaginary dialogue that follows. Having been introduced at a noisy reception the night before, they are envisaged as agreeing to meet the next afternoon for tea in the lounge of the comfortable hotel in which they are both staying. In 1911, a Scottish tea would have consisted of a substantial repast with all kinds of delicious treats, but it is unlikely that either Russell or Cantor would have felt like eating much at 5 o'clock in the afternoon.

Dialogue

Cantor and Russell are settled at a table in their hotel lounge with much ceremony. Tea is served, and they are at last left in peace to continue the conversation that proved impossible to sustain the previous evening as the noise level at the reception where they were introduced rose along with the quantity of Scotch whisky consumed by the assembled crowd of academic celebrities.

CANTOR: It was a privilege to attend yesterday's events marking the 500th anniversary of the founding of the University of St Andrews. Before my invitation, I had no idea that Scotland boasted such ancient universities. But the noisy reception at which we were introduced was too much for my ageing bones. It was kind of you to agree to meet me here in the quiet of the hotel lounge. The British habit of taking tea in the afternoon is very civilized.

RUSSELL: You asked me yesterday about how to reach a popular audience—how to make your ideas on the infinity of infinities created by God available to the masses. You probably know that I do not share your religious sentiments, although I am aware that mathematical insights sometimes feel like shafts of blinding light from another world. Nor do I believe that you need fear for your reputation, in spite of the shameful abuse to which you have been subjected, and your subsequent history of illness. You will be remembered for ever as a great mathematician and philosopher. As my grandmother used to say, when your opponents resort to abuse, it shows you have won the argument.

CANTOR: Your remarks are kind, but the fact remains that my road to advancement in the German mathematical world continues to be blocked by my philosophical enemies. So the project of attempting a popular work while I am still capable remains attractive to me. Did you come up with any thoughts overnight on how to put my ideas across without my getting too tangled up in technicalities?

RUSSELL: Here are my thoughts for what they are worth. You need first to explain that we use ordinary finite numbers like 5 or 23 for both ordinal and cardinal purposes—for counting and for saying how many items there are in a set. For example, a farmer who finds it hard to keep track of how many sheep he has in a field might count them by painting numbers on their backs. If the last number he paints is 47, then he knows his flock contains 47 sheep because the act of painting a number on each sheep establishes a one-to-one relationship between the sheep and the numerals 1 to 47. This will seem hardly worth saying to most people, but what if the same procedure is applied to infinite sets? I suggest approaching this question using David Hilbert's popular notion of a hotel with an infinite number of rooms.

CANTOR: David Hilbert is a great mathematician and a stout defender of my ideas, but I do not know about his hotel.

RUSSELL: You surprise me! Hilbert's story is that each room has a number painted on its door, so establishing a one-to-one relationship between the set of all ordinary numerals and the rooms in the hotel. So there are the same number of rooms in the hotel as there are numerals—they have the same cardinality. But the hotel never need turn a new customer away! If every room is occupied and new guests arrive, the manager can simply move all his current guests into the rooms with even numbers, leaving the odd numbers free for the new guests. The guest currently in room 1 goes into room 2, the guest currently in room 2 goes into room 4, the guest currently in room 3 goes into room 6, and so on. The point is that we thereby establish a one-to-one correspondence between the set of all numerals and the set of even numerals. So an infinite set can retain the same cardinality even after an infinite number of its members have been thrown away.

CANTOR: Your point is that all this can be explained without any formulas. This requires a talent that I am not sure I possess.

RUSSELL: You would now need to explain how the ordinal and cardinal roles of finite numbers need to be separated for infinite numbers.

CANTOR: I am thinking of saying transfinite numbers instead of infinite numbers. Or is this too technical?

RUSSELL: Not at all! People love such fancy jargon. Everybody knows that God says "I am the alpha and the omega" in the Book of Revelation. So they will fall over themselves with delight that the first transfinite ordinal is called omega after the Greek letter ω. As for the first transfinite cardinal being called aleph-zero and denoted by the Hebrew letter $\aleph_0$, we might as well be introducing our readers to the Kabbalah! What we must not do is to expect our readers to use such symbols for any precise purpose. We include them for the same reason that astrologers have fancy symbols for the planets—to impress our customers.

CANTOR: I am not sure that I care to be compared with astrologers or insurance salesmen. God has gifted me with genuine insight into his infinite Nature as the

Absolute Infinity beyond all transfinite infinities. Nothing but the Truth will suffice in communicating what He has taught me. You will reply that a popular account need not tell the whole truth, but only enough of the truth to get a hearing—but how is it possible to explain transfinite ordinals without precise definitions and formulas?

RUSSELL: There are many distinct ways to count the rooms in Hilbert's hotel. The simplest way is paint a finite number $1, 2, 3 \ldots$ on each door. We call them numerals when using them as ordinals to count with in this way. To signal that all the rooms have been counted, we need a new transfinite ordinal ω.

But one could use up all the finite numbers by painting every other door. We would then reach ω with an infinite set of rooms still uncounted. To count these rooms, we need more transfinite ordinals, $\omega + 1, \omega + 2, \omega + 3, \ldots$. When all the rooms have been counted this way, we will have reached the transfinite ordinal $\omega + \omega$. There are obviously an infinite number of other distinct ways that one could count the rooms of Hilbert's hotel, each of which will need a new transfinite ordinal.

CANTOR: I see how this would go, but such a lot is being left out. In particular, your story proceeds as though a mathematician would need actually to perform an infinite number of counting operations rather than simply to exhibit a one-to-one correspondence between a set of rooms in Hilbert's hotel and the set of ordinals with which they are counted. It was this misunderstanding that led to my being called a lunatic and a madman.

RUSSELL: I think this point would perhaps be too subtle for the generality of readers. However I am sure that they would readily understand that the cardinality of a set does not depend on how it is counted. So we could identify the cardinality of Hilbert's hotel with the first transfinite ordinal ω to register that its rooms can be put into one-to-one correspondence with the set of all finite numerals. But who can resist using the more exotic $\aleph_0$ for the cardinality of this set?

CANTOR: But then people will inevitably want to know what $\aleph_1$ is. Do we say that this can be identified with the first transfinite ordinal that comes after those that are needed to count Hilbert's hotel in all the infinite number of ways that it can be counted?

RUSSELL: This would perhaps be to pile Pelion upon Ossa! But we should be pleased that readers ask about $\aleph_1$ because it is important that they understand that there is no biggest cardinality. Your theory identifies an infinity of infinities! In particular, they can be told that the set of all decimal expansions cannot be put into a one-to-one correspondence with the set of all finite numerals, and so must have a larger cardinality. If you could count the real numbers between 0 and 1 using the finite numerals, their decimal expansions would thereby be arranged in a sequence from which you could construct a decimal expansion not in the sequence by making it differ in its nth digit from the nth term in the sequence.

CANTOR: This glib version of my diagonalization argument fails to make it clear that it can be applied to a set of any cardinality to construct a new set with even larger cardinality. I note also that you skate over the fact that we do not know whether the cardinality of the real numbers is $\aleph_1$ or not. It looks more and more to me that a popular account of my theory is not feasible—certainly not for someone with my limited literary talents.

RUSSELL: I share your doubts about the feasibility of the book you have in mind. It seems as though you want to explain more than can be explained without assuming some mathematical sophistication. Moreover, I have to admit that I do not myself understand your notion of an absolute infinity that somehow transcends all transfinite infinities. Are we now talking about the cardinality of the set of all sets? It cannot be meaningful to speak of such a set because there cannot be a set with greater cardinality than the set of all sets, but your diagonalization argument shows how to construct one. Hence my theory of types, in which a collection of sets does not itself count as a set. I believe it is you yourself who first drew attention to the fact that paradoxes arise if any proposition whatever is allowed to determine a set.

CANTOR: It is inevitable that the Nature of God be shrouded in mystery and paradox. Who are we to fathom the Mind of God? But I understand that such arguments are doomed to fall on stony ground when talking to an atheist. Let us therefore turn to the question of who deserves the credit for discovering the existence of these paradoxes of the infinite. I naturally feel that the tide of abuse that greeted my discovery of transfinite numbers also washed from view my own part in denying that we can meaningfully speak of a set of all sets.

RUSSELL: I believe the tide has receded and that your reputation is now secure. But the beach remains littered with paradoxes—and also the wreckage of Frege's attempt to reduce mathematics to logic. When I wrote to him to tell him of what the world now calls Russell's Paradox, he responded with integrity and grace. There is nothing in my knowledge to compare with Frege's dedication to truth. His entire life's work was on the verge of completion, much of his work had been ignored to the benefit of men infinitely less capable, his second volume was about to be published, and upon finding that his fundamental assumption was in error, he responded with an intellectual pleasure clearly submerging any feelings of personal disappointment. I am similarly disappointed with the lack of enthusiasm with which my theory of types has been received, but Frege is an example to us all on how to cope with such disappointments.

CANTOR: I agree that Frege is an example that we should seek to emulate. As for Russell's Paradox, this has the advantage that it does not depend on problems with the infinite. Does the set of all sets that do not belong to themselves belong to itself? If I were still contemplating writing a popular book, you would doubtless advocate explaining that your argument is no different from the story of the barber who shaves everybody in a town who does not shave himself. There can be no such barber, because both the assumption that he shaves himself and the assumption that he does not shave himself lead to contradictions. Similarly, there can be no set of all sets that do not contain themselves.

RUSSELL: For your book, I would rather offer the paradox of a benevolent and efficient God who helps all those mortals and only those mortals who do not help themselves!

CANTOR: A good place for us to end our discussion! Our conversation has been very useful to me. You have lifted a load from my shoulders. I see both that my reputation is safe in hands such as yours, and that my project of writing a popular book is impractical.

Chapter 23
Bertrand Russell versus John Dewey

Context

There was a famous debate between Bertrand Russell and John Dewey in the early twentieth century. It was ostensibly about how children should best be educated. Both men had helped their wives run experimental schools, and then used their philosophical careers as platforms from which to preach their favored methodologies. Looking back on their debate from a hundred years in the future, it is their similarities rather than their differences that strike the eye. So what generated their sometimes heated exchanges? It is usually thought to be their attitude to truth.

In an essay on the occasion of his eightieth birthday, Russell writes, "I wanted certainty, in the kind of way in which people want religious faith." On other hand, Dewey was the embodiment of pragmatism in his time, which held that certainty is unavailable, and that usefulness should be the criterion of what we count as true. However, it looks to me as though the real issue was that Russell—who felt that everybody should do their own thinking for themselves—interpreted Dewey's enthusiasm for democracy as an invitation to follow the herd wherever it might go. Dewey, on the other hand, perhaps thought that Russell's extravagant individualism would be a disaster for society if widely adopted.

Pragmatism was a home-grown American philosophy whose standard bearers were successively Charles Sanders Peirce, William James, and John Dewey. They were not only influential in education, but also in the new subject of psychology that was just getting going. Nowadays, it seems that Peirce and James are rated above Dewey, but it was Dewey who won most applause in their own time. One extravagant tribute observed that Dewey was to his age what Aristotle was to the later Middle Ages, not just a philosopher, but *the* philosopher.

John Dewey (1859–1952) had a classical American childhood in Vermont, followed by an orthodox career as a professor of philosophy in universities of increasing grandeur that culminated in his becoming a public intellectual with a global reputation. Like Russell, he sought to reconcile the naturalism of his age with the more traditional philosophical issues of how we should live our lives. Some significance may perhaps be found in the fact that Russell was originally inspired by Leibniz, and Dewey by Hegel.

Bertrand Russell (1872–1970) was born to a famous family of English aristocrats, becoming Earl Russell after the death of his older brother. He was orphaned as a child, and brought up by his very strict grandparents and a line of private tutors. It is no wonder that he became somewhat wild when allowed a little freedom. He fell in love with the deductive logic of Euclidean geometry as a boy, and sought to bring the certainty of logic to the foundations of mathematics as a man. He went on to be regarded as a pillar of analytic philosophy. In his maturity, he became a public figure for espousing unpopular liberal causes. He was imprisoned in the First World War for his pacifism; his advocacy of free love was an ongoing scandal; he was a leader in the later movement for nuclear disarmament. Two episodes in his ramshackle life will have to serve for many more. The experimental school he ran with the second of his four wives was not put at risk when she found he was sleeping with the governess of their children, but finally collapsed when she gave birth to a second child by a lover of her own. In a second episode from the year 1940, he was dismissed from a professorship at the City College of New York after a scandalous court case, in which he was vilified for both his atheism and his sexual liberalism. Although the entirely respectable John Dewey did not care for Russell personally, he spoke up publicly in his defense, arguing that the dismissal was a case of pure prejudice.

Russell and Dewey first met at Harvard in 1914, but their imaginary dialogue is set in Beijing, China where they were both visiting in 1921. They were supposedly always cordial to each other when meeting face to face, but we know that Russell formed a dislike to Dewey at that time from a letter he wrote to one of his various mistresses. Dewey apparently reciprocated the dislike, finding Russell's aristocratic manner difficult to bear. I have invented an occasion for their meeting when both are enjoying the hospitality of Hu Shih, one of John Dewey's fervent Chinese admirers.

Dialogue

Dewey and Russell are both visiting in China. Russell is a new arrival but Dewey has been there for some time. Russell is accustomed to being the center of attention, so his equanimity is disturbed when it turns out that Dewey and the pragmatic philosophy that he promotes have already won the hearts of the Chinese intellectual elite. He is nevertheless delighted to accept an invitation to a reception in what was then called Peking hosted by Dewey's disciple, Hu Shih. However, he had not anticipated that he would be expected to debate with Dewey in the presence of an audience waiting with baited breath to hear the wisdom of such famous western philosophers—nor that the shafts of wit with which he normally carried all before him would fail to hit the spot in an environment where sages were expected to maintain a certain dignity in public.

HU SHIH: I have set aside a little time in which I hope our two distinguished guests will clarify how they differ on their attitudes to how philosophers should think about truth. Am I wrong in thinking that the fault line is to be found where Immanuel Kant drew the line between pure and practical reason?

RUSSELL: There is perhaps something to your suggestion. But we first need to emphasize how much Professor Dewey and I have in common. Neither of us subscribe to the idealism of philosophers like Bradley. We do not think truths are to be found by adopting the posture of Rodin's *Thinker* and waiting for inspiration. The knowledge-as-certainty claimed by idealists is beyond human reach. Professor Dewey and I belong to both the empirical and naturalist traditions. We do not believe it makes sense to look for more than knowledge-as-commitment. Where we differ is in what it is reasonable to take as basic commitments or axioms. But here again I think we can limit the area of disagreement to exclude putative axioms that can be refuted by scientific means.

DEWEY: I would not follow Professor Russell in speaking of axioms, but we are indeed broadly in agreement on the basic issues he mentions. Pragmatists like myself are particularly hostile to the armchair reasoning of traditional philosophy. We think real-world verification of any principles that may be proposed is essential to any reasonable approach to the world.

RUSSELL: Where we differ is in what should be allowed to count as verification, where I think we only differ at the extremes. Professor Dewey is doubtful that the research into the foundations of mathematics to which I devoted my youth is capable of uncovering genuine truths about the universe because of the paradoxes that people like myself have discovered. But I freely concede this point. Mathematicians do not see themselves as one more sect of armchair metaphysicians. The truths on which they insist are merely that some propositions follow logically from other propositions. I think we should therefore focus on what counts as verification at the other extreme—particularly in a social context. Is it enough that some principle should be generally thought to work out well in practice for it to be regarded as true, or should we insist on the more demanding requirements of professional scientists?

DEWEY: Here I think Professor Russell refers to our disagreement about the education of children. I believe that what works for a democratic society is that all children be treated the same—no child should be treated as inferior. I agree that some children are cleverer than others, but the evidence shows that it is not good for society that they be singled out for special treatment.

RUSSELL: There are things to be said on both sides of this question. Where I disagree is in calling something true without appealing to objective criteria. The danger is that we then legitimize the rule of the herd—that we restrict the opportunity of children to think their own thoughts by denying them a language within which they can express anything unconventional. Surely we can find a word less sharp than truth for what are really social conventions.

DEWEY: The difference between us dates back at least as far as the Fifth Century BC to a challenge made by the sophist Antiphon to Parmenides' assumption that truth is nothing more than correspondence to reality—that *nomos* needs to be considered alongside *physis*. Pragmatists agree with Antiphon that some truths are indeed true whatever people may believe, but others are true because people believe them. For example, it is true as a matter-of-fact that it is wise to drive your automobile on the left in England because everybody believes that it is safer to drive on the left in England.

RUSSELL: Our audience may not be aware that Antiphon's *On Truth* is one of the Oxyrhynchus Papyri excavated not so long ago from an ancient garbage heap in Egypt. It is as ancient perhaps as the *Analects* of Confucius. But I am not a naive follower of Parmenides. I do not deny that some truths are true because people believe them to be true. The problem that troubles me is whether the criteria that determine such social truths are adequate for the purpose. Let me propose what I hope is a non-controversial example derived from a dull weekend spent with folk who breed dogs. What counts as a prize-winning Afghan Hound turns out to depend on who is chosen to judge at a particular dog show, with the result that dog-breeders devote much effort to the politics of deciding who the judges should be.

DEWEY: I agree that we do not want what counts as true to become a political football, but there are also problems in the purest of pure mathematics—especially in recent developments in set theory, which abounds with paradoxes. Are infinite sets real or are they not? You have already staked out a neutral position for yourself, but other mathematicians seem willing to argue both sides of the question.

RUSSELL: Neither you nor I are responsible for the reckless claims of some of our colleagues. We can perhaps also agree that the fact that imperfect criteria are not perfect should be insufficient to justify their wholesale rejection.

DEWEY: What of the possibility that the pragmatist position might treat as true propositions that contradict each other? For example, nobody denies that the notion that we have free will works because we take this claim for granted when going about our daily affairs. But materialists argue that the laws of physics apply even to our brains.

RUSSELL: One day we will understand why models postulating free will work in practice. A similar situation arises with the ancient principle that Nature abhors a vacuum, which works perfectly well under normal circumstances, but turned out to fail when tested by the barometers of Torricelli and Pascal. The theory of relativity recently invented by Albert Einstein—this year's winner of the Nobel Prize for physics—makes it clear that we have to be ready to revise even what we thought were the most solid laws of physics. In brief, your example of free will from human psychology is another warning that we need to be careful in what we choose to call true. We need a more flexible vocabulary. It is a practical necessity that we sometimes behave *as though* certain propositions are true—that is what is meant by knowledge-as-commitment. But knowledge-as-commitment is only provisional. Knowledge-as-certainty is unattainable, but it can serve as a ideal toward which to strive—although even the notion that the universe is sufficiently simple that it can be fully described in terms of a collection of propositions that can be classified as true or false is doubtful.

DEWEY: Pragmatists share your skepticism about whether absolute truth is even possible. Perhaps it is therefore a good point on which to end our debate. I am also in agreement that there are many shades of meaning to the word *truth* as used by philosophers, and that it would be helpful to find a commonly accepted vocabulary to distinguish these meanings. But I guess you are no more optimistic than I that the philosophy profession will put aside its differences to create such a vocabulary, nor that it will give up its addiction to the notion of absolute truth.

HU SHIH: Let me express the thanks of all present for this enlightening exchange of views. It is of the greatest importance as we build a new China that we take serious account of all views that are in contention in the west. I hope now that our guests will be prepared to respond to a few questions.

The English in which the questions are asked is often hard to follow, but Russell quickly learns both that the audience has been won over in advance to pragmatism, and that they feel he should have been more respectful of their hero. However, Dewey's success in 1920's China will count for nothing after the future triumph of Marxism.

Chapter 24
Ludwig Wittgenstein versus David Hilbert

Context

People sometimes say that Ludwig Wittgenstein was the greatest philosopher of the twentieth century. He is credited with having made important contributions to logic, the philosophy of mathematics, and the philosophy of language.

Wittgenstein (1889–1951) was born into a seriously rich family in Vienna, the youngest of eight children, all of whom were mixed-up in one way or another. Wittgenstein himself was relentlessly serious, and subject to periodic rounds of depression, but he did not commit suicide like three of his brothers. After redistributing his inherited wealth to his siblings, he decided to become a philosopher, finding his way to Cambridge, where he was taken under the wing of a welcoming Bertrand Russell. However, his philosophical career was interrupted by various unsuccessful efforts to make a mark elsewhere. His career itself was also turbulent, with switches in direction sometimes leading him to repudiate his earlier work. However, he never repudiated the view he expresses in the coming imaginary dialogue, which reflects his enduring distaste for anything but the most matter-of-fact of philosophies. The invention of transfinite numbers by Georg Cantor—making sense of the issues that got William of Ockham and Duns Scotus into a tangle in an earlier imaginary dialogue—would therefore have been a natural target for Wittgenstein.

David Hilbert (1862–1943) was born in Königsberg, where he attended the same school as Immanuel Kant. His contributions to mathematics were so extraordinary that after he was made a professor at Göttingen University, it became the leading center for mathematics in the world until destroyed by the Nazis. Only two of his many achievements will be mentioned. The first was his rewriting Euclid's axioms for geometry after he discovered that they lacked a formal treatment of betweenness.

© The Editor(s) (if applicable) and The Author(s), under exclusive license to Springer Nature Switzerland AG 2021
K. Binmore, *Imaginary Philosophical Dialogues*,
https://doi.org/10.1007/978-3-030-65387-3_24

The second was his invention of Hilbert Space, which is nowadays the mathematical backdrop for quantum physics.

The 1930 meeting of the Society of German Natural Scientists and Physicians was held in his birthplace, Königsberg. It was therefore appropriate to make it the occasion for honoring his retirement in the same year. Among other things, he gave a radio broadcast that is still remembered for its stirring conclusion in which he denied that there are matters beyond human understanding. As he put it: We *can* know, and we *must* know. The meeting was to prove even more famous because it was here that Kurt Gödel made the first tentative announcement of the undecidability results that eventually put an end to Hilbert's aspirations for the foundations of mathematics.

Gödel spoke up during a round-table discussion at a conference on epistemology held alongside the main event. Other participants included John von Neumann and Rudolf Carnap. It seems that von Neumann immediately grasped at least some of the implications of Gödel's discoveries, but it was some time before Gödel published his second incompleteness theorem that makes it explicit that the answer to the second of Hilbert's famous list of 23 unsolved problems is that no finitistic proof of the consistency of arithmetic is possible.

It is not clear whether Hilbert was in Gödel's audience, or whether he was ever reconciled to his hopes being dashed. But the following imaginary dialogue assumes that he was present, and understood immediately the implications of what he was hearing. There is no reason to suppose that Wittgenstein ever came anywhere near Königsberg, but an epistemology conference would have been his kind of thing. If he had been there, it would have been like him to approach the leading mathematician of the day to explain why mathematics is "ridden through and through with the pernicious idioms of set theory", which are not only "utter nonsense" but "laughable" and "wrong". However, to be fair to Wittgenstein, his views on the philosophy of mathematics evolved over the years, and it is not clear that he would have been so brash at the age of 41 as he is represented in the dialogue. To be fair to Hilbert also, he would probably not have teased the implacably serious Wittgenstein by saying that mathematics is just a game that mathematicians play. However, he would certainly not have taken too seriously being told how mathematics should be done by somebody who had never done any serious mathematics.

Dialogue

There is a mid-morning break during a conference on epistemology attended by Hilbert and Wittgenstein in 1930—the year of Hilbert's retirement from Göttingen. Wittgenstein approaches Hilbert with a view to explaining why the way Hilbert thinks about mathematics is wholly mistaken. He finds Hilbert in a vulnerable state after hearing Gödel make a tentative announcement of the results that destroyed his hopes for a firm foundation for mathematics. Something in the way of a diversion is therefore welcome when Wittgenstein introduces himself, and proposes that they linger over their coffee rather than attend the next session.

Wittgenstein versus Hilbert

WITTGENSTEIN: It is gracious of you to give time to a philosopher of mathematics, albeit a one-time student of Bertrand Russell. I am anxious to seek your opinion on the reasons for my opposition to the innovations of Georg Cantor in set theory. In particular, his treating infinity as though it were a real entity rather than a way of saying that certain operations cannot be completed.

HILBERT: Do you have more to contribute than the abuse we heard from the mathematicians Kronecker and Poincaré? Cantor's state of mind was always uncertain, and it certainly did not help his mental equilibrium to be denounced as a lunatic or madman. Let me repeat what I have said before in public: Nobody shall expel us from the paradise that Cantor has created for us.

WITTGENSTEIN: I hope you will regard my criticisms as being more principled. I start from the nominalist premise that there is no such thing as an integer like 4, merely collections of four objects. I even differ from my mentor Russell in denying that 4 can be defined as the set of all sets with four members, because such a definition would require quantifying over an infinite set, which is a task that cannot be completed in reality.

HILBERT: Let us separate the two points you have made. The first is that the integers do not really exist as abstract objects in their own right. Like other empiricists, notably John Stuart Mill, you probably also think that addition tables are simply human inventions which summarize the physical laws that govern what happens when groups of pebbles on a table-top are pushed together. At the other end of the spectrum are the philosophical rationalists, who believe that the addition tables were always awaiting our discovery in a Platonic limbo of which the world of our experience is a mere shadow. Some mathematicians hold to each of these views. I suspect that you belong to the constructivist branch of the empiricist sect. Cantor himself would count as a rationalist, believing to his death that his researches into the infinite had deep religious significance. A more modern view is to deny that metaphysics has any role to play in pure mathematics—that mathematical models are just formal games that mathematicians play in which symbols are manipulated according to fixed rules. There is then no need to insist either that the axioms in such formal models are self-evident, or that they are induced from empirical laws.

WITTGENSTEIN: You have changed your opinion? I have here a record of something you said in 1919: "Mathematics is not like a game whose tasks are determined by arbitrarily stipulated rules. Rather, it is a conceptual system possessing internal necessity that can only be so and by no means otherwise."

HILBERT: You may recall that I gave a list of 23 problems in the year 1900 at a mathematical congress in Paris. Yesterday, we heard Kurt Gödel announce results that imply my second problem is impossible—that no proof of the consistency of arithmetic can be found without bringing in new principles. He says his claim is only tentative, but I found his brilliant argument very convincing. Who would have thought the Liar Paradox could be used in such a way? My old certainties have had to be discarded overnight. But when I now say that mathematics is a formal game played by mathematicians, I do not mean that it is not a serious activity—only that proofs should not depend on particular interpretations of the symbols used in mathematical models.

WITTGENSTEIN: So the problem of interpreting the symbols in a formal model when an application is proposed is something that mathematicians can leave to the scientists who are proposing the application? But surely the whole interest of a model lies in how the symbols are to be interpreted?

HILBERT: It is true that models are usually constructed with an application in mind, but the difficulty in proving theorems gives the models a life of their own. People ask themselves how things would be with different axioms. Sometimes the new models invented in this way then turn out to have unexpected applications elsewhere. For example, nobody expected group theory to be relevant to seating people around a dinner table so that men and women alternate, but no wife sits next to her husband.

WITTGENSTEIN: But mathematicians playing with their models can still only do a finite number of things. They cannot count all the integers, and so find that there are ω of them. So even Cantor's first transfinite ordinal ω is an impossible fancy.

HILBERT: This brings us back to the second point you made earlier. Mathematicians do not need to do an infinite number of things to handle infinite sets. For example, we can prove that something is true of every integer using Mathematical Induction.

WITTGENSTEIN: But you thereby own up to the fact that you are not really handling an infinite set as such, but an algorithm—a rule for generating the next member of a sequence. Constructivists have no problem with uncompleted infinities.

HILBERT: You would presumably say that the sequence of prime numbers is the algorithm that proceeds by keeping on adding one to whatever is the current prime until you reach a larger number divisible only by itself and one? What do you say to Euclid's proof that this algorithm always generates a successor prime—that there is an infinity of prime numbers?

WITTGENSTEIN: If there were a finite number of primes, we could multiply them together and add one to obtain an integer that does not have any of the primes we multiplied together as a factor. I say that it is not a proof at all because it relies on obtaining a contradiction from the hypothesis that there are only a finite number of primes.

HILBERT: Spoken like a true constructivist! Proof by contradiction is not allowed. But we can treat the proving of theorems as a branch of formal mathematics in which the Principle of Contradiction becomes an axiom alongside the Principle of Mathematical Induction. Dealing with sets as completed infinities then becomes part of the game that mathematicians play. I use the term metamathematics to refer to the branch of mathematics in which we study how mathematicians play this game. Just as you insist that arithmetic is merely the science of rearranging sets of pebbles on a table-top, so metamathematics is just the science of rearranging sets of symbols on a blackboard according to certain rules. But now we find an area where we agree, since I have argued that metamathematics should be restricted to constructive methods of proof.

WITTGENSTEIN: Such an approach would admittedly rescue the argument by contradiction by which Cantor shows that one cannot count the real numbers using the integers. You might then interpret this result as showing that some infinities are larger than others, but all you would really have done is to show that a finite set of operations can transform one collection of symbols into another. What relevance would such an exercise have to whether infinities actually exist in the real world?

HILBERT: None at all! There is no place in mathematics for metaphysics. Metaphysicians have to do their own metaphysics for themselves. They can use our models if they like, but how they interpret the symbols they contain is their own responsibility.

WITTGENSTEIN: What of the first of your 23 problems—that there is no infinity larger than that of the integers and smaller than that of the real numbers? What if it turns out to be impossible to decide this question?

HILBERT: The Continuum Hypothesis! It will certainly put the cat among the pigeons if this turns out to be independent of the other axioms of set theory.

WITTGENSTEIN: At least we would then be in agreement in denying that it makes sense to postulate a Platonic universe in which the theorems of mathematics lie waiting to be discovered. if we accept that completed infinities are to be part of formal mathematics, it would then be open to us to invent an infinity of Platonic universes.

HILBERT: Indeed! A veritable paradise for mathematicians to play in! And you would confine us to shifting pebbles around on a table.

WITTGENSTEIN: Your paradises are mere fantasies. They cannot all be true because they contradict each other.

HILBERT: What do mathematicians care what is said to be "true" by philosophers? As Russell remarked: Mathematics is the subject where we do not know what we are talking about, and do not care whether what we say is "true". Are our activities therefore worthless? There may be philosophers like yourself who think so, but physicists think otherwise. Even theologians are sometimes willing to agree that God must be a mathematician.

So their session ended with Hilbert in better humor than before their conversation, and Wittgenstein feeling a bit like the victim of a confidence trick. After all, Hilbert had told him nothing that he did not know already.

Afterword

The Continuum Hypothesis is that the cardinality of the set of real numbers is $\aleph_1$. Its independence of the other axioms of set theory was proved by Paul Cohen in 1963, completing earlier work by Gödel in 1934. As a graduate student of mathematics in the late sixties who had just read Cohen's excellent book, I had the opportunity to ask him how he got interested in set theory. He replied that he had no particular interest in set theory; it was just that the Continuum Hypothesis seemed the easiest of Hilbert's famous 23 unsolved problems. I was left dumbstruck at being in the presence of somebody who could look at Hilbert's problems, and have an opinion on which might be easiest.

The ancient Liar Paradox is attributed to Epimenides of Crete, who said that Cretans always lie. Philosophers of language sometimes rule out all such self-referential sentences—and hence Gödel's insights—on the grounds that they notoriously lead to contradictions. But this sentence is grammatical.

Chapter 25

Oskar Morgenstern versus John von Neumann

Context

John von Neumann's 1928 invention of game theory was just a sideline for him. It remained unappreciated until the economist Oskar Morgenstern persuaded him that they should write a book together that was eventually published as *The Theory of Games and Economic Behavior* in 1944. Economists greeted the book at first with great enthusiasm, but lost interest when they discovered that only zero-sum games were analyzed in detail.

John Nash extended the scope of game theory to games that are of more interest to economists by redirecting their attention to the idea of a Nash equilibrium, but more than twenty years passed before economists realized that they now had a viable way of thinking about imperfectly competitive markets. It is interesting that von Neumann and Morgenstern anticipated Nash's definition, but not the fact that this was going to be the way forward for applying game theory in economics.

John von Neumann (1903–1957) was the ultimate polymath. His extraordinary talents were evident from a very young age. His father was a banker who was wealthy enough to buy the family's *von* from the Hungarian government. He also ensured that von Neumann was educated to the highest level alongside a constellation of other gifted boys that Budapest somehow generated at that time. He was only 19 when he rewrote the foundations of Cantor's theory of transfinite numbers in a way that remains the standard treatment. I will not attempt to enumerate his major theoretical contributions across a wide spectrum of disciplines ranging from mathematical logic to quantum mechanics, as several pages would be necessary for this purpose. If that were not enough, he was also a pioneer in computer science, and a leading figure in the Manhattan project that produced the first atomic bomb.

He became politically influential after the Second World War—one of the hawkish advocates of a pre-emptive strike against Russia. As a result, he is sometimes named as the inspiration of the crazed Dr Strangelove in the famous movie. But he was not at all uptight as a person, enjoying a good time, and apparently happy to get on with his work however chaotic the environment. But he must have been a daunting companion, so quick and clever that people thought he was perhaps from another planet.

Oskar Morgenstern (1902–1977) was born in Germany, but grew up and was educated in Vienna. Adolf Hitler took over Austria in the Anschluss of 1938 while Morgenstern was visiting the USA, after which he decided not to return to Austria, but to accept an offer from Princeton's Economics Department. However, he felt most at home in the atmosphere of Princeton's famous Institute of Advanced Studies, where he met John von Neumann. He must have exercised all his considerable charm to persuade von Neumann that they should write a book together that would explain the potential of game theory to revolutionize economic theory.

Von Neumann was dead by the time Morgenstern's prediction that game theory would revolutionize economics finally came true. Morgenstern is then said by detractors—who regard him as nothing more than a Watson to von Neumann's Holmes—to have waited by his telephone at the time Nobel Prizes are awarded in case a call should come for him, a possibility that was never to be realized but which does not seem so unreasonable to me. His influence on von Neumann is transparent in *The Theory of Games and Economic Behavior*, where the abrupt transitions from passages written by Morgenstern to those written by von Neumann are plain to see. It is a pity that Morgenstern obviously did not follow all of von Neumann's mathematics. If he had, he would perhaps have restrained von Neumann from sometimes losing his way—especially towards the end of the book—in developing his ideas beyond any possible economic application. But I do not see that it is reasonable to criticize Morgenstern for not being a better mathematician. I am a mathematician by training myself, but I did not find it at all easy to follow von Neumann's analysis of his simplified model of Poker when preparing my own—even more simplified—Poker model for a textbook.

When they were writing their book, Morgenstern turned up one afternoon at von Neumann's Princeton house to argue that they needed a better explanation of the payoffs in the games they were analyzing. Von Neumann had been taking for granted that players would seek to maximize the long-run average of these payoffs, but the orthodox opinion among economists at the time was that it is unscientific to identify a player's utility with such payoffs. Von Neumann then sat right down and wrote an axiomatic theory refuting this philosophical position on the spot.

It is ironic that this incident is likely to be the major reason that Morgenstern is remembered in the future. Von Neumann and Morgenstern utility remains the standard textbook approach to this day. John Harsanyi, for example, uses it as the obvious substitute for the vague happiness notion of Bentham and Mill when discussing utilitarianism with John Rawls in a later imaginary dialogue. Von Neumann's explanation of the maximin criterion in the current imaginary dialogue is also relevant to Rawls' reply.

The real-life story of the invention of von Neumann and Morgenstern utility is the basis for the imaginary dialogue that follows. I do not suppose that the real von Neumann would have listened as patiently as his imaginary counterpart to Morgenstern's explanation of why they needed to respond to what was then the orthodox economic position. Still less do I suppose that my fictional Morgenstern will get a hearing from those utilitarian philosophers of today who proceed as though modern economists still hold fast to the Benthamite orthodoxy that preceded the Robbins orthodoxy that von Neumann is about to explode. It is now more than seventy years since Von Neumann increased the number of orthodoxies by which such philosophers are behind the times from one to two.

Dialogue

It is a sunny afternoon in the Fall of 1943. Morgenstern arrives at von Neumann's Princeton home to keep an appointment to review their progress on the book they are writing together. He has summoned up his courage, and is very determined not to have his philosophical problems with their project dismissed again as mere philosophy. However, he begins diplomatically by softening von Neumann up with some lesser points that he hopes will prove uncontroversial.

MORGENSTERN: I was told yesterday that we need to give credit to the mathematician Émile Borel for anticipating your 1928 paper on game theory.

VON NEUMANN: Émile Borel was certainly a great mathematician, and it is true that I did not know in 1928 that anyone had thought about game theory before me. He certainly had the idea of a pure strategy as a complete plan of action for a player in a game that tells the player what to do under all possible contingencies that might arise. He also understood that the solution of some games will require a rational player—let us call her Alice and her opponent Bob—to randomize over her pure strategies to keep Bob guessing. Our draft says that when Alice randomizes in this way, she is using a mixed strategy. He also saw that a rational solution of a zero-sum game between Alice and Bob would necessarily require each to use their maximin strategy.

MORGENSTERN: I want to press you shortly on how I should rewrite our explanation of maximin strategies, but please continue with what you were saying about Borel.

VON NEUMANN: Borel's contributions thus far seem trivial to me. Borel thought the same. He could see that they lead nowhere unless the minimax theorem is true, but guessed it to be false. I never thought I had made any progress at all until I had proved that the minimax theorem is true.

MORGENSTERN: It is a pity we are confined to zero-sum games. It doubtless makes it easier to prove theorems to assume that, whatever Alice wins, Bob will necessarily lose, but such games are rare in economic applications, where Alice and Bob usually both expect to profit from trading with each other.

VON NEUMANN: I have tried hard to extend my notion of a rational solution to games that are not zero-sum, but here I have to join Borel in thinking that perhaps we ask for too much in seeking a concept of rationality that solves all games.

MORGENSTERN: The minimax theorem says that a player's minimax payoff is equal to his maximin payoff if mixed strategies are allowed. The philosopher Jeremy Bentham, who invented the words *maximum* and *minimum,* would have been delighted by *maximin* and *minimax.* But how are we to explain these exotic concepts to economists who seldom know much mathematics? Why should Alice and Bob play their minimax strategies?

VON NEUMANN: They certainly should *not* play their minimax strategies! That would be really stupid! If Alice and Bob are rational, they should play their maximin strategies in a zero-sum game.

MORGENSTERN: It is certainly easy to confuse maximin with minimax! It is hard to remember that mathematicians read such formulas from right to left. It would have helped if your minimax theorem had been called the maximin theorem, but I guess it is too late now to change how people talk about your 1928 paper.

VON NEUMANN: To find her maximin strategy, Alice first works out the worst that could happen for each of her mixed strategies, which is that Bob will then choose whichever of his strategies minimizes her expected payoff. Alice's maximin strategy is whichever of her own strategies secures the maximum of these minimum payoffs. By playing her maximin strategy, she thereby guarantees getting no less than her maximin payoff.

MORGENSTERN: But how do we explain why it is rational for Alice to play her maximin strategy? It seems overly cautious on the face of it.

VON NEUMANN: This is where the minimax theorem comes in. In a zero-sum game, Bob can guarantee that Alice gets no more than her minimax payoff by playing his maximin strategy. To see why, just redo Bob's maximin calculation in terms of Alice's losses instead of his gains. But Alice's minimax payoff equals her maximin payoff.

MORGENSTERN: By playing their maximin strategies, Alice and Bob therefore guarantee both that their own payoff will be no less its maximin value, and that their opponent's payoff will be no more than its maximin value.

VON NEUMANN: Precisely! We can explain further by asking what should be written in an authoritative dictionary of all possible games as the rational way for each player to play each game. For two-person, zero-sum games, the answer is that the players should choose one of their maximin strategies. Alice and Bob will then each be making a best reply to the choice of the other—which is a necessary requirement if the book is to be authoritative. If Alice, for example, had a better reply, she would not follow the book's advice.

MORGENSTERN: All this holds together very well as a piece of theory, but we need examples to lighten things up. Your second model of Poker would be ideal for this purpose if its analysis were not so mathematically dense. Who would have thought that optimal play in Poker would require the players to bluff so much? Who would have thought that optimal play requires players to bluff only with very bad hands, and not at all with middle-range hands?

VON NEUMANN: The betting opportunities in my second Poker model are very restricted, but I think it captures the essence of Poker. Most of the mathematics could be eliminated by allowing only three cards in the deck—say the King, Queen and Jack of Hearts—from which Alice and Bob are dealt one card each. If Alice has to open the betting with a high or a low bet, she will obviously always bet high when holding the King. But nobody will guess that she should never bet high when holding the Queen, and only bluff when holding the Jack.

MORGENSTERN: It would be great if you could write up this three-card Poker model for our book!

VON NEUMANN: The probability with which Alice should bluff when holding the Jack will depend on the size of the high and low bets in the model. The calculation would be trivial, but I would rather spend my time working on the problem of coalition formation in multiplayer games for the cooperative part of our book, which has still to be finished.

Morgenstern thinks to himself that few of their readers will agree with John von Neumann on what counts as trivial! However he is pleased that von Neumann seems willing to consider additions to the current draft. Now is perhaps the time to broach the philosophical question of how to model the preferences of the players in a game.

MORGENSTERN: There is no problem with interpreting our payoffs in Poker. We simply identify them with money, and assume that the players try to make as much money on average as they can. But there is a problem if the stakes get very high. The St Petersburg Paradox shows that psychologically absurd outcomes can then result from assuming that people care only about their expected monetary gain.

VON NEUMANN: Is the St Petersburg Paradox something serious, or just more philosophical juggling with words?

MORGENSTERN: The paradox was invented by the Swiss mathematician Nicolaus Bernoulli.

VON NEUMANN: One of the famous Bernoulli family!

MORGENSTERN: It was actually his brother Daniel who published the paradox in a St Petersburg journal at the beginning of the eighteenth century. The brothers proposed dealing with the problem by replacing the expected value of money by the expected value of the utility of money. Their basic idea is that the utility of an extra dollar paid to a millionaire is a lot smaller than the utility of an extra dollar to a beggar. If the utility of each extra dollar—the marginal utility of money—decreases fast enough, the St Petersburg Paradox disappears.

VON NEUMANN: So why do we not simply replace dollars by units of utility—let us call them utils—citing the Bernoullis as our authority?

MORGENSTERN: The economists we are trying to reach will care nothing about some family of Swiss mathematicians! But they do care about the jeremiads of an English guru called Lionel Robbins, who is famous for his banal definition of economics as a science which studies human behavior as a relationship between ends and scarce means which have alternative uses.

VON NEUMANN: What does he say that denies us the use of Bernoulli utilities?

MORGENSTERN: His jeremiads are directed against following the utilitarians of the last century in treating happiness as an unproblematic concept. For them, a util was just a unit of happiness. But how do we measure happiness? Are we to assume that people have happiness meters inside their heads? How is economics to become a science if it is based on such dubious psychological foundations?

VON NEUMANN: How can economists get by without modeling people as utility maximizers?

MORGENSTERN: It turns out that models of markets do not need such a strong assumption. It is enough to be able to say whether people would prefer a little bit more of this to a little bit less of that, without having to say by how much they prefer one to the other. Robbins is tireless in advocating our giving up the utilitarianism of our Victorian ancestors in favor of this so-called marginalist revolution. Cardinal utilities like those of Bentham or the Bernoullis must be abandoned altogether. We must give up the idea that all the utils people accumulate as they become richer can be counted as being worth the same. Only ordinal utilities make sense because they do not pretend otherwise. Not only are cardinal utilities unscientific, they are said to be philosophically incoherent. Robbins waxes particularly strong on the impossibility of comparing the utils of different people. How are we to evaluate how much more Alice is suffering in the dentist's chair than Bob?

VON NEUMANN: The fact that we study zero-sum games in the non-cooperative part of our book makes it look like we are comparing Alice and Bob's utils, but we could double all of Bob's utils without making any difference to our conclusions. We only need that Alice's preferences are the opposite of Bob's. But I see no way to satisfy a tub-thumper like Robbins in the cooperative part of our book. In our cooperative games, players not only compare their utils, but pass them from one person to another like dollar bills.

MORGENSTERN: We cannot avoid controversy in the cooperative part of our book, in which we also assume that people can write binding pre-play contracts. But I have hopes that we can escape criticism in the more fundamental non-cooperative section. Is it possible that we could justify using Bernoulli-stye utilities there by following the methodology of the mathematician Frank Ramsey? He showed that if Alice is consistent in how she makes risky choices, then she necessarily behaves as though probabilities can be used to quantify the risks she faces. Ramsey's assumptions about Alice's preferences are admittedly primitive, but perhaps a souped-up version of his consistency assumptions can be made to imply that Alice necessarily behaves as though cardinal utilities can be used to quantify her preferences?

VON NEUMANN: Ramsey was full of good ideas! But we do not need to soup-up his axioms. We can simplify our task by assuming that the risks our players face are already quantified with probabilities. It may well then be easy to come up with consistency axioms that do the trick. Why not take a walk in the garden while I think how we might go about it?

When Morgenstern returns, von Neumann has scribbled a list of hard-to-deny consistency axioms on a piece of paper which imply that a rational person has no choice but to behave as though maximizing the expected value of an abstract something that he proposes to call utility. His proof is a knock-down refutation of Robbins' claim that cardinal utility can never make any sense, since one can check whether Alice or Bob satisfy von Neumann's axioms simply by observing their choice behavior in risky situations. It is a pity that experiments show that real people are seldom as rational as von Neumann's axioms require.

Afterword

The St Petersburg Paradox is only one of many psychological paradoxes of the infinite that can be constructed unless a player's utilities are confined between upper and lower bounds, but only philosophers seem to care about this problem. It is a shame that philosophers are less careful about the distinction between cooperative and non-cooperative game theory, which are *not* characterized by differing assumptions about how nice people are assumed to be. From a philosophical point of view, John Nash's ideas on how to reconcile the two approaches are perhaps as important as his contribution to equilibrium theory. In brief, cooperative game theory is a branch of non-cooperative game theory that applies when some very strong simplifying assumptions are made. It is admittedly confusing that non-cooperative game theory should allow the possibility that the players might cooperate in games that are not zero-sum. But to say that a game theory is non-cooperative only means that cooperation is not taken for granted, but has to be explained as individually rational behavior when it occurs.

The reference to Émile Borel is probably anachronistic. Von Neumann's response to the suggestion that he was anticipated by Borel is quoted from a 1950's paper in which the mathematician Frèchet makes this accusation.

The three-card simplification of von Neumann's Poker model that he proposes in the dialogue is actually taken from my own *Playing for Real*, where the details of a very elementary analysis are to be found. The same book has an even more elementary simplification of the argument that deduces von Neumann and Morgenstern utilities from appropriate consistency assumptions.

On this last topic, our imaginary dialogue allows von Neumann to short-circuit Morgenstern's suggestion that they might extend Frank Ramsey's consistency approach to quantifying subjective probabilities to the case when preferences also need to be quantified. In a later dialogue, Leonard Savage discusses his real-life solution of the actual problem Morgenstern proposes to von Neumann with Rudolph Carnap.

Chapter 26

Karl Popper versus Ludwig Wittgenstein

Context

Various accounts of a 1946 meeting between Popper and Wittgenstein appear in a lively book called *Wittgenstein's Poker* by David Edmonds and John Eidinow.

According to Popper, the poker was supposedly flourished by Wittgenstein at a meeting of the Moral Sciences Club held in the Cambridge rooms of Richard Braithwaite (perhaps the first philosopher to think that game theory might be relevant to human morality). In accordance with his belief that the great philosophical problems to which metaphysicians devote their lives are mere bagatelles created by a failure to use language adequately, Wittgenstein had invited Popper to give a talk on how to resolve some philosophical puzzle. But Popper had his growing reputation as a philosopher of science to consider. So he challenged Wittgenstein by taking for granted that genuine moral problems do indeed exist. The relentlessly serious Wittgenstein was incensed. "Give me an example of a moral rule!" he supposedly demanded, while stirring the open fire with a poker. Popper is said to have responded with what he would have regarded as a joke: "Not to threaten visiting speakers with pokers!" Whereupon Wittgenstein stalked out of the room, slamming the door behind him.

This childish confrontation says a lot about the huge egos of both philosophers, neither of whom had much of a sense of humour. Wittgenstein was at that time basking in his fame. Not only had he displaced his mentor Bertrand Russell as the Cambridge philosopher to watch, but his disciples accepted his own estimation of himself as a philosophical genius. His students even copied his eccentric mannerisms and style of dress. Carnap's account of his meeting with Wittgenstein and Schlick—founder of the famous Vienna Circle—says all that need be said. He reports that insights came to Wittgenstein "as through a divine inspiration, so that we could not help feeling that any sober rational comment or analysis of it would be a profanation."

Other philosophers were less polite in expressing their disapproval of the Wittgenstein phenomenon. I guess Ernest Gellner is now largely forgotten, but he was once sufficiently well-known that I was delighted to find myself placed next to him at a dinner. He taught me how to sing the last sentence of Wittgenstein's absurdly pretentious *Tractatus Logico-Philosophicus* to the tune of Good King Wenceslas. Try it for yourself. In German, it goes

> *Wovon man nicht sprechen kann, darüber muss man schweigen.*

When translated into English as

> *Whereof one cannot speak, thereof one must be silent,*

the euphony is lost. But Wittgenstein famously disowned the *Tractatus*. So it seems to me now that Gellner's ridicule was unfair. The later Wittgenstein deserves credit, not only for seeking to prick the pretentious bubbles of others with his common-sense brand of philosophy, but for pricking his own bubble too.

A previous imaginary dialogue between Wittgenstein and David Hilbert summarizes Wittgenstein's history, but something needs to be said about Popper, to which more will be added when introducing a later imaginary dialogue between Popper and Imre Lakatos.

Karl Popper (1902–1994) was born in Vienna to a well-off Jewish family that had converted to Lutherism before his birth. He described his upbringing as bookish, but left school early, presumably to participate in the continuing unrest promoted by Marxist parties of the time. But he became disillusioned after the police shot eight of his comrades dead at a demonstration. In later life, he became a social liberal, very vocal in arguing that Marxian historical materialism has no better claim to be regarded as scientific than Freudian psychoanalysis. His attempts to make a living, first in proletarian jobs, and later in the teaching profession were not very successful, but he managed to get himself an education of sorts that included picking up the ethos of the Vienna Circle mentioned again in the debate between Carnap and Savage. His unconventional background made it difficult for him to find an academic position, but he was finally appointed to a post in New Zealand, from which he was headhunted by Lionel Robbins—the leading intellectual figure at the London School of Economics in those days—where he eventually headed up its Department of Philosophy, Logic and Scientific Method.

The coming imaginary dialogue is to be thought of as replacing the 1946 confrontation reported in *Wittgenstein's Poker,* but without an audience, so that both Wittgenstein and Popper are freed from the necessity of playing to the gallery. Popper seeks to tease Wittgenstein more subtly than in real life by restating the most basic of all philosophical problems—why is there something and not nothing? Wittgenstein does not understand that he is being teased, and attempts to reduce the problem of existence to a mere puzzle by picking holes in the language in which Popper seeks to update Leibniz on this issue. He is successful in this enterprise, but seemingly unaware that his failure to translate Popper's language into terms that allow an easy analysis implicitly concedes Popper's point that some philosophical problems are indeed problems, and not mere puzzles.

Wittgenstein's observations nevertheless remain relevant today to the claims of those modern physicists who think they can answer Leibniz's question of why there is something and not nothing. When their answers are rejected by philosophers, they become frustrated—you say our definition of nothing is no good, so what is your definition? But if you could define nothing, it wouldn't be no thing! The definition would make it a thing—the thing that the definition defines.

Dialogue

Wittgenstein atypically agrees to meet Popper in his Cambridge rooms to discuss their differences. It is the winter of 1946, and the weather is nearly as cold as it will be in the famously cold winter of 1947. Popper's welcome is appropriately frosty, but the Cambridge tradition of offering sherry has captured even Wittgenstein. With glasses in hand, they then sit by the blazing fire, which Wittgenstein stirs occasionally with a poker that is actually his own. They are to discuss whether all meaningful problems said to be philosophical are really problems, or whether they are merely puzzles that can be sorted out by avoiding confusing language. Popper proposes that they use as an example Leibniz's famous questioning of our existence. He knows that it is commonplace in certain circles to assert that the question is meaningless, but he finds that Wittgenstein is uninterested in such evasions.

POPPER: Perhaps we can center our discussion around Leibniz's famous question: "Why is there something and not nothing?" Is it a genuine philosophical problem, or is it just a puzzle to be sorted out by getting our language straight?

WITTGENSTEIN: We need to begin by echoing Parmenides' observation that nothing is not a thing. What we mean when we say *nothing* is *no thing*. By running the *no* and the *thing* together to make *nothing*, we do not create a thing, but merely set up the opportunity for metaphysicians to confuse themselves with a contradiction.

POPPER: So Leibniz's question becomes: "Why is there something, and not no thing?" But then Leibniz would merely be repeating the same phrase twice.

WITTGENSTEIN: It is not even clear that we are allowed to eliminate a double negative in metaphysics. Even the mathematician Hilbert accepts that proof by contradiction should be disbarred in metamathematics. So why should we allow it in metaphysics?

POPPER: But we can rephrase Leibniz's question to: "Something exists. Why?" Or better still: "Something exists. How come?"

WITTGENSTEIN: What does it mean for something to exist? For example, the mathematician, John von Neumann takes for granted the existence of the empty set ∅ when apparently constructing the whole numbers from nothing. The number zero is identified with ∅. The number one is identified with the set that contains only ∅. Having defined 0 and 1, he then identifies 2 as the set containing only 0 and 1. The number 3 is defined as the set containing only 0, 1 and 2. And so on.

POPPER: You are going to deny that the symbol Ø has any metaphysical significance—that it is merely a mark on piece of paper—that von Neumann may have found a neat way of embedding numbers in the formalism of set theory, but the idea that there is a thing Ø that represents *no thing* does not survive serious scrutiny.

WITTGENSTEIN: I do not deny that set theory has useful applications, but they all take for granted the prior existence of some local universe of discourse, so that it is always meaningful to ask of the empty set—empty of what? For example, a baker who has sold out his stock of bread, may say that his shelves are empty. Similarly, one may always ask of zero—zero on what scale?

POPPER: The ancient Greeks apparently used a kind of abacus in which pebbles—calculi—were placed in a sand tray marked out into columns. The origin of the symbol 0 can then be explained as the mark in the sand left behind when a pebble is removed.

WITTGENSTEIN: I had not heard of this pleasing speculation before—although the concept of zero supposedly originated in India rather than Greece. But the important thing is that regarding the empty set or zero as a free-standing metaphysical objects gains no respectability from the success of models in which they are used.

POPPER: I accept that the success of Ø and 0 in mathematical modeling is without metaphysical significance, but it does not follow that Leibniz's question is therefore meaningless. What of Leibniz's theory of possible worlds from which God chose the best possible world?

WITTGENSTEIN: You are perhaps going to argue that we should regard *nothing* as one of the possible worlds that God might have chosen? I am surprised that a philosopher of science should be religious.

POPPER: I am not religious. It seems to me that Voltaire was amply justified in making fun of the idea that the world in which we live is the best of all possible worlds. However, it does not follow that skeptics like ourselves should regard the arguments theologians use as being entirely without merit. For example, discarding St Thomas Aquinas on the logic of possibility and necessity would certainly be to throw a very useful baby out with the bathwater.

WITTGENSTEIN: I agree. But the set of all possible worlds would be as much a thing as the set of no things at all. We cannot take its existence for granted in arguing against the possibility that there might have been nothing. In fact, if there were no things at all, it would not be possible to say anything at all—least of all what I just said. It therefore does not help to seek to examine Leibniz's question using a model of possible worlds in which one of the possible worlds contains no things, because such a model of possible things is itself a thing.

POPPER: But the possible world that actually exists does contain a model of all possible worlds. What does it matter that the same may not be true of possible worlds that do not exist?

WITTGENSTEIN: Again you use difficult words as though their meaning is clear. To return to Leibniz's story of God's choosing which world to create—which world to bring into existence—from a set of all possible worlds, what would be the point? If His infinite power is indeed without limitation, he perceives each of the infinity of possible worlds perfectly in all of its infinite detail—way beyond the fall of any tiny sparrow. God will necessarily be aware of which world is best according to all the infinite number of definitions of 'best" that may be possible. Why "create" one of these worlds? How would this differ from simply identifying it as being distinguished from other possible worlds?

POPPER: Such an approach would certainly settle the question: "Why does this particular world exist, and not some other world?" With your story, no such question need be answered. What we call existence may be no more than existence-as-a-possibility. Why does it seem to us that we exist in some stronger sense? With the religious interpretation, we are just thoughts in the mind of God, and when He thinks of us, He effortlessly reproduces all the thoughts that we have in the possible world of which we are a part. In particular, God reproduces our feeling that we exist in some deeper sense. How could we feel otherwise when we have no direct experience of any possible world other than that in which we are embedded?

WITTGENSTEIN: You will perhaps say next that we do not need to postulate the prior existence of God to tell the same story.

POPPER: You guess rightly. I was about to suggest that the ontological argument for the existence of God works better if it is employed only to demonstrate the necessary existence of something. Descartes' version certainly works better if so interpreted. It cannot be denied that the existence of something is contained in the concept of the necessary existence of something—that something must exist in all possible worlds. Nor need the concept be held to have some necessary existence of its own. It is enough that it be held to exist in this possible world right now.

WITTGENSTEIN: You are something of a metaphysician yourself, in spite of your scientific credentials! Let us suppose for the moment that your argument demonstrating the necessary existence of something could be made to work in some possible world without some substitute for the perfection supposedly implicit in the concept of God. If necessity is taken to mean "true in all possible worlds", then it follows that it is impossible that *nothing* is a possible world. Very neat!

POPPER: But you will not grant my premises?

WITTGENSTEIN: You would still be relying on the conventional understanding of how to reason with the notions of possibility and necessity—and I am not even willing to grant the principles of standard logic. It is not for nothing(!) that I end my *Tractatus* by saying that we are forced into silence on questions about which it is impossible(!) to say anything.

So they end on a guarded but amicable note. Popper accepts that Wittgenstein got the better of him, but he had dealt himself a busted flush by trying on the metaphysical role of Plato, and allowing Wittgenstein to play the skeptical role of Diogenes. On the other hand, Wittgenstein did implicitly accept that existence is a problem rather a puzzle, albeit one about which nothing can usefully be said.

Afterword

The question of whether numbers exist as metaphysical objects goes all the way back to Pythagoras, and remains controversial to this day. The previous dialogue between Eudoxus and Aristotle is largely focussed on this issue.

In this dialogue, Wittgenstein seems to have taken on board what he learned from Hilbert about the formalist philosophy of mathematics in their earlier imaginary dialogue.

What Wittgenstein says about the assumption of the prior existence of sets in applying set theory in new contexts is incorporated in modern set theory by denying that new sets can defined except as subsets of sets that already exist. The paradoxes of the infinite discussed in the imaginary dialogue between Cantor and Russell need then not be addressed.

Popper is relying on the version of the ontological argument for the existence of God proposed by Abelard in his imaginary dialogue with St Anselm.

The idea that all possible worlds exist in some sense is the subject that Nozick and Lewis move onto after the recorded part of their imaginary dialogue later in this book. Physicists tell a similar story known as the many-worlds interpretation of quantum mechanics.

The idea that we exist only as thoughts in the mind of God is ancient. A new version that is nowadays popular among physicists replaces God by some giant alien computer. I particularly like the idea that the mysteries of quantum mechanics are to be explained by a desperate programmer making up the details of the subatomic world in a hurry as his creations explore parts of his simulation for which he had not thought it necessary to provide any micro foundations.

Chapter 27
Jean-Paul Sartre versus Simone de Beauvoir

Context

The obsessive affair between Jean-Paul Sartre and Simone de Beauvoir provided copy for French newspapers for more than fifty years. They certainly went to bed together, but they were by no means rivals to Abelard and Héloise. Their imaginary dialogue is therefore realistic to the extent that it sidelines this aspect of their relationship. It is used instead to exemplify a continental style of philosophy that is totally alien to the analytic style that all the other protagonists in this book take for granted. The aim of Continental Philosophy is not so much to give arguments why one way of thinking makes more sense than another, but to establish an attitude to life that is revealed as much in poetry, novels and plays as in conventional works of philosophy.

In retrospect, Sartre and de Beauvoir's famous joint venture into the realm of existentialism and phenomenology seems no more than an attempt to find some metaphysical clothing in which to dress up their urge to break free of the chains of bourgeois convention that they felt left them with no room to do their own thinking for themselves. It is ironic that they shared this imperative to be your own person with philosophers like Epicurus or Hume, who are usually placed at the other extreme of the philosophical spectrum. What is held in common is the belief that the so-called natural laws of morality are not natural, but are no more than cultural inventions. We are therefore not bound to obey them, but are free to do our own thing. This seems to be the fundamental content of Sartre's much-quoted mantra that existence precedes essence.

Where Sartre and de Beauvoir differ from the likes of Epicurus or Hume is in what they thought that philosophy teaches us about how best to live our lives.

Sartre and de Beauvoir believed that we should strive for Authenticity—which seems to require advertizing your freedom from conventional constraint by shocking the world with what it regards as bad or squalid behavior, rather like Diogenes and his followers in ancient Athens. Those who broke free of convention altogether, like the Marquis de Sade or Jean Genet, were therefore to be admired—not in spite of their flouting the sexual mores of their time—but because they supposedly recognized that the opinions of what existentialists call the Other count as nothing against the Authenticity of the Self. Epicurus or Hume—who lived apparently sexless lives directed at quiet contentment out of the public eye—could not have been more different in what they deduced from the need to separate your own individuality from the demands of the herd.

The way Sartre and de Beauvoir lived their own lives is revealed in their letters to each other, freely available now that both are dead. They were students together—rivals for the prize as best student—then lovers, and finally intellectual companions revealing all to each other in an open relationship that lasted until Sartre's death in 1980. As with the *Confessions* of Jean-Jacques Rousseau, one sometimes wonders whether they really were as heedless of the pain they caused their victims as they boasted in these letters. They certainly went out of their way not to take account of each other's feelings when writing to each other in a kind of *folié á deux*. The ultimate irony is that they succeeded in creating a new cool Other that snared the young and naive who thought they were learning how to transcend the Other altogether by living Authentic lives. Nowadays the same youngsters would be looking for a new and cooler herd to join in the world of pop music.

Where Sartre and de Beauvoir differ most from Epicurus and Hume is in their attitude to sex, which should not be taken to mean that they were knee-jerk hedonists dedicated to the mindless pursuit of pleasure. Their sex was a kind of sexless sex. They seemed more interested—especially Sartre—in the pursuit and conquest of their many sexual partners than the sex act itself. For this reason, the imaginary dialogue that follows is not about the metaphysics of Heidegger or Husserl, or any of the other high priests of existentialism or phenomenology. I do not suppose even Sartre understood Heidegger any better than the rest of us, although he famously devoted his time while a prisoner-of-war to studying Heidegger's *Sein und Zeit*. Indeed, the last place to look for enlightenment would seem to be in the works of a Nazi who thought it amusing to say that it is suicide for philosophy to make itself intelligible. They discuss instead de Beauvoir's 1951 essay *Must We Burn Sade?* in which she assesses the claims of the Marquis de Sade to be a counted as a philosophical hero.

Jean-Paul Sartre (1905–1980) had a difficult childhood in which he was introduced to scholarly pursuits by his grandfather after the death of his father when Sartre was very young. He made it to the École Normale Supérieure alongside the cream of the young French intelligentsia, where he met Simone de Beauvoir in 1929. They all flirted with Hegel, who was then enjoying a revival in France. Their admiration for the works of Marx remained *de rigeur* among French intellectuals until relatively recently.

Sartre's interest in existentialism was picked up in a German prisoner-of-war camp from which he was repatriated to Paris in 1941 for reasons of ill-health.

He was then active among the intellectual elite in promoting action against the French who chose to collaborate with the German occupation, but nothing came of his urging for action. After the war, he made a living by teaching until he was eventually able to devote himself full-time to his writing and political activism. The latter is typified by the much-quoted line *Il ne faut pas désespérer Billancourt,* which is interpreted as meaning that French workers—like those Renault workers on strike in Billancourt—need not be told the truth lest it dampen their revolutionary fervor. But he was never a Stalinist, or even a member of the Communist Party. He described himself as a special kind of anarchist.

How much Sartre actually influenced the politics of his time is hard to assess, but he was certainly widely thought to matter, especially in Moscow and Havana. He refused both the Legión d'Honneur and the Nobel Prize for Literature—although he was awarded the latter anyway. It is perhaps significant that he should be honored for literature, since it is his novels and plays that got most attention. His 1943 philosophical work *Being and Nothingness* is nowhere near as impenetrable as Heidegger's *Being and Time,* but it does its best.

It is frustrating for feminists that the author of *The Second Sex* should be treated as a mere adjunct to Sartre. Simone de Beauvoir (1908–1986) did not help her case by denying that she was a philosopher at all. In doing so, she was merely recognizing that—like Sartre—she was most effective in her literary writing. However, the claim that Sartre's *Being and Nothingness* borrows from de Beauvoir's novel *She Came to Stay* should not be classified alongside the claim I read a little while ago that Charles Darwin borrowed his ideas on evolution from his wife Emma. It is not for nothing that the plot of de Beauvoir's novel was notoriously characterized as existential ambiguity trumping Hegelian clarity.

Sartre and de Beauvoir always read each other's work, and their letters make it clear that their influence on each other went both ways. Why else would Sartre have maintained his increasingly fractious relationship with her until his death? In any case, feminists need not fear that Sartre will be allowed to patronize de Beauvoir in their coming debate. Like Héloise, she was well able to hold her own in any dispute with anyone.

Perhaps de Beauvoir's most effective contribution to philosophy is her *Ambiguity of Ethics,* in which she is more honest than Sartre in acknowledging the origins of their dissatisfaction with society. She tells us that children are born into a "serious world" in which obedience to ready-made values and established authority is taken for granted. Such restrictions on our freedom are not problematic for children, who express the human need for creativity and meaning in their play, inventing imaginary worlds in which they act out the fundamental truth that is only we ourselves who invest the world with meaning and value. Free from responsibility, children are metaphysically privileged in not having to account for these imaginary worlds, so they are able to experience the joys of freedom without the overpowering angst that de Beauvoir believes afflicts adults who realize that they have not been assigned a secure role in the world by God or by Nature, but have nobody to blame for who they turn out to be than themselves.

Adolescence brings an end to the childish joys of freedom, but most of humanity remain trapped as *serious men.* Serious men are people of whatever sex who still inhabit the serious world in which the moral responsibility for the Self to make its own choices for itself remains devolved on the Other. De Beauvoir compares her serious man with a series of other invented types, including the *artist-writer*, with whom she clearly identifies herself. The passion that motivates the ethics of an artist-writer is founded on the kind of generosity of spirit that recognizes that other people have their own way of expressing their individuality, and so resists the urge to treat them as means-to-an-end rather than ends-in-themselves. Nobody would deny that she was both an artist and a writer, but her life story certainly leaves room for a good deal of skepticism about the extent to which she fits her own stereotype of the artist-writer!

Why is the ethics that is created by those who escape the trap of the serious man necessarily ambiguous? It seems to me that de Beauvoir retreats into a kind of high-flown folk psychology at this point. She doubtless felt the same kind of ambiguity about moral issues as the rest of us, but why should we favor her rationalization of the reasons why? In brief, the intentionality of consciousness is said to be split between the need to bring meaning to being, and the need to bring meaning to the world. Each intentionality is said to correspond to a mood. Bringing meaning to being corresponds to feeling joyful. Bringing meaning to the world corresponds to feeling both hopeful and dominant. I guess it is significant that she should regard dominance as a mood one feels when Self explains itself to Other. It certainly explains why she should have been motivated to write about the Marquis de Sade.

Dialogue

It is a gloomy afternoon in the winter of the year 1950. Paris has yet to recover from the atmosphere of mutual suspicion that accompanied the widespread collaboration of French defeatists during the German occupation of World War II. At least nobody is hungry any more. Simone de Beauvoir has agreed to meet Jean-Paul Sartre to discuss the current draft of an essay she has written on the Marquis de Sade—the man who gave his name to sadism. It is to serve as an introduction to a new edition of de Sade's notorious *Justine*. Such meetings to discuss their writings will continue for another thirty years.

The venue is a famous café called Les Deux Magots, which was the favorite hang-out of the Parisian literary and intellectual elite in those days. Over the course of time, it will welcome a host of celebrities—not just French celebrities like Albert Camus—but foreign visitors like Pablo Picasso, James Joyce, Bertolt Brecht and Ernest Hemingway, for whom Paris remained the center of the civilized world. When she arrives, she finds Sartre impatient at being kept waiting. There are no celebrities to keep him occupied at such an unfashionable hour.

Les Deux Magots café is not the kind of establishment in which you sit at one end of a zinc-topped bar wondering how the old guys drinking rough brandy at the other end can find so much to talk about. A waiter therefore appears even before de Beauvoir has got out of her wet things. When Sartre and de Beauvoir were students, their meetings were always fuelled by alcohol, but today they order Deux Magot's excellent coffee—in those days made in France simply by pouring boiling water over freshly ground coffee in a jug. What a pity that this is one more pleasure lost to the advance of technology!

SARTRE: I have here your draft for *Must We Burn Sade?* I like your choosing to begin by quoting Sade's own description of himself as "imperious, choleric, irascible, extreme in everything, with a dissolute imagination the like of which was never seen." But why write about such a person? Should we not dismiss him as just another madman?

DE BEAUVOIR: There is a commercial reason and a philosophical reason. I was commissioned to tell Sade's life story, and to comment on its relevance to existentialism by a publisher planning a new edition of Sade's *Justine*. Have you read it? It is relentlessly pornographic. No wonder taking pleasure in the pain of others is nowadays called sadism! I guess I am being paid to write an introduction so that a book that people will buy for salacious reasons can be passed off as a work of philosophical significance.

SARTRE: But you carry off the task with some élan. I think perhaps you genuinely believe that Sade is philosophically significant.

DE BEAUVOIR: What interests me about Sade is that he poses the problem of the Other in an extreme form. He therefore gives me the chance to re-examine the problem of artistic responsibility I raised in my *Ethics of Ambiguity*. It is true that treating Sade as a possible example to follow will raise the hackles of the bourgeoisie, but we have our own Authenticity to consider. Why should we allow the Other to censor truths revealed to the Self?

SARTRE: I see no need for the Self to tell Truth to the Other. One manifests a generosity of spirit in telling them whatever lies will advance their own quest for Authenticity.

DE BEAUVOIR: It was also an occasion to review my own attitude to sex. I once thought that to be an existentialist was to be insulated against the intimacy of the sex act—that knowing the Self is free to be whatever it chooses automatically immunizes the Self against the intrusion of the Other during copulation. But I have since learned that this naive belief is false.

SARTRE: I have marked the place in your draft where you give expression to this revelation: "The sexual act creates the illusion of sovereign pleasure which gives it its incomparable value in Sade's eyes; for all his sadism strove to compensate for the absence of one necessary element which he lacked. The state of emotional intoxication allows one to grasp existence in one's self and in the other, as both subjectivity and passivity. The two partners merge in this ambiguous unity; each one is freed of his own presence and achieves immediate communication with the other. The curse which weighed upon Sade—and which only his childhood could explain—was this "autism" which prevented him from ever forgetting himself or being genuinely aware of the reality of the other person." But it is not from me that you learned that it is possible to lose yourself in sex!

DE BEAUVOIR: Indeed not! You are the coldest fish with whom I have ever shared a bed. There is no ambiguity in you at all. You echo my *Ethics of Ambiguity* in speaking of generosity of spirit, but I doubt that generosity of spirit has ever motivated any of your actions ever.

SARTRE: When we agreed to an open relationship in which we would be utterly frank with each other, I never thought that I would actually enjoy your insults. There must be some of the masochism in me that you also find in Sade! But I am doubtful that you really did succeed in turning off your critical thinking in the sex act. Are you not deceiving yourself in thinking that you have sometimes lost yourself in the intoxication of satisfying your lust?

DE BEAUVOIR: There is perhaps something of Sade in all men. Never in Sade's stories does sensual pleasure appear as self-forgetfulness, swooning, or abandon. Compare, for example, the brutal pleasures of Sade's lesbians with Rousseau's *Confessions,* or the flutters of the Mother Superior in Diderot's *La Religieuse.* The male aggression of the Sadist hero is never softened by the usual transformation of the body into flesh. He never, for an instant, loses himself in his animal nature; he remains so lucid, so cerebral, that philosophic discourse, far from dampening his ardor, acts as an aphrodisiac.

SARTRE: Let us move on from the failings of the male sex to your philosophical claims for Sade.

DE BEAUVOIR: My draft ends by denying that Sade can be regarded as either a consummate artist or a coherent philosopher. But he deserves to be hailed as a great moralist.

SARTRE: Épater la bourgeoisie! But will the bourgeois appreciate the magnificence of your paradox? They will say that a morality not held in common by a whole society is pointless. They will not understand that existentialists believe that a free man constructs his own ethics for himself. A free man will necessarily be aware of the fact that he is free in this aspect of his being—as in every other aspect of his being. Sade not only satisfies this primary requirement for an ethically free man, but trumpets it to the skies. But why do you differ from other apologists for Sade in denying their claim that he is worthy of admiration as a writer-artist?

DE BEAUVOIR: No one could be genuinely serious in ranking *Justine* with erotic works like *Les Liaisons Dangereuses.* Sade did not have the perspective essential to an artist. He lacked the detachment necessary to confront reality and recreate it. He did not confront himself; he contented himself with projecting his fantasies. His accounts have the unreality, the false precision, and the monotony of schizophrenic reveries. He struggles to escape the chains that bind the serious man described in my *Ethics of Ambiguity,* but ultimately fails.

SARTRE: What of his ventures into metaphysics?

DE BEAUVOIR: They are entirely cosmetic—feeble attempts to justify his self-indulgence. People who are anxious to get on with the pornography doubtless find their obsessive repetition very tiresome.

SARTRE: Sade still seems to have had women running after him, even after his fearsome reputation had become a public scandal. How come?

DE BEAUVOIR: Perhaps for the same reason I took up with you when we were students together. After all, you were then no more an embodiment of Adonis than you are now. Or to put the same point in existential terms, serious women bear heavier chains than serious men. Women are deprived of the opportunity to exercise power, and so seek to share in the autonomy of powerful lovers.

Sartre feels no inclination to defend either his physical attractiveness or his slovenly appearance, so he closes their discussion of the Marquis de Sade by calling for the waiter. It is now about the time when Les Deux Magots begins to play host to the intellectual elite of Paris, and therefore of the world. In the meantime, Sartre explains again his plan to abandon writing novels in favor of plays. The craft of drama compels us to show man directly through his actions. Husserl's phenomenology demands no less! De Beauvoir listens patiently. Perhaps André Gide will shortly appear.

Afterword

I have failed in this dialogue to capture the atmosphere of Les Deux Magots as it must have been. Nor have I come near capturing the in-your-face rudeness of some of the letters Sartre and de Beauvoir exchanged in later life. Anglo-Saxon prejudice will also be evident in my not taking either existentialism or phenomenology very seriously. It seems to me that one can assess the philosophy of Sartre and de Beauvoir much as Bertrand Russell assessed the philosophy of Nietzsche. Why not just say that you wished you had been brought up in the Athens of Pericles or the Florence of the Medicis, rather than the stifling atmosphere of provincial France in the interwar years?

Chapter 28
John Nash versus John von Neumann

Context

Von Neumann and Morgenstern's 1944 *Theory of Games and Economic Behavior* was initially thought to herald a revolution in economic theory, but disillusion soon set in when it was realized that only zero-sum games were adequately covered. John Nash redirected the subject in a more profitable direction by focusing attention on what came to be known as a Nash equilibrium, although it took more than twenty years before economists were willing to pay attention to game theory again.

Von Neumann and Nash did actually meet at the Institute of Advanced Studies in Princeton, when Nash visited von Neumann in his office to tell him about his work on game theory. However, von Neumann was reportedly dismissive for reasons that they discuss in their imaginary dialogue. It is imaginary because philosophical views are attributed to Nash that he endorsed in later life, but which he told me that he certainly had not envisaged at the time of his meeting with von Neumann. The youthful Nash would have been simultaneously brash and awkward, and it is easy to see why von Neumann would have been unwilling to give him much time. Albert Einstein was apparently more patient when Nash visited him in his office around the same time to tell him his ideas on physics.

John Nash (1928–2015) was yet another exotic character. After a classical American childhood similar to that of Dewey, he originally intended to become an engineer like his father, but his advisors recognized his extraordinary mathematical talent, and he ended up as a somewhat childlike graduate student at Princeton at a time when it was buzzing with new ideas. His thesis proved the existence of Nash equilibria in finite games, but the imaginary dialogue also mentions his simultaneous invention of the Nash bargaining solution, which he thought up while taking an ancillary course on economics while still studying engineering. His thesis on Nash equilibria won him a Nobel prize, but he might equally well have been awarded another for his work on bargaining.

However, these triumphs in economics were incidental to his primary objective, which was to excel in mathematics. He succeeded here too, eventually being awarded the prestigious Abel prize in 2015 for his solution of Hilbert's nineteenth problem on partial differential equations, although he might equally well have been honored for his contributions to algebraic geometry. He was killed with his wife Alicia when their taxi crashed on the New Jersey Turnpike while returning to Princeton after the award of the Abel prize.

Nash is widely known to the public because of the movie *A Beautiful Mind* that recounts the story of how he was brought low by a schizophrenic illness that put him out of action for more than thirty years, recovering just in time to be included among the three winners of the 1994 Nobel prize for game theory.

Both von Neumann and Nash would have thought of themselves as problem-solvers rather than philosophers, but—like Darwin or Einstein—they contributed more to philosophy than most of those who appear in lists of celebrated philosophers. I hope their shades will forgive my having them talk as though they cared what philosophers thought. I once tried to explain to Nash why his work was relevant to the ideas of David Hume, but I am pretty sure that he had never heard of Hume before. Purists may think I go too far in attributing the evolutionary interpretation of Nash equilibria to Nash himself, but the paragraph in his thesis in which he actually makes this proposal was deleted as being of no interest by the journal editor that published the rest of his thesis!

Dialogue

It is perhaps 1949 when Nash calls on von Neumann in his office at the Advanced Institute in Princeton to tell him about his work on game theory. Von Neumann is more patient in this imaginary version of their dialogue than he apparently was in real life, and Nash very much more eloquent. Their debate has something of the flavor of the imaginary dialogue between Pascal and Fermat on how probability should be interpreted, but with probability replaced by game theory.

NASH: Can you spare some time for me? I have just finished writing my thesis on game theory in which I extend your work on two-person, zero-sum games to finite games in general. I prove that all such games have what I call an equilibrium point.

VON NEUMANN: What is an equilibrium point?

NASH: An equilibrium point is a strategy profile—one for each player—that arises when each player is making a best reply to the strategy choices of the other players. I prove the existence of such equilibrium points using Brouwer's fixed-point theorem.

VON NEUMANN: Oh yes—a fixed-point argument. One of the proofs of my minimax theorem for zero-sum games uses the same method. Perhaps you do not know that the mathematician Kakutani has produced a version of Brouwer's theorem that is much easier to apply. I met him in the corridor when on my way to give a seminar on the minimax theorem, and persuaded him to join the audience. At the end, he rose, and asked why I did not prove it using what is now known as the Kakutani fixed-point theorem, which he had invented on the spot.

NASH: What do you think of my idea that we can sometimes replace your maximin strategies by the notion of equilibrium strategies when a game is not zero-sum?

VON NEUMANN: Morgenstern and I observe in our book that if a game has a rational solution, it must be what you call an equilibrium point, but the converse is not true. The fact that a strategy profile is an equilibrium point does not imply that rational players will play a game that way.

NASH: I do not claim otherwise. But there are games that have only one equilibrium point, or in which a single equilibrium point dominates all its rivals. I have a simple model of three-person Poker which exemplifies the first case.

VON NEUMANN: I grant that such special cases are of interest, but I am not convinced that we are entitled to call an equilibrium point the rational solution of a game, even when it is unique. We might do better to admit that such games sometimes do not have a rational solution at all.

NASH: Yes—but I have an alternative interpretation of my notion of an equilibrium point. We do not need to confine our attention to what happens in games played by omniscient rational players. It is also of interest to study what happens in an evolutionary context. Suppose the players adjust their strategy choices in the direction of increasing payoffs in a game that they play repeatedly against new opponents each time. If their behavior converges at all, it can only converge on an equilibrium point. Only when all players are making an optimal reply to the combined choices of their opponents will no player have an incentive to make a further adjustment. I call this the mass-action interpretation.

VON NEUMANN: Your evolutionary story is very abstract. Do you have any empirical applications from biology?

NASH: Not as yet. The truth is that my ambitions lie elsewhere. My plan is to build a career as a pure mathematician.

VON NEUMANN: I see your notion of an equilibrium point as a negative condition that excludes irrational strategy profiles from consideration, but what is needed are positive conditions that tell rational players how they should play. If you are unable to give positive reasons why players should use one equilibrium point rather than another, I do not see that your existence result is very significant.

NASH: It is true that one would also need social conventions to select among equilibrium points in the manner pioneered by the philosopher David Hume. For example, the two-person Driving Game has three equilibrium points: both choose left; both choose right; or both choose at random. In America, we use the convention of always driving on the right.

VON NEUMANN: Both your biological and your social stories need a great deal of ancillary work before a viable alternative to my rational approach would be possible. Come back and tell me when you have made some progress in this direction.

NASH: May I also mention a contribution I have made to the theory of bargaining that you and Morgenstern classify as a problem for psychologists?

VON NEUMANN: It is true that we see no role for rationality in what is essentially a question of how good different people are at haggling.

NASH: My approach assigns a role to rationality in the case when the bargainers face a risk of ending up with nothing if they are unable to agree on how to divide a surplus. Since the theory of cardinal utility you offer in your book with Morgenstern measures how much utility something is assigned by the size of the risk a person is willing to take to get it, your theory is ideal for my purpose.

VON NEUMANN: I was astonished when Morgenstern told me that cardinal utilities were deemed impossible by economists. How do you use our utility theory in your approach to bargaining?

NASH: I offer both an axiomatic treatment along the lines of the part of your book with Morgenstern that deals with cooperative games, and also a model of an actual bargaining game. The equilibrium points of the bargaining game approximate the same outcome as an analysis of the axioms. I call this outcome the bargaining solution of the bargaining problem.

VON NEUMANN: How do you handle the problem of incomplete information, which is hard enough in the case of Poker, let alone in a general bargaining problem?

NASH: My approach only applies in the case when the players have no secrets from each other.

VON NEUMANN: Again I have to say, come back when you have something more than the beginnings of a theory.

Afterword

Nash is disappointed not to have made a better impression on von Neumann, whose criticism of Nash's failure to take account of the problem of incomplete information in bargaining has still to be dealt with adequately by the many scholars who have followed his lead. On the other hand, his notion of an equilibrium point—nowadays called a Nash equilibrium—has been wildly successful in both economics and evolutionary biology. In the latter case, the payoffs in a game are identified with how fit the players are. Adjustment processes that favor the more fit at the expense of the less fit will stop working when we get to a Nash equilibrium, because all the survivors will then be as fit as it is possible to be in the circumstances. Biologists are then able to evade having to take account of all the immensely complicated twists and turns that an evolutionary process might take, and simply argue that the result will be *as if* the players had reasoned their way to a rational outcome.

Nash's use of a non-cooperative bargaining game to support the result of applying his bargaining axioms exemplifies what is nowadays sometimes called the Nash program for keeping the imagination of mathematicians in check. Von Neumann and Morgenstern's invention of cooperative game theory opened the flood gates for a plethora of rival axioms systems intended for applications in cooperative contexts. The Nash program suggests that the only axiom systems worth taking seriously are those that come accompanied by at least one example of a non-cooperative game with a Nash equilibrium outcome that coincides with the outcome predicted by the axioms.

I once presided at a dinner for Kakutani after he had given a very mathematical seminar at the London School of Economics. He asked me why his audience was so large. I replied that most of those present were economists keen to see the guy who proved the Kakutani fixed-point theorem. His response left me speechless: "What is the Kakutani fixed-point theorem?"

Chapter 29
Rudolph Carnap versus Leonard Savage

Context

Logical positivism is an extreme variety of empiricism which holds that all propositions that cannot be verified through direct observation or logical proof are without meaning. It flourished in the 1930s, when its chief proponents were known as the Vienna Circle, whose leading member was arguably Rudolph Carnap. His reputation later went into eclipse along with logical positivism itself, but Carnap's philosophical position constantly evolved throughout his life, although he always remained a stout defender of knowledge-as-commitment over knowledge-as-certainty. He would perhaps have expressed this position himself by saying that our view of the universe is not discovered but constructed—that what we take as axiomatic is not self-evident or given by nature, but is something provisional that we have to specify when attempting to create rational models of the world around us. Other philosophers whose ideas have gone out of fashion should take heart from the fact that he has been restored to the pantheon of great philosophers now that nobody feels the need to trample logical positivism to death any more.

Leonard (Jimmie) Savage was a mathematician rather than a philosopher, and he would probably have resisted being shoe-horned into one philosophical Ism rather than another. His imaginary dialogue with Carnap continues the earlier debate imagined between Pascal and Fermat on the philosophical basis of probability. What they discuss is the currently fashionable doctrine known as Bayesianism that was just getting started in the 1950s when they are envisaged as meeting. Savage is nowadays famous for providing firm foundations for Bayesian decision theory, but his 1954 book *Foundations of Statistics* is very clear that the kind of probability he is talking about is subjective probability rather than the logical probability of Carnap's

1950 *Logical Foundations of Probability*. Jack Good jokingly distinguished 46,656 possible varieties of Bayesianism, and it is not clear to which variety Carnap should be assigned. However, in the debate, Savage forcefully argues against treating his foundations for subjective probability as though they will also serve as foundations for Carnap's various approaches to logical probability—a confusion that continues to plague philosophical discussions of probabilistic matters to this day.

Carnap's (1891–1970) early career in Germany left him poised between physics and philosophy. He came down in favor of the latter as a consequence of being taught by Gottlob Frege, who introduced him to the works of Bertrand Russell. After being recruited by Moritz Schlick to his department in Vienna, Carnap became a prominent member of the Vienna Circle that Schlick had founded. The advent of the Nazis led to Carnap's emigrating to the USA, where he was first a professor of philosophy at Chicago, and then at UCLA. He was the object of much philosophical criticism during this time, but nowadays his efforts to build structures within which scientific philosophies can flourish are better appreciated.

Leonard Savage (1917–1971) preferred to be called Jimmie in his private life. His early education was a disaster, perhaps partly due to his poor eyesight. He was sometimes even thought to be backward, but he finally bloomed under the guidance of an inspiring teacher of mathematics at the University of Michigan. He eventually became a polymath whose talents were widely recognized. He served, for example, as John von Neumann's statistical assistant during the Second World War. He wrote his famous *Foundations of Statistics* while at the University of Chicago, where he was a close associate of the economist Milton Friedman. He moved on to Michigan, and then to Yale, where he was still relatively young when he died. I met him briefly during his time in Michigan.

It is possible that Carnap and Savage never actually met in real life, but I imagine them together in Chicago in 1954. Savage's book was about to appear, and Carnap would have made an effort to talk to him about it if he had been visiting his old department at the University of Chicago. To paraphrase a recent philosophical commentary, Carnap would have wished to compare Savage's new contribution to logical or epistemic probability with his own work, and that of such other pioneers as Ramsey, de Finetti, Good, and Jeffrey—except that Savage's contributions were to subjective probability, and not to logical probability.

Dialogue

There is a tap on Savage's office door in the Statistics Department at the University of Chicago. Savage opens the door to find Carnap there. Carnap has walked over from the Philosophy Department in the hope of persuading Savage to discuss his forthcoming book, which Carnap's old philosophical friends tell him is going to get a thumbs-down from classical statisticians for turning their view of things upside-down. They have told Carnap that Savage's theory is going to be called Bayesianism to make fun of its relying so much on Bayes' rule for working out conditional probabilities. Little do the classicists know that the certainties of Bayesianists are eventually fated to displace their own philosophical certainties in the not-so-distant future. In any case, Savage invites Carnap to join him for coffee in the faculty club, where they enjoy a convivial afternoon. Neither is interested in exchanging further meaningless courtesies, and so they get straight down to business. Savage thinks he will persuade Carnap not to confuse Savage's subjective probabilities with Carnap's logical probabilities, but he will not be successful.

CARNAP: I am hoping you will tell me something about the book you have written providing axiomatic foundations for what I guess is going to be called Bayesian decision theory—that rational choice reduces to maximizing the long-run average of a utility function relative to subjective probabilities that people invent for themselves even if no objective information is available.

SAVAGE: In my book, rationality is reduced to nothing more than consistency of choice.

CARNAP: So you follow Frank Ramsey in arguing that a person will necessarily behave as though operating with probabilities provided that they would always respond in the same way no matter how a decision problem is formulated—that they will not make the common mistake of failing to recognize that two decision problems are really the same even though they are expressed in different terms.

SAVAGE: My aim was to combine the insights of Ramsey and others with the expected utility theory of von Neumann and Morgenstern by explaining how the probabilities the latter take for granted can be derived from a person's choice behavior.

CARNAP: I am excited at the prospect that your work will provide the foundations for a scientific theory of logical probability that philosophers have been seeking since the time of Laplace. Instead of limiting logic to statements that can be classified as true or false, we will be able to discuss the degree of belief it is rational to assign to statements given the available evidence.

SAVAGE: I am sorry to disappoint you. I have not found the statistical equivalent of the Philosopher's Stone that transforms base metal into gold. My theory is not about logical or epistemic probabilities, which would be the same for everybody with the same evidence. My theory is about subjective or personal probabilities that are likely to be different for different people. I am talking about how people bet at a racetrack rather than how scientists should update their theories in the light of new experimental results. The fact that an opinion might be offered consistently does not convert it into a rational degree of belief.

CARNAP: So you deny that there is only one rational way to think about probability?

SAVAGE: We all agree on what the mathematical criteria should be for something to be called a probability. The question is how the mathematical concept of probability should be interpreted in practice. It seems to me that at least three interpretations should be distinguished.

CARNAP: I guess you are going to say that there is the objective interpretation, the subjective interpretation, and the logical interpretation. We can perhaps dismiss the objective interpretation of probability as long-run frequency since it can be absorbed into the other interpretations in a rational context. And it would be irrational to assign a subjective probability to something different from its logical probability even at the race-track.

SAVAGE: You remind me of de Finetti, who says IN CAPITAL LETTERS that only what he calls subjective probability makes sense! If a theory of logical probability were available, it is perhaps true that there would be no need for a theory of subjective probability—but I have grave doubts about whether a viable theory of logical probability is even possible. We would need to replace the mathematical definition of a probability by something much more complicated to sustain the logical interpretation. The mathematical definition of a probability was designed for use with objective probabilities for which it is ideally suited. Even its reinterpretation as a subjective probability is a bit of a stretch.

CARNAP: Why can I not interpret your subjective probabilities as logical probabilities? You only seem to demand consistency as a requirement.

SAVAGE: The difference is that consistency is to be taken for granted with the logical interpretation of probability—just as in classical logic. My way of thinking about subjective probability makes consistency something that is hard to achieve— something that a person must struggle towards by comparing the choices they would make in different hypothetical situations, and adjusting them until they become consistent with each other when they are found to be inconsistent. Because this task will be impossible in practice if the class of hypothetical situations is too large, I insist on page 16 of my book that it would be "utterly ridiculous" to use my theory outside what I later call a small world. You want to argue that the universe of all conceivable decision problems can be regarded as small. I think it is impossibly large for my theory to be adequate for its analysis.

CARNAP: Philosophical critics made essentially the same point about Ramsey's consistency assumptions. Doubtless Aristotle was similarly plagued by critics who said the same of his invention of formal logic. Mountains always seem impossible to climb before someone climbs them. On the other hand, I see that you will be misunderstood—as Ramsey continues to be misunderstood—because the dynamic process you envisage as converging eventually on consistent choice behavior is not part of your formal model. People using your formal model, as I hope to do, will not feel bound to honor the interpretation you prefer—any more than you felt bound to honor the objective interpretation that motivated the mathematical definition of probability on which we all agree.

SAVAGE: It is really important that people who want to use my theory understand that it is a *descriptive* theory rather than a *prescriptive* theory of the kind you are seeking. If the unmodeled dynamic process by means of which consistency is achieved is neglected, my theory offers nothing more than a way of describing the choice behavior of somebody who chooses consistently. The difference between my descriptive theory and the various attempts that have been made at constructing a prescriptive theory are most evident in their treatment of prior probabilities.

CARNAP: I agree that the question of where prior probabilities come from is vital. Once they are determined, the later posterior probabilities that reflect new evidence are simply deduced using Bayes' rule. But ever since Laplace proposed that equal prior probabilities should be assigned to two events if no reason exists to think one is more likely than the other, we have been plagued by a variety of paradoxes that can be constructed using this or other similar principles. I hope to handle such problems by inventing artificial scientific languages within which the ambiguities that lie the root of such paradoxes cannot be expressed.

SAVAGE: You have not yet appreciated the extent of the gulf between us. Untroubled by the ancient maxim that *ex nihilo nihil fit*, you envisage priors being formulated in some imagined initial state of complete ignorance. My position on this subject could not differ more. I think everything a person supposes might conceivably matter will inform the adjustment process by means of which he contrives to come up with a consistent set of hypothetical decisions in whatever small world is relevant. One might express what I have in mind crudely by saying that my priors are actually determined by my posteriors—but only after they have been massaged into consistency. Such priors then serve only to summarize the result of the massaging process. The fact that Bayes' rule can then be used to determine the massaged posteriors from these priors merely confirms that the massaging process converged on a consistent system.

CARNAP: You have a gift for paradox yourself! Who is going to be persuaded that that posteriors come before priors! I see now where you are coming from, but I do not see that a theory with so little substance is worth pursuing. All the learning in your interpretation occurs during your unmodeled adjustment process, but it is essential that Bayes' rule be seen as the engine of rational learning. In your set-up it is reduced to nothing more than an accounting tool, with no more substance than double-entry book-keeping.

SAVAGE: I see that we now understand each other. Your incredulity at my approach is matched by my own incredulity that the trivial manipulation of the mathematical definition of a conditional probability called Bayes' rule should not only be said to be a theorem, but be thought adequate to describe rational learning.

CARNAP: We shall have to agree to disagree. But I hope you will not resent your theory being put to a use that you did not intend.

Afterword

The failure of most of the philosophy profession to distinguish between subjective and logical probability continues to this day. In large worlds, it is not even clear that prioritizing consistency in modeling rational learning is a good idea. After all, relativity and quantum mechanics are not consistent where they overlap, but physicists do not think this a good reason for throwing them away.

Chapter 30
Imre Lakatos versus Karl Popper

Context

Karl Popper and Imre Lakatos became my colleagues at the London School of Economics when I joined its new Mathematics Department in 1969. Both are leading names in the philosophy of science. At that time, Popper was sometimes said to be the greatest living philosopher. His major claim to fame was his denial that scientific propositions can ever be proved to be true. The best we can do is refute those which are false. Theories that cannot be refuted are not scientific at all. Popper was particularly hostile to psychoanalytic theories for this reason. They have an explanation for any human behavior whatever, and so cannot be refuted—therefore they are not scientific. Marx's historical materialism was to be thrown out of the window for the same reason.

Popper's *Open Society and its Enemies* expresses his contempt, not just for Karl Marx, but also for Plato and Hegel as well. I must have expressed my admiration for this unpopular book, because the only time he spoke to me at any length was to complain bitterly about the difficulty he had found in getting the book published. Even at the time, I thought it naive to imagine that it was possible to rubbish Plato, and simultaneously retain the respect of the philosophical establishment.

Lakatos (1922–1974) was born to a Jewish family in Hungary at a more dangerous time than Popper. His mother and grandmother died in Auschwitz. He himself contrived, not only to escape the Nazi death camps, but to join a Marxist resistance group. After the war, he rose in the Communist hierarchy until accused of revisionism, for which thought crime he was imprisoned for several years in the early 1950s. After the Soviet Union invaded in 1956, he seized the opportunity to join the failed Hungarian rebels in fleeing over the border into Austria. By this time, his enthusiasm for Marxism was over, and he began a new career by studying for a doctorate in philosophy at Cambridge, England.

I came to know him quite well. I heard his own version of his life story when I persuaded him to join me for a drink at a small pub in a back street behind LSE. I think this must have been his first experience of British pub culture. He was surely the first man ever to sit at the bar in the White Hart pub with a crème de menthe before him! The whole pub was held spell-bound as he offered his own version of his life story, in which he fled across the border into Austria pretending to be a rebel as result of the failure of his Machiavellian plot to move up the Communist hierarchy. Once in Austria, how was he to make living? He decided to pretend to be a philosopher of mathematics—and see how he now fools the whole world into thinking that he knows what he is talking about!

In claiming to have fooled the whole world, he was talking about the collection of essays he published as *Proofs and Refutations*, whose title deliberately echoes Popper's famous *Conjectures and Refutations*. I recall thinking at the time that his essay on Fourier series did indeed reveal that he knew next to nothing about the subject, but his essay on Euler's theorem was a brilliant exercise in the use of the dialogue style. Looking back at this and other occasions, he puts me in mind of Leibniz in an earlier imaginary dialogue, and Nozick in a later one. Did he really hold the views he expressed, or was he always just playing?

If this last assessment is true, Lakatos needed to walk on eggshells when interacting with Popper, who was his polar opposite in this regard. Lakatos certainly did his best to avoid letting his ebullient character spill over into any confrontation with Popper—which was doubtless wise, since Popper belied his writings by being seriously authoritarian in policing his philosophical followers. I recall being tearfully told by his devoted disciple and successor as head of the LSE Philosophy Department that Popper had cut him dead after he had said something heretical at an international conference—and it was not easy to bring tears to the eyes of John Watkins, who had commanded a destroyer in World War II. However, as Lakatos acquired an independent reputation of his own, he became increasingly unwilling to toe the official Popperian line.

I have dramatized the division between Lakatos and Popper by proceeding as though their differences were concentrated into single imaginary dialogue that takes place after Lakatos has accepted an invitation to visit Popper in his LSE office some time in the early 1970s. One can dramatize their meeting further by thinking of it as yet another skirmish in the never-ending war between nomos and physis, with Lakatos defending knowledge-as-commitment, and Popper offering a last ditch defence of knowledge-as-certainty in the form of an unattainable ideal. Both would probably have said that philosophy was long past the stage when such issues could profitably be debated, but we do not have to agree with them.

At the personal level, Lakatos and Popper would perhaps have understood each other better if Lakatos had been willing to provoke Popper by acknowledging his attraction to the ideas of Thomas Kuhn—Popper's new rival as the world's predominant philosopher of science. Ten years or so before our imaginary dialogue, Kuhn had written a book that succeeded in switching the focus of philosophers of science away from the preoccupations of Carnap and the Vienna Circle. Instead of vainly telling scientists how science ought to be done, the new style was to learn from scientists how science is actually done. However, Lakatos never got round to adopting the new style in his approach to mathematics. He continued to follow Wittgenstein in telling mathematicians how mathematics ought to be done, rather studying what mathematicians actually do.

Dialogue

Lakatos enters the lion's den expecting a difficult interview. He guesses that Popper has belatedly taken a look at the paper "Popper on Demarcation and Induction" that is to be Lakatos's contribution to a book of commentaries celebrating Popper's philosophy. Its divergence from Popper's ideas is sufficiently wide that an open breach is now on the cards. But Lakatos is determined to remain respectful while minimizing the extent of his heresy. His immediate response to Popper's not-very-polite opening challenge is taken almost verbatim from his summary of the paper that has brought their differences to a head.

LAKATOS: Your ideas represent the most important development in the philosophy of the twentieth century—an achievement comparable to that of Hume or Kant. My debt to you is immeasurable. More than anyone else, you changed my life. I was nearly forty when I was attracted into the magnetic field of your intellect. Your philosophy helped me to make a final break with the Hegelian outlook which I had held for nearly twenty years before. More importantly, it provided me with an immensely fertile range of problems, indeed, with a veritable research program. But work on a research program is a critical affair, and it is inevitable that somebody working on Popperian problems should sometimes feel the need to refine Popper's own solutions.

POPPER: I do not see that there is any need to refine what is a very simple criterion for what divides science from pseudo-science. Either propositions are refutable by experiment, or they are not. If they are not, then the system from which they are derived is not scientific.

LAKATOS: Let me first register my agreement that the problem of scientific induction that David Hume thought insoluble is actually reducible to the question of where the line should be drawn between science and non-science. As you say yourself, "The problem of induction is only an instance or facet of the problem of demarcation." Your solution to the problem of demarcation is certainly a great achievement, but I did not expect to be thought disrespectful in thinking that it could be improved upon. Indeed, my proposed refinements open up new areas that cry out for further Popperian analysis.

POPPER: Why are refinements necessary at all?

LAKATOS: The Popperian criterion for an interesting theory to be good science is not only that it be refutable, but that it have survived extensive experimental attempts to refute it that the theory might easily have failed. I think this criterion is perhaps too strict. The observation of the precession of the orbit of Mercury refutes Newtonian mechanics, but do we really want to say that physicists should therefore have abandoned Newton's theory of gravitation? Was not the fact that Newton's theory provides a good approximation to the data in other contexts a good reason to continue using it as a model until Einstein came up with a model that works for Mercury as well as it does for the other planets?

POPPER: Physics has at least two roles. My own work is concerned with the discovery of Truths about the universe. A second role lies in providing ammunition for the kind of engineers who put the Earth's first artificial satellite into orbit not so long ago. For the second purpose, the models physicists use do not need to be attempts at Truth. It is enough that experiment shows that they predict with sufficient accuracy for engineering work. The simplicity of the Newtonian model then becomes a virtue that can outweigh the increase of accuracy of the Einsteinian alternative. So I think physicists preoccupied with their second role were right not to abandon Newton's theory, even after Einstein's theory survived all attempts at refutation. My own emphasis on refutation is directed at physicists who are concerned with their primary role in discovering Truth—the same physicists who will have to think again once the contradictions between the continuous nature of Einstein's theory of relativity and the discrete nature of quantum mechanics are manifested in experimental data from situations where both theories are predicted to have significant effects.

LAKATOS: I wonder how many physicists would endorse the correspondence theory of Truth you have borrowed from Alfred Tarski. I think they would mostly regard it as a naive metaphysical concept on which no opinion is necessary. Who is to say that the universe is organized in a way that can be adequately described by assigning truth values to some list of basic propositions?

POPPER: What of psychoanalysis and other pseudo-sciences? Are they to be regarded as respectable after Truth has been thrown out of the window?

LAKATOS: By no means! My proposal retains your emphasis on refutation while abandoning what I see as its metaphysical trappings in favor of following the skeptical practice of actual scientists. You need not fear that psychoanalysis and other pseudo-sciences will be somehow rehabilitated by such a skeptical reassessment of your theory.

POPPER: Tell me more about how we are to proceed without the concept of Truth to act as a possibly unattainable ideal to light the way forward.

LAKATOS: I argue that instead of thinking in terms of one conjectural theory at a time in isolation from other theories, we can instead think of a sequence of theories in which each new theory is constructed in response to an experimental refutation of its predecessor. What links the theories in a sequence is a hard core of axiomatic material—the basic structures that the scientific culture of the time is unable or unwilling to question. Refutation of one theory in the sequence will therefore lead only to a revision of how the auxiliary parameters of the theory are conceived or computed. I call the whole sequence of theories a research program, and think of progress in the human scientific endeavor as an evolutionary process in which rival research programs compete for survival.

POPPER: It sounds like you are dressing up Thomas Kuhn's notion of normal science in Popperian clothing. But I am decidedly hostile to Kuhn's idea that we should reduce the philosophy of science to the history of science. If we are not careful, we will thereby lay ourselves open to the same criticism I directed against Hegel and Marx in my *Poverty of Historicism*. But you never seem to have given up your youthful enthusiasm for Hegel in spite of joining me in turning your back on Marxism.

LAKATOS: It is true that I remain enamoured with Hegel's rhetorical gifts, but I now see Hegel as nothing more than a magnificent showman. What chutzpah to write a sentence that supposedly achieves the ultimate aim of the evolution of the human spirit!

POPPER: What teleological nonsense! To admire Hegel is to flutter like a moth around a flame. We must be as scientific in our attitude to philosophical theories as we are to physical theories. However, our discussion has cleared the air for me. You want to reduce the philosophy of science to studying the games that scientists play when following what Kuhn calls normal science. I do not think it is enough that we follow Hegel in asking where evolution will take us when such games are played. However one chooses to think about truth, nothing says that evolution will necessarily take us there. My theory transcends such attempts to model normal science. It is about what Kuhn calls extraordinary science—what happens when a scientific revolution substitutes new axioms for what you call the hard-core axioms of a research program.

LAKATOS: I nevertheless retain your belief that the replacement of Newton's axioms by those of Einstein should be regarded as the basic paradigm of a scientific advance.

POPPER: I see that I must reconcile myself to your abandoning the tradition of Rudolph Carnap and the Vienna Circle. It seems obvious to me that the decision on which research program should triumph ought to be made on rational grounds rather than being left to the vagaries of social evolution. But you are prepared even to leave to social evolution the decision on which research program to follow in studying research programs. This is blow from which I shall find it hard to recover.

Afterword

The split between Lakatos and Popper actually opened up more gradually than their imaginary dialogue suggests. While it was going on, Lakatos engineered another dialogue with his close friend Paul Feyerband, whose line was that we should allow no constraints at all in what we regard as science. It says something of Lakatos's approach to life that he chose to defend rationality in this celebrated public debate. It is also instructive that critics of their sometimes hilarious exchanges have suggested that the whole event was nothing more than a publicity stunt contrived by the protagonists to promote their careers.

The theorem of Euler mentioned in the introduction says that the number of faces and the number of vertices of any polyhedron sum to the number of edges plus two. It follows that there are no more than the five regular polyhedra called the Platonic solids discovered by Theaetetus.

Newton's theory predicts that the orbit of Mercury is an ellipse with the sun at one focus. (The other planets are too far off for their influence to be significant.) The ellipse should be stable, but the data shows that the point in Mercury's orbit at which it is nearest the sun rotates over time. The phenomenon is very much stronger in recent observations of the orbits of objects orbiting black holes. The fact that Einstein's theory predicts this procession of the perihelion, was very important in gaining acceptance for his ideas.

Chapter 31

Robert Nozick versus David Lewis

Context

The 1969 publication of "Newcomb's Problem and Two Principles of Choice" brought Robert Nozick to the attention of the world of philosophical controversy with an almighty splash. The paper claimed to have found a contradiction in orthodox decision theory! Nozick had originally included the problem in his dissertation after learning at a cocktail party of its invention by a Californian physicist named William Newcomb.

In the same 1969 publication, David Lewis wrote a response claiming that Newcomb's problem is really two versions of a game called the Prisoners' Dilemma written back-to-back, but he was soon joined by a multitude of philosophers proposing different resolutions of the problem. The excitement generated at the time was aptly described as Newcombmania. A recent commentary observed that the paradox remains just as perplexing as when first conceived. It is curious that nobody seems willing to listen to the simple resolution that a contradiction is obtained because the assumptions of Newcomb's problem are contradictory—that it to say, there is no Newcomb's problem requiring resolution.

The imaginary dialogue takes Newcomb's problem and the Prisoners' Dilemma as the topic of discussion—the latter having also been a subject of continuing philosophical controversy. A version of the Prisoners' Dilemma can be very simply described. Alice and Bob are each given a dollar. They then both independently decide whether to use one of two strategies. The *hawk* strategy is to selfishly keep your dollar. The *dove* strategy is to behave cooperatively by contributing your dollar to a common pot. The amount contributed to the pot is then increased by half as much again. Equal shares are then returned to both players, whether or not they made a contribution.

Philosophers are interested because they see *dove* as representing cooperation in general, and *hawk* as representing selfishness in general. But to play *hawk* in the Prisoners' Dilemma is a dominant strategy—you get a higher payoff by playing *hawk* whether or not your opponent plays *hawk* or *dove*. But if both Alice and Bob play *hawk*, they will each end up with only $1.00 rather than the $1.50 they would each get if both played *dove*. This conclusion is said to be a paradox of rationality because, if the same logic were applied generally, societies could not survive. All kinds of arguments have therefore been invented why game theorists analyze the game wrongly. Nozick's favorite was the Fallacy of the Twins, which is discussed in the dialogue. Game theorists are untroubled by all the fuss, because they do not think the Prisoners' Dilemma is a good model for studying how societies hold together. They follow David Hume in thinking that only repeated games make sense in such a context, since only then can reciprocity be brought into play.

I shall explain Newcomb's problem in a manner that makes it obvious why Lewis thought it reduced to two Prisoners' Dilemmas written back-to-back. It involves two boxes that may have money inside. Alice is free to take either the first box or both boxes. If she cares only for money, what choice should she make? This seems an easy problem. If *dove* represents taking only the first box, and *hawk* represents taking both boxes, then Alice should choose *hawk*, because this choice always results in her getting at least as much money as *dove*. That is to say, *hawk* dominates *dove*. The catch is that although it is certain that there is one dollar in the second box, the first box contains either nothing or two dollars. The decision about whether to put money in the first box is made by Bob, who knows Alice so well that he can always make a perfect prediction of what she will do—whether or not she behaves rationally. Like Alice, he has two choices, *dove* and *hawk*. His dovelike choice is to put two dollar bills in the first box. His hawkish choice is to put nothing in the first box. His motivation is to catch Alice out. He therefore plays *dove* if and only if he predicts that Alice will choose *dove*. He plays *hawk* if and only if he predicts that she will choose *hawk*.

Alice's choice of *hawk* now looks dubious. If she chooses *hawk*, Bob predicts her choice and puts nothing in the first box, so that Alice gets only the single dollar in the second box. If Alice chooses *dove*, Bob predicts her choice and puts two dollars in the first box. Alice then gets two dollars, but is left regretting the dollar in the second box that she failed to choose. Nozick argues that the principle of eliminating dominated strategies is therefore inconsistent with the principle of maximizing expected utility. If true, Samson's bringing down the temple upon the heads of the Philistines would be as nothing compared with the consequences for game theory! However, in their imaginary dialogue, Lewis tries to persuade Nozick that he is no Samson.

Robert Nozick (1938–2002) was born in Brooklyn to a Russian Jewish immigrant family. He studied philosophy at Columbia and Princeton before securing a permanent position at Harvard in 1969. He became widely known through his 1974 book *Anarchy, State and Utopia*, which adopts a Lockian approach to Natural Rights to engineer a libertarian denial of John Rawls' immensely successful *Theory* of Justice (discussed in the next dialogue). Was Nozick actually a libertarian, or did he really hold by the socialism that he espoused earlier? It is perhaps significant that he always refused to discuss *Anarchy, State and Utopia* after its publication. He was perhaps something of a modern Leibniz—brimming over with ideas on many topics, including Leibniz's notion of possible worlds, but holding fast to none. He was not as clever as Leibniz by any means, but he made up for this lack by being gifted with a genuinely charismatic personality. However, his later work never got the same attention as either his venture into game theory, or his criticism of Rawls.

David Lewis (1941–2001) was born to academic parents in Ohio. His brilliance was obvious from an early age, but he only decided to go into philosophy after spending a year at Oxford, which perhaps explains why he became the standard bearer for analytic philosophy rather than one of the other branches of philosophy. He is best remembered for his development of Leibniz's idea of possible worlds, taking this idea much further than most people are willing to go. This is one way in which he followed a parallel line to Nozick. The other is in his early book *Conventions*, in which he exploits the ideas of Tom Schelling to put flesh on the bones of David Hume's observation that languages are gradually established by human conventions without any need to postulate the existence of a binding social contract.

Nozick and Lewis must have met many times. For their imaginary dialogue, I have them meeting for lunch at a small restaurant in Cambridge in 1995, where Nozick once entertained me. The joke about vegetarianism he told me had the air of being much repeated, and so I have him telling it to Lewis as well. Lewis is supposedly visiting Harvard to give a seminar. He has just read Nozick's *Nature of Rationality* in which Nozick retells Newcomb's problem with what he feels to be a more plausible background story, but Lewis remains unconvinced that there is any problem with orthodox decision theory. I imagine that Lewis has also revised his 1969 views so as to recognize that the assumptions of Newcomb's problem contradict each other.

Dialogue

Nozick has been a gracious host in a small restaurant in Cambridge to which he has invited Lewis for lunch. They leave any serious discussion till their coffee arrives. However, before they begin to discuss Newcomb's problem, Lewis cannot resist teasing Nozick about his having eaten meat.

LEWIS: I noticed that you ate meat with your main course, but I seem to recall that your *Philosophical Explanations* argues that morality demands that we be vegetarian.

NOZICK: Oh yes—but I divorced that wife!

LEWIS: Very good! Your *Nature of Rationality* also revises your original approach to Newcomb's problem by relaxing the requirement that Bob can predict Alice's choice perfectly. Now you offer the hypothesis that Bob's predictions have been successful in the past, and so are likely to be successful in the future, but might be wrong with some small probability. I do not see that you thereby rescue your claim that orthodox decision theory contains a fundamental contradiction. However, before discussing this point, I would first like to confess that I too have revised my original take on modeling Newcomb's problem.

NOZICK: You have revised your claim that Newcomb's original problem consists of two back-to-back Prisoners' Dilemmas?

LEWIS: Yes. In following the standard assumption in game theory that rational players can predict the rational play of their opponents, I failed to recognize that your formulation of Newcomb's problem requires the much stronger requirement that Bob would predict Alice's choice even if she chose irrationally.

NOZICK: Let us pursue this last point in the simpler context of the Prisoner's Dilemma without the extra complications involved by embedding the game in Newcomb's problem. But I would first like to hear your current views on my original formulation of the Newcomb problem.

LEWIS: There cannot be a contradiction between choosing a dominating strategy and maximizing expected utility. The latter tells you to choose whatever strategy maximizes your expected utility given your beliefs about what your opponent is going to do, and the former tells you that a dominating strategy maximizes your expected utility whatever your beliefs may be. You obtain the appearance of a contradiction by starting with assumptions that already contain a contradiction—and we were all taught in Logic 101 that anything can be deduced from a contradiction.

NOZICK: What do you regard as the assumptions for Newcomb's problem that you think contradict each other?

LEWIS: The three assumptions are first that Alice is free to choose, the second is that she chooses after Bob has made his prediction, and the third is that Bob's prediction is always correct whatever Alice may choose.

NOZICK: You are going to say that it is impossible for Bob always to be right if Alice is free to choose after he has made his prediction, because she would not then be free to choose what he did not predict. Theologians have put a lot of effort into denying this argument in reconciling their faith in the omniscience of God and the existence of human free will.

LEWIS: I think your exposition of Newcomb's problem can best be seen as a contribution to this theological debate. It demonstrates that orthodox decision theory has to be abandoned if the theologians are right. But I think that you have no more confidence in the reasoning of theologians than I do.

NOZICK: You are right that I am a skeptic about religious matters, which is one reason that I modified the hypothesis of perfect prediction to prediction with high probability in my recent book.

LEWIS: I see that your modification removes the outright contradiction in the assumptions of Newcomb's problem, but it makes no essential difference. A game theorist can model the new situation by denying Alice the freedom to deviate from Bob's prediction except with some small probability when she exercises her free will. In the subgame in which she exercises her free will, she will simply choose the dominant strategy.

NOZICK: I agree with you to the extent that we can focus on whether it makes sense to choose the dominant strategy in the simpler Prisoners' Dilemma. I think you will probably say that my Paradox of the Twins also incorporates a fallacy.

LEWIS: If I recall accurately, your Paradox of the Twins offers an argument why it is rational for the players in the Prisoners' Dilemma to cooperate by playing *dove*. Alice reasons that Bob is her twin, since he is in the same position as herself. So he will do whatever she does. If she chooses *dove*, he will choose *dove*. If she chooses *hawk*, he will choose *hawk*. Of these two possibilities, she prefers that they both choose *dove*. Bob reasons the same, and so their expectations are realized in their both choosing *dove*.

NOZICK: I do not say this reasoning is correct—only that it is a viable alternative to the reasoning that game theorists prefer.

LEWIS: It is true that if there is a unique rational solution of a symmetric game, then a rational Alice and Bob will independently both choose the same strategy. But it does not follow that whatever Alice chooses, Bob will choose the same. Alice will certainly think about playing irrational strategies to check that they are indeed irrational. But she will not think that Bob's thoughts move in lockstep with hers. His thoughts are independent of hers. But it does not matter how his thinking goes because he is assumed to be rational, and so he will end up choosing whatever the rational strategy turns out to be. She should therefore choose whatever strategy is her best reply to his rational strategy. Since the same reasoning works for Bob, each will make a best reply to the other's choice by playing *hawk* because this is the best reply whatever strategy the other chooses.

NOZICK: Why then do biologists sometimes endorse the idea that evolution will generate cooperation in the Prisoners' Dilemma?

LEWIS: There are two reasons. The first is a failure to distinguish between the *one-shot* Prisoners' Dilemma that we have been talking about up to now, and the *indefinitely repeated* Prisoners' Dilemma, in which the strategic issues are very different. Robert Axelrod's *Evolution of Cooperation* extols the virtues of the strategy *tit-for-tat* for the latter. It is indeed a Nash equilibrium in the indefinitely repeated Prisoners' Dilemma for both players to use *tit-for-tat,* provided the probability that the game will be played at least once more is always sufficiently high.

NOZICK: As I recall, *tit-for-tat* requires a player to begin by cooperating, and then simply copy whatever the other player did in the previous round. The players will then cooperate forever. Neither will want to cheat because they will only provoke their opponent into cheating until they stop cheating themselves. The indefinitely repeated Prisoners' Dilemma therefore provides a model that supports David Hume's contention that reciprocity can support cooperation in repeated situations without the necessity for any external enforcement.

LEWIS: But there is nothing very special about the particular strategy *tit-for-tat*. The folk theorem of repeated game theory says that cooperation can be maintained in many different ways by many different strategies.

NOZICK: So why do evolutionary biologists endorse Axelrod's claims for *tit-for-tat*?

LEWIS: You are perhaps referring to John Maynard Smith apparently joining Axelrod in claiming that *tit-for-tat* is an evolutionary stable strategy? But it is obvious that this is false. Evolutionary stability requires that a population of animals all programmed to play *tit-for-tat* will be able to repel any mutant invasion that might occur. But such a population cannot even repel a mutant that always cooperates no matter what. In fact, no pure strategies whatever can pass the evolutionary stability test in a repeated game. The definition of evolutionary stability only works properly in the games for which it was designed, which have only two strategies for each player.

NOZICK: I guess it is enough for philosophers like ourselves that game theory endorses David Hume's intuition. But Axelrod has also written with the evolutionary biologist William Hamilton.

LEWIS: Yes—and Hamilton's work is immediately relevant to your Paradox of the Twins.

NOZICK: I guess we are now talking about the one-shot Prisoners' Dilemma again. You are going to say that if Alice and Bob really are twins, then my argument is no longer fallacious.

LEWIS: Yes—provided that Alice and Bob's choices of strategy are genetically programmed. Since their genes are then identical, so will be their strategy choices.

NOZICK: What if Alice and Bob are only brother and sister?

LEWIS: Hamilton has this all worked out too. I doubt that he read your ideas on the Paradox of the Twins in advance of his research, but it turns out that the ideas are relevant whenever related players whose behavior is genetically determined play games together. The consequences for sex ratios in species with unusual genetics—like bees and ants—are the most convincing argument I know for why evolution must be right.

NOZICK: It is a pleasure to learn that you think my efforts on this front were not entirely in vain! I hope you will think the same of my recent thoughts on evolution in the space of all possible worlds.

LEWIS: Evolution in the space of all possible worlds! People are going to think this even wilder than my contention that all possible worlds really exist.

NOZICK: I certainly hope so! Let me tell you all about it.

They linger over their coffee for an hour or so more, taking delight in their creativity in pushing the notion of possible worlds so far that they strain the credulity of even the most determined of metaphysicians. However, Nozick does not forget the crushing blows that Lewis delivered earlier to his analysis of Newcomb's problem.

Afterword

Newcombmania is still not entirely dead nowadays, and so it may be of interest that the Paradox of the Twins and a variety of other related fallacies are discussed at length in *Playing Fair* (pages 173–254), which is the first volume of my *Game Theory and the Social Contract*.

Chapter 32

John Rawls versus John Harsanyi

Context

John Rawls is regarded as the leading moral philosopher of the twentieth century. His *Theory of Justice* is a counterblast against utilitarianism that redirected political liberalism onto a new path. His continuing success in reaching hearts and minds is even enshrined in an all-singing, all-dancing musical *A Theory of Justice: The Musical!*, which had some success in the UK in 2013. Rawls' basic idea is that justice is no more than fairness, which is to be judged using the "original position" in which we imagine ourselves behind a "veil of ignorance" that conceals our identities from ourselves while we bargain our way to solutions to our social problems.

In spite of his Nobel Prize in Economics for his Bayesian solution to the problem of incomplete information in game theory, John Harsanyi is largely unknown to philosophers, presumably because he couched his ideas in mathematical terms, although nothing very deep is involved. His contribution to philosophy was to offer answers to all the problems with utilitarianism left hanging in the air by Bentham that are usually thought to have been solved by Mill. Mill's much cited "proof" of utilitarianism just consists of an unconvincing chapter devoted to the claim that what people desire is happiness. But what we want to know is whether happiness is really something that can be sharply defined. How do we measure it? How do we add it up? Why substitute the sum of everybody's happiness for our own? In offering answers to these questions, Harsanyi invented the original position independently of Rawls at about the same time in the 1950s, but paradoxically used it to arrive at the very utilitarian conclusion that Rawls wrote his famous book to deny. How and why they differ on this subject is part of what they discuss in their imaginary dialogue. I have allowed myself to appear toward the end of the dialogue offering my own solution to their differences from my book *Natural Justice*.

John Rawls (1921–2002) ended up as a much-loved philosophy professor at Harvard, but his early career was not all plain sailing. He was apparently much affected by the death of two of his brothers after they contracted illnesses from him. His service in the Second World War as an enlisted man in the appalling trench war during the retaking of the Philippines was traumatic. His later observation of the aftermath of the nuclear bombing while serving during the later occupation of Japan completed his conversion from a one-time devout Christian to atheism. He is described as being of a retiring nature, plagued with a stutter. He was certainly almost absurdly modest in my own experience, although I found his stutter hardly noticeable in the few conversations I had with him. I remember thinking at the time that if everybody were like John Rawls, there would be no necessity for moral philosophy at all.

I knew John Harsanyi (1920–2000) a lot better. We often disputed his very determined attachment to Bayesianism. He was a much more aggressive personality than Rawls, perhaps because his life was more of a struggle. As a Jew in Hungary, he escaped disaster by the skin of his teeth not once, but twice. Having evaded the death camps of the Nazis, he was then forced to cross illegally into Austria with his wife to escape persecution by the Communists who followed. And once in the West, he had to build his career again from scratch, beginning with a factory job in Australia. In spite of his Nobel prize, his work in ethics will probably never get the recognition it deserves. Perhaps things would have been different if he had finished the philosophical book on which he was working when he died. As with David Hume, to accept his common-sense insights requires junking centuries of earnest scholarship as worthless—and which of us is ready to dump our own books first?

I do not think Harsanyi and Rawls ever met in person, although they certainly exchanged letters. I have seen copies of Harsanyi's not-very-polite contributions to this exchange, so it is clear where they saw the fault-line as lying. I have set their imaginary dialogue at a 1996 conference on *Justice, Political Liberalism, and Utilitarianism* held in honor of Harsanyi and Rawls at the University of Caen in Normandy, France. The plan was that both Harsanyi and Rawls would receive honorary doctorates, but Rawls was prevented from attending by the first of several strokes that eventually led to his death. The celebration of their achievements was therefore tinged with regret. It was particularly sad for me, as I had hoped to show Rawls my own evolutionary slant on his ideas in which he had encouraged me over several years, in spite of his holding—alongside Harsanyi—that the original position is best seen as an operationalization of Kant's categorical imperative.

Dialogue

The sun is peeping through the rainclouds on a June day in Normandy as the conference participants return from lunch to a much-awaited session in which Harsanyi and Rawls are to debate their opposed views on utilitarianism. The chairman invites

Rawls versus Harsanyi

them to begin by discussing who holds priority in inventing the notion that Rawls calls the original position.

HARSANYI: It is clear enough that we invented the original position independently. In any case, we were both anticipated by a remark of William Vickrey, who just died three days after learning he had won the Nobel Prize in Economics for his work on auctions.

RAWLS: I agree that disputing priority is unprofitable, but if we were to go down that road, it would be necessary to mention the philosopher Robert Hare, who attributes his own version of the original position to Clarence Lewis. I sometimes ask classical scholars if they know of any hint of the idea among the ancients, but so far they have nothing to say.

HARSANYI: We are asked to debate our differences on utilitarianism. Perhaps I might begin by summarizing my approach, although I know that my use of modeling techniques is not always popular with moral philosophers.

RAWLS: I am no mathematician, but I am no less enthusiastic than Spinoza about adopting the precise methods of geometry into foundational issues in philosophy. Indeed, my notion of reflective equilibrium might reasonably be regarded as a general defense of scientific model-building in general.

HARSANYI: I model the original position as a bargaining problem in which each participant seeks to maximize his or her individual expected utility. I do not follow Bentham or yourself in proposing some index of goods in measuring utility. Economists no longer find such an approach adequate. Instead of telling people what they ought to want, economists think we should take as basic what they actually would choose for themselves if they were given the opportunity. If these hypothetical choices are consistent, people will behave as though maximizing the average value of something that we call utility. Philosophers often fail to understand that this new approach to utility turns Bentham and Mill's concept of utility-as-happiness on its head. In the modern theory, people do not choose one thing rather than another because it makes them happier—utilities are assigned to outcomes to make people's choices accord with maximizing the long-run average of an abstract something that we call utility, which is what is necessary if their choices are to be consistent with each other.

RAWLS: You appeal here to the version of subjective Bayesianism that Savage defended so effectively in his *Foundations of Statistics*. The price of following this line is that one has to give up any *explanation* of why people do one thing rather than another in favor of a mere *description* of what people actually do—or what they would do if they were sufficiently rational not to be inconsistent in how they would make different choices. What of the problem of comparing the utilities of different people that many economists insist is impossible?

HARSANYI: It is said that Alice may complain more than Bob in the dentist's chair, but who is to say who is really feeling more pain? Economists who argue in this way appeal to the outdated concept of utility-as-happiness so that they can argue that fairness has no role in economic analysis—and it is true that if one could not compare who gets how much after some economic transaction, then fairness would cease to be meaningful.

RAWLS: We agree then that we have to look beyond the naive economics of the Chicago school who think that markets are the solution to everything?

HARSANYI: We do indeed—but because the Chicago school are wrong about fairness, it does not follow that they are wrong about everything else. However, the immediate point is that people in the original position need to be able to attach utilities to the various possible outcomes of their bargaining problem in the original position. One might call such utilities ethical because they necessarily describe a person's attitude to how they would feel if they turned out to be Alice rather than Bob when emerging from behind the veil of ignorance. Applying standard Bayesian theory to such ethical utilities, I find that maximizing expected utility in the original position corresponds to behaving as a utilitarian who weights Alice and Bob's everyday utilities according to their ethical preferences.

RAWLS: I am pleased to have the opportunity to congratulate you on your bold resolution of the classical problems with utilitarianism that Mill neglected—but the price that has to be paid is high. In particular, we have to take Bayesianism for granted as the only rational way for decisions to be made.

HARSANYI: I am a Bayesian to my roots, but it is true that Savage warns against using his theory in large worlds. In such large worlds, he argues that it would be impossible to attain the kind of consistency necessary to justify expected utility. However, the conditions of the original position make it almost as small a world as one can conceive. The only uncertainty lies in who will turn out to be who when the veil of ignorance is lifted.

RAWLS: Here we disagree on two levels. I disagree that the only source of uncertainty in the original position that needs to be considered is who will turn out to be who when the veil of ignorance is lifted. But at a deeper level, we differ in what we are trying to achieve in thinking about the original position. You aim at a deductive analysis that proceeds from Bayesian axiomatic principles that you take to be self-evident. My notion of reflective equilibrium allows give-and-take between what we take to be axiomatic and our basic moral intuitions. It is repulsive that utilitarianism allows minorities to be sacrificed so that the majority may flourish. What axioms allow this conclusion to be denied in a coherent system? The answer I offer is that we should use the maximin criterion rather than maximizing expected utility. With the maximin criterion, each person bargains in the original position on the assumption that, when he emerges from behind the veil of ignorance, he will find himself occupying the role of the least-favored citizen in the society to which they have agreed.

Harsanyi looks impatient at Rawls' response, and the chairman can see that he is probably about to patronize Rawls by explaining that the maximin criterion only makes sense in zero-sum games when people have nothing to gain by cooperating.

So he decides that this is a good time to open the discussion to the floor. Ken Binmore is anxious to speak, but the chairman would like what Harsanyi and Rawls have discussed so far to be chewed over before more revolutionary proposals are made. But when the chewing over runs out of steam, he turns to Binmore to liven things up.

BINMORE: The paper I shall give tomorrow argues that we do not have to choose between Harsanyi's very sound Bayesian foundations and Rawls' moral intuitions about how fairness norms work in practice. But—as both commented in their own remarks—there is always a price to be paid. The price in this case is that it is necessary to abandon the Kantian metaphysics that both espouse in favor of an evolutionary explanation of the origin of fairness norms. I know that moral philosophers typically react with horror at such a suggestion. Can it really be that David Hume was right—that the iron laws of morality are no more than social conventions that might vary from one society to another?

RAWLS: I am willing to suspend disbelief while you explain how it is possible to reconcile my position with Harsanyi's.

BINMORE: For this purpose, it is necessary to pay attention to the sword in the hand of the statues of Justice with which we embellish our courts of law. Her scales represent how she weighs one person's welfare against another's. I borrow Harsanyi's theory for this purpose. Her blindfold represents the veil of ignorance for which you are jointly responsible. However, you both neglect the question of enforcement. Why should someone neglect their own interests in favor of whatever their society regards as fair? You both resort to standard metaphysical skyhooks for this purpose. Rawls calls his skyhook Natural Duty. Harsanyi calls his Moral Commitment. In my view, we have to dispense with such metaphysical skyhooks altogether. As Jeremy Bentham said of Natural Rights, such skyhooks are not just nonsense, but nonsense upon stilts!

HARSANYI: But the alternative is to give up any rational approach to morality. My theory recognizes that people have two kinds of preferences: their everyday preferences and their ethical preferences. They use their everyday preferences when shopping at the supermarket. They use their ethical preferences when adjudicating fairness issues. But why should they care about fairness at all if they have no reason to believe that morality matters?

BINMORE: The evolutionary reason that people sometimes play fair is that they have to take account of the behavior of the other people with whom they interact. Game theory models this issue by assuming that people will coordinate on one of the Nash equilibria of their game of life—in which case, each person will be selfishly optimizing given the behavior of their fellows. That is to say, morality did not evolve as a substitute for the exercise of power as you imagine, but as a device for balancing power.

RAWLS: So you follow David Hume in regarding morality as no more than a system of social conventions for selecting one of the many equilibria in the game of life.

For you, morality has no more significance than the traffic signals that tell us when to stop or go. But I guess you will reply that to say fairness norms have no more significance than traffic signals is like saying that Shakespeare is no different from a comic book because they are both printed on paper.

BINMORE: A big difference between traffic signals and fairness norms is that we understand how traffic signals work, but fairness norms remain a mystery to which our intuition is no reliable guide. But I think the original position hits the spot with most people when they hear of it for the first time because they recognize an idealization of an equilibrium selection device that they use all the time in solving everyday coordination problems, like who should wash the dishes tonight, or who should get how much of a treat in short supply at the dinner table.

HARSANYI: I see where you are coming from in endorsing Rawls' moral intuition, but it seems your approach leaves no room for utilitarianism.

BINMORE: Not so! When outside enforcement is genuinely available rather than as an invented skyhook, your argument applies unaltered. My approach therefore endorses utilitarianism as an instrument of public policy. But it supports Rawls' position when outside enforcement is unavailable—as in everyday applications of fairness norms or, at the other extreme, in discussions of constitutional issues.

RAWLS: I do not think I will ever be persuaded to abandon my Kantian foundations, but I am attracted by the fact that an evolutionary approach can explain how everybody in a society might come to have the same ethical preferences about how one type of person is to be compared with another. It is essential for both Harsanyi and myself that people do in fact hold such ethical preferences in common, but neither of us offer any explanation why.

HARSANYI: I have no time for this evolutionary nonsense at all. The moral relativism that follows is abhorrent. We need to find rational arguments that will eventually convince everybody to adopt the same moral absolutes independently of our evolutionary history. Binmore speaks slightingly of the metaphysical attitude necessary to formulate the axioms from which such absolutes can be deduced, but someone with his mathematical training should know better.

The chairman now thinks that this discussion has not only gone on too long but shows signs of getting heated, so he takes the opportunity of changing the subject by calling upon another person who has been seeking to attract his attention for some time. He also interrupted the discussion of whether Rawls is entitled to throw away Bayesian decision theory in favor of the maximin criterion. This issue is taken up again in the next imaginary dialogue.

Afterword

Harsanyi's simple resolution of the problem of interpersonal comparison of utility that economists used to say is impossible goes like this. He begins with the requirement that we are all able to express preferences that say, for example, whether we would prefer to be Alice drinking a cup of coffee, or Bob downing a glass of whisky. He then adds the requirement that we are fully successful when we seek to empathize with Alice or Bob. If so, we will substitute their everyday preferences for our own everyday preferences when identifying with them. For example, I might prefer coffee to whisky, but if Alice prefers whisky to coffee, I will accept that I would share her preference for whisky over coffee if I were her. Some truly minimal algebra then shows that the von Neumann and Morgenstern utility I attach to being Alice drinking a cup of coffee is her everyday von Neumann and Morgenstern utility for a cup of coffee times a weight (plus an irrelevant constant). There will be different weights for different people. These weights determine how my ethical preferences value Alice's everyday utils in comparison with Bob's everyday utils.

Chapter 33
Derek Parfit versus John Rawls

Context

The preceding dialogue between Harsanyi and Rawls took place in Normandy, where they are imagined to have both flown from America to receive honorary doctorates from the University of Caen. In real life, Rawls was unable to come, having been struck down by the first of a number of strokes that largely confined him thereafter to his bed. Our next imaginary dialogue is similarly unrealistic in assuming that he is sufficiently well to receive Derek Parfit in his sickroom some years later. Parfit is hoping to get some endorsement from Rawls of his interpreting Rawls' *Theory of Justice* as a defense of a moral principle that Parfit calls prioritarianism.

Derek Parfit (1942–2017) was born in China of parents who were there to teach preventive medicine in missionary hospitals. After his birth, the family moved back to England, where Parfit benefited from an elite education at Eton College and Oxford. He switched from history to philosophy in 1966 while holding a Harkness Fellowship at Columbia and Harvard. His special interests were in personal identity, rationality, and morality. His 1984 book *Persons and Reasons* was described at the time as the most important work of moral philosophy since the 1800s. I met him briefly, but our conversation was not productive, since he took exception to someone with a mathematical background thinking he could contribute to moral philosophy. It was for the likes of Parfit that the poet Auden wrote the immortal lines:

> Thou shalt not sit
> With statisticians nor commit
> A social science.

Parfit appears in this book as a consequence of a recent report from the World Health Organization (WHO) that offers a minimal consensus on what a panel of 22 health gurus thought acceptable as fairness principles to guide the design of public health systems. Partly as a consequence of Parfit's successful agitation, they saw their problem as a Trilemma, in which they had to choose between naive versions of utilitarianism, egalitarianism, and Parfit's prioritarianism. They followed Parfit in ruling out egalitarianism, but his strictures against utilitarianism seem to have left them unmoved. They ended up endorsing an incoherent mixture of utilitarianism and prioritarianism that is unlikely to impress any reformers looking for practical advice on how to proceed.

The efforts of this particular WHO committee may lack conviction, but they show that philosophers cannot always be dismissed as impractical dreamers who count how many angels can dance on the end of a pin. When their claims are backed by the prestige of an ancient university like Oxford, they have the potential to influence who gets to live, and who gets to die. As John Maynard Keynes said of the ideas of economists and political philosophers, "The world is ruled by little else. Practical men, who believe themselves to be quite exempt from any intellectual influences, are usually slaves of some defunct economist."

Dialogue

Derek Parfit remained a Visiting Professor at Harvard until his death. On one of his visits in perhaps the year 2000, he is imagined to seek an interview with John Rawls to discuss the transcript of a 1995 lecture *Equality or Priority*, in which he rubbishes egalitarianism, and invokes the authority of Rawls in advocating that it be replaced by prioritarianism. Rawls is not pleased to be thought hostile to egalitarianism, and so agrees to an interview in his sickroom on the understanding that it will have to be cut short if he gets too weak to continue. One might reasonably suppose that Rawls' illness would have made him grumpier than those who knew him remember, but it is unlikely that he would ever have been as assertive as he is represented in the coming imaginary dialogue. However, Parfit remains undaunted at finding Rawls does not share his unquestioning allegiance to physis in the ancient nomos versus physis debate.

RAWLS: I have read the transcript of your lecture *Equality or Priority*. I wrote my *Theory of Justice* partly to provide a coherent alternative to utilitarianism, so I feel no urge to disagree with your conclusion that utilitarianism fails to capture how real fairness norms work. But I think the arguments you use in rejecting it are too quick. I debated the issue with the late John Harsanyi a few years ago. The philosophy profession ignores him, but we ought to congratulate him on replacing Bentham and Mill's shaky foundations by something that holds together much more successfully.

PARFIT: I suspect John Harsanyi is just one more of those mathematical folk who hide their ignorance of what really matters in life behind a smoke-screen of equations and formulas. Not for one moment do I imagine that he has an answer to what I call the repugnant conclusion in my *Persons and Reasons*. You will recall that I explain why it does not matter to a utilitarian how low the utility of the citizens in a society may be if there are enough of them. Whatever society you propose, I can make a repugnant society whose sum of utilities is greater than yours by making its population size very large.

RAWLS: I do not think mathematicians should be accused of ignorance because we cannot understand their arguments. On the contrary, I follow Spinoza in believing that we should strive for arguments as sound as the proofs of geometers. In the case of Harsanyi—who is apparently no great shakes as a mathematician—he would doubtless respond to your repugnant conclusion by saying that you set up a straw man only to knock it down. His formal defense of utilitarianism takes the size of the population as fixed. He could therefore say that those utilitarians who differ from him in being prepared to apply their doctrine to population size do not have serious arguments to support their doing so. So you fail to follow the philosophical principle that we should attribute the strongest arguments we can find to our opponents in seeking to refute their positions. We are not evangelists seeking to discredit what we regard as heresies with whatever rhetorical devices come to hand.

PARFIT: You will perhaps be more kind in assessing the arguments that I use to argue that egalitarianism should be replaced by prioritarianism. Instead of vainly striving for equality, we should instead prioritize relieving the suffering of our least well-off citizens.

RAWLS: Let me first deny the classification you offer in *Equality or Priority* of the possible metaphysical moral positions from which one might evaluate fairness issues. I am neither a telic nor a deontic egalitarian, and I take exception to being shoe-horned into one or the other category. I am certainly not the kind of prioritarian you suggest at the end of your lecture. It is not even necessary to take a metaphysical position at all to have an opinion on fairness issues that is worthy of respect. One could, for example, simply regard society's current fairness norms as the product of biological and social evolutionary forces operating in tandem. My notion of the original position is certainly consistent with this position. The standard metaphysical method of testing people's intuitions with fictional examples—like Philippa Foot's famous trolley example—then ceases to have any bite. An evolutionist has no difficulty in explaining why different people respond differently to such exotic moral problems. It is not because of a clash between rival metaphysical principles, but because the fairness norms that actually govern their choices are adapted to sharing problems that frequently arise in real life, rather than fables that have been invented by metaphysicians to make metaphysical points.

PARFIT: I am certainly guilty of promoting what you call a metaphysical fable in using the standard example that presupposes a new surgical technique that allows a living eye to be transferred from one person to another, but I do not see that any apology is due. The example allows us to make the point that utilitarians would argue that people with two eyes should be chosen at random to have one eye surgically removed so that it could be transferred to a blind person. But who would be willing to sacrifice an eye so that another can see without being compelled by force? Only a saint!

RAWLS: There is no harm in using such fables to illustrate how different moral principles work in simplified situations from which all the complications of real life have been removed—although the real-life case of saints who volunteer to give up one of their kidneys for a stranger without expecting anything in return is worthy of our attention. And I certainly agree that a moral system which insists that some citizens must submit to being sacrificed for the general good is abhorrent. This was my major motivation for writing *The Theory of Justice*—to show that rational foundations can be found for egalitarianism that are no worse than the foundations of utilitarianism of which it proponents are so proud. Where we differ is that I do not think it adequate to rely on people's intuitive responses to invented moral fables in formulating a coherent moral position. I certainly do not think it serves any useful purpose to discredit egalitarianism by inventing a version that leads to the absurd conclusion that everybody should submit to being blinded in the eye-transfer fable!

PARFIT: But is not your original position just the kind of moral fable whose use you wish to deny to me?

RAWLS: It is true that I described my original position at first as an operationalization of the Kantian categorical imperative, but even in those early days I did not think of the categorical imperative as a primitive moral axiom. I took Kant at his word that it could be deduced from a system of rational principles that share with logic the property of being beyond dispute. But the rational analysis of the Prisoners' Dilemma recently offered by game theorists puts this position in serious doubt. I now prefer to think that Kant was an unconscious pioneer in constructing a model of morality using my notion of a reflective equilibrium. I remain a Kantian, but my philosophical position on the status of the original position puts me closer to the model-building ethos of scientists than the metaphysical reasoning of more orthodox moral philosophers like yourself.

PARFIT: I certainly think it true that exponents of the absurd notion that ethics could possibly be an evolutionary phenomenon are best ignored. Your willingness to tolerate them comes as a considerable surprise—even more than your regarding reflective equilibrium as no more than a tool for building models.

RAWLS: I am certainly much less ambitious than metaphysicians like yourself. My notion of reflective equilibrium is merely a method to investigate the coherence of our moral intuitions. Perhaps contradictions are lurking in the intuitions of our fellow philosophers when they dispute moral positions so fiercely. But if a coherent model can be fitted to a set of moral principles, we can at least reject the hypothesis that the disputants have arrived at different conclusions because anything can be deduced from a contradiction.

PARFIT: Can you give an example of a case to which this unorthodox story applies?

RAWLS: Your *Equality or Priority* provides a simple example. Towards the end, you discuss what my attitude might be to what economists call Pareto efficiency. Am I in favor or not of Pareto's principle that one outcome should be preferred to another if nobody is worse off in the second outcome, and some people are better off? As the eye-transfer fable illustrates, the Pareto principle can lead to outcomes being favored that are decidedly unequal.

PARFIT: How is this relevant?

RAWLS: My original position is generally agreed to capture our fairness intuitions in at least some situations where limited resources are to be shared. One cannot go along with this view—as you seem to do—and simultaneously remain in doubt over the Pareto principle. If people bargain in the circumstances of the original position, it would be irrational of them to agree on a Pareto inefficient outcome. Economists call this the Coase theorem. It would therefore be incoherent of an egalitarian like myself to advocate that everybody be blinded in the eye-transfer fable, and hence to subordinate the Pareto principle to equality.

PARFIT: Another theorem to confuse the issue!

RAWLS: Actually the so-called Coase theorem is neither due to Ronald Coase, nor is it a theorem in the sense of having a formal proof. It is simply the observation that two bargainers who care only about their own welfare would be irrational to agree on one outcome knowing that a Pareto-improvement is available.

PARFIT: What of my taking on board your use of the maximin criterion in analyzing the bargaining problem in the original position. Surely you see that the maximin criterion supports prioritarianism better than egalitarianism?

RAWLS: I certainly see that people with egalitarian intuitions will support prioritarianism as a step on the way to true equality. I also see that prioritarianism is nothing other than the maximin criterion applied to the case in which we evaluate each possible outcome in terms of those who would be made worse off if that outcome were implemented. But I did not choose to analyze the original position using the maximin criterion for the metaphysical reasons you want to attribute to me. In using the method of reflective equilibrium to investigate my egalitarian intuitions, I could see that something other than orthodox Bayesian decision theory is necessary if a utilitarian outcome is to be avoided. So I substituted the maximin criterion. Harsanyi does not understand my motivation here any better than you.

PARFIT: I do not care to be compared with the likes of a mathematician like Harsanyi. But are you really saying that you have no better reason for applying the maximin criterion than that the alternative leads to a conclusion you wish to avoid?

RAWLS: There are better reasons. Bayesianism has feet of clay, which Bayesians are determined not to see. There is in fact a small community of economists and statisticians who advocate using the maximin criterion when it is manifestly absurd to imagine that rational people will be able to assign probabilities to events about which they are entirely ignorant.

PARFIT: Bayesianism does indeed seem absurd in such cases. So why are we not justified in throwing it away, along with Harsanyi's mathematical defense of utilitarianism?

RAWLS: How irresponsible that would be! Do we really want to advocate one moral principle rather than another on the basis of whether we like one decision theory rather than another in analyzing some abstract formulation of how fairness norms work? What we say on such matters has the potential to influence policy in deciding between rival political approaches to health and other life-and-death issues. It seems to me immoral to pretend that we have sound foundations for defending one policy rather than another when all we really have are better formulated prejudices than those without a philosophical training.

Parfit remains utterly unconvinced. How sad that illness and old age should have stolen the great man's capacity to reason! But the thought belatedly draws Parfit's attention to the fact that Rawls has clearly over-extended himself. So Parfit makes his excuses, and leaves.

Afterword

The Coase theorem was anticipated in Edgeworth's 1881 *Mathematical Psychics*, of which Parfit would not have approved at all. Nor would be have approved of the work of Gilboa and Schmeidler, who are perhaps the leading economic exponents of the use of the maximin criterion as an alternative to the Bayesian principle of maximizing expected utility.

Index

Abel prize, 164
Abelard, 33–36, 45, 56, 154, 155
absolute, 5, 25, 194
Absolute Infinity, 126
Academy, Plato's, 7, 8, 11, 12, 15, 21
Achilles and the Tortoise, 5, 21
Agora, 7, 19, 21
alchemy, 40
Alcibiades, 2
Alexander the Great, 8, 11, 12, 16, 17
Alexandria, 29, 83
algorithm, 138
alienation, 104
American War of Independence, 89
Analects, of Confucius, 132
analytic philosophy, 130, 183
analytical geometry, 49, 53
Anselm, 33–35, 37, 45, 49, 51, 56, 154
Antiphon, 132
antithesis, 118
Aquinas, 39–43, 45, 47, 51, 52, 85, 105, 106, 152
Archimedes, 15
Archytas, 8
Aristagoras, 16, 20
Aristarchus, 16
Aristippus, 14, 19, 23
aristocrat, 93
Aristotle, 8, 10–21, 39, 40, 46, 47, 57, 73, 107, 129, 172
Arnold, Thomas, 96
asceticism, 23
astrology, 40
atheism, 70, 78, 85, 108, 127, 190
Athens, 3, 7, 11, 15, 21, 93, 156, 161
Augustine, 29–32, 40, 83
Aurelian, 30
Austria, 175, 190
Authenticity, 156, 159
automaton, 72
Averroes, 40
Axelrod, 185
axiom, viii, 18, 52, 56, 70, 74, 131, 138, 147, 166, 169, 178, 192, 194

baboons, 119

Bacon, Roger, 39–43
bargaining, 191
bargaining game, 166
barometer, 55, 57
Bayes' rule, 170, 173
Bayesian decision theory, 169, 171, 201
Bayesianism, 169, 170, 190–192, 201
Bayle, 25
Beagle, the, 107, 108
Beauvoir, Simone de, 155–161
Bec, Abbey of, 34
Beijing, 130
belief, 3, 171
Bentham, 95–99, 103, 142–144, 146, 189, 191, 193, 198
Berkeley, 63
Berlin, 84
Bernoulli, Daniel, 145
Bernoulli, Nicolaus, 145
best reply, 144
Billancourt, 157
Binmore, 193, 194
bluffing, 145
Bolivar, Simon, 96
Bonaparte, Napoleon, 90, 102
Borel, 143, 144, 147
Boswell, 97
bourgeoisie, 118, 120, 160
Bradley, 131
Braithwaite, 149
Brecht, 158
Bristol, 89
Brno, 108, 119
Brouwer, 164
Brussels, 101, 102
Buccleuch, 84, 85, 87
Budapest, 141
Burke, 89–94, 102, 120

Caen, 190
calculus, 56, 70
Caligula, 26
Callias, 2
Calvinism, 85
Cambridge, 151
Camus, 158

© The Editor(s) (if applicable) and The Author(s), under exclusive license to Springer Nature Switzerland AG 2021
K. Binmore, *Imaginary Philosophical Dialogues*,
https://doi.org/10.1007/978-3-030-65387-3

Cantor, 46, 48, 123–127, 135, 137, 139, 141, 154
capitalism, 103, 118, 120
cardinal utility, 146, 147, 166
cardinality, 125, 126, 139
Carnap, 136, 147, 149, 150, 169–171, 173, 176, 179
Cartesian axes, 49
categorical imperative, 85–87, 190, 200
Catullus, 97
causality, 77
certainty, 4, 56, 74, 120, 137
Chaerephon, 3
Chagas disease, 108
Charles I, King, 80
Charles II, King, 50
Chicago, 170, 192
Christina, Queen, 50
Chrysippus, 8
Cicero, 25
City College of New York, 130
coalition formation, 145
Coase theorem, 201, 202
cogito ergo sum, 49, 51
Cohen, Paul, 139
Coleridge, 97
Commodus, 26
Communism, 157, 175, 176
Communist League, 102–104
Communist Manifesto, 102, 116, 119
comparison of utilities, 191
conditional probability, 58, 170, 173
Confucius, 132
consequentialism, 85
conservatism, 90
consistency, 146, 147, 171–173, 191
constructivism, 138
Continental Philosophy, 155
Continuum Hypothesis, 139, 140
contradiction, 4, 74, 75, 106, 115–118, 120, 132, 138, 139, 151, 178, 184
convention, 5, 80, 93, 102, 131, 165, 183, 193
cooperative game theory, 147
cooperative games, 145, 146, 166
Copenhagen, 87
Copernicus, 16
Crates, 22
Cromwell, 92, 93
cynicism, 7, 24
Cyril, St 29

Darwin, Annie, 117
Darwin, Charles, 102, 107–112, 115–120, 157, 164
Darwin, Emma, 117, 157
Darwin, Erasmus, 117
de Finetti, 170, 172

death, 9, 27, 108
Dedekind, 16
deism, 90
demagogue, 93
democracy, direct, 89, 93
democracy, representative, 89, 92, 93
Democritus, 4, 13, 21, 63
deontologism, 85
Descartes, 49–52, 56, 70–72, 77, 153
Dewey, 129–133, 163
diagonalization argument, 126
dialectic, Hegelian, 118
dialectical materialism, 103, 116, 118
dictatorship of the proletariat, 105, 120
Diderot, 78, 160
Didius Julianus, 26
Diogenes, 7–10, 13, 14, 21, 153, 156
Dion, 13
dominant gene, 108, 110, 111
dominant strategy, 182, 184
Dominican Order, 40
Down House, 115, 117, 121
Dr Mirabilis, 40
Dr Pangloss, 71
Dr Strangelove, 142
Driving Game, 165
dualism, 72
Duc de Roannes, 57
Duns Scotus, 45–48, 135

Edgeworth, 202
Edmonds, 149
egalitarianism, 93, 198–201
Eidinow, 149
Einstein, 53, 116, 132, 163, 164, 178, 179
electron, 112
empiricism, 21, 24, 51, 56, 63, 70, 74, 77, 83, 85, 89, 131, 137, 169
empty set, 151
Encyclopedists, 78
enforcement, 193, 194
Engels, 101–106, 116, 119
English Civil War, 92
enlightened self-interest, 101–104, 119
enlightenment, viii, 25, 39, 78, 79, 84, 88, 97
Epictetus, 22, 25, 26, 69
Epicureanism, 21, 25, 27
Epicurus, 15, 21–24, 27, 28, 30, 31, 51, 63, 69, 74, 97, 155, 156
epicycles, 16
Epimenides, 140
epistemic probability, 60, 170, 171
epistemology, 136
Equality or Priority, Parfit's, 198, 200
equilibrium, 78, 80, 81, 93, 102, 164, 166
equilibrium selection device, 194
ethical utility, 192

ethics, 72
Euclid, 16, 52, 72, 138
Euclidean geometry, 84, 130, 135
Eudoxus, 12, 15–18, 70, 154
eugenics, 109
Euler, 88
Euler's theorem, 176
Euripedes, 36
Euthyphro, 7
evolution, 119
evolutionary biology, 166, 186
evolutionary stable strategy, 186
examined life, 6, 9, 14, 19, 22, 24, 27, 74, 97
exchange-value, 41, 105
existentialism, 155, 156, 159, 160
expected utility, 79, 171, 182, 184, 191, 192, 202

fairness, 189, 192–194
faith, 10, 35, 39, 47
Fallacy of the Twins, 182
farmer's dilemma, 81
felicity, 98
feminism, 157
Fénelon, Archbishop, 91
Fermat, 55–60, 70, 164, 169
Fermat's last theorem, 56
feudalism, 118
Feyerband, 179
First-Cause Argument, 46
Fisher, 112
Florence, 161
folk theorem, 186
Foot, Philippa, 199
forms, theory of, 11, 19, 33, 47
Frèchet, 147
Franciscan Order, 40, 45, 51
Frankenstein, 91
Franklin, Benjamin, 90
Frederick the Great, 77, 84
free will, 31, 70–72, 74, 87, 132, 184, 185
freedom, positive and negative, 72
Frege, 123, 127, 170
French Revolution, 89, 92, 120
frequency, long-run, 55, 59, 60, 172
Freud, 55, 150
Friedman, 112, 170

Galapagos, 107, 120
Galileo, 50
Galton, 108–113, 117
game of life, 93, 102, 193
game theory, 81, 142, 163, 164, 193
Garden, of Epicurus, 21, 24
Gassendi, 51
Gaunilo, 34
Gellner, 150

gene, 110
General Will, 79, 86
Genet, 156
genetics, 107
Geneva, 84
geometry, 10, 14, 18, 52, 56, 69, 191
Louis XIV, King, 70
Gibbon, 25
Gide, 161
Gilboa, 202
giraffe's neck, 107
Glorious Revolution, 89, 92
Gödel, 136, 137, 140
Godwin, 89–91, 94, 103
Good, Jack, 170
Good, the, 14, 19, 23, 30, 31
Göttingen, 135, 136
Great Library of Alexandria, 29
Green, Joseph, 87
Gregory, Pope, 34

Hamilton, 186
happiness, 98, 146, 189
Hare, 191
Harsanyi, 95, 99, 142, 189–194, 197–199, 201
Hartshorne, 34
Harvard, 190, 197
hedonism, 21, 23, 97, 156
Hegel, 115–118, 120, 130, 156, 157, 175, 177, 179
Heidegger, 156, 157
Héloise, 33, 78, 155, 157
Helvétius, 95
Hemingway, 158
Henry I, King, 33
Heraclitus, 15
heresy, 32, 36, 41, 46, 47, 110
Herodotus, 2
Herschel, 61
Hilbert, 125, 135, 136, 139, 140, 150, 151, 154, 164
Hilbert Space, 136
Hippo, 29
Hippocrates, 2
historical materialism, 116, 118, 150, 175
Hitler, 142
Hobbes, 49–53, 63, 80, 119
Holbach, Baron de, 79
Hu Shih, 130, 133
Hume, 63, 77–81, 83–85, 87, 93, 102, 104, 107, 119, 155, 156, 164, 165, 177, 182, 183, 185, 186, 190, 193
Hungary, 190
Husserl, 156, 161
Huygens, 70
hybrid, 111
Hypatia, 29–32

idealism, 131
Ilissus, 16
immoral, 79
immortal, 10, 27, 51
induction, scientific, 77
infinite, 46, 59, 125, 132, 137, 138
infinite regress, 46, 47
infinity, 46, 47, 123, 137, 139
infinity of infinities, 123, 126
Institute of Advanced Studies, 163, 164
interpersonal comparison of utility, 146, 194
invisible hand, 103

Jacobins, 90
James, 129
Jansenism, 56
Japan, 190
Jefferson, 90
Jeffrey, 170
John XXII, Pope, 46
Johnson, Samuel, 97
Jowett, 2
Joyce, 158
Julius Caesar, 30
just price, 39, 41, 64, 105
justice, 79, 80, 189, 190, 193
Justine, Sade's, 158–160

Kabbalah, 125
Kakutani, 165, 167
Kant, 63, 78, 83, 84, 86–88, 131, 135, 177, 190, 193, 194, 200
Kapital, Marx's, 101, 102, 115–117
Keynes, 198
kibbutz, 117
knowledge, 3, 4, 70
knowledge-as-certainty, 4, 9, 18, 35, 70, 131, 132, 169
knowledge-as-commitment, 4, 10, 18, 19, 26, 35, 70, 131, 132, 169, 176
knucklebones, 59
Königsberg, 83, 87, 135, 136
Kronecker, 16, 137
Kuhn, 176, 179

labor theory of value, 101, 105, 120
Lakatos, 150, 175–179
Lamarck, 107
Lamarckism, 107
Laplace, 61, 83, 171, 173
large worlds, 192
Law of Ancestral Heredity, Galton's, 109, 112
Law of Independent Assortment, Mendel's, 111
Law of Large Numbers, 59, 60
Law of Segregation, Mendel's, 111
laws of nature, 23, 24
Laws, Plato's, 12

Leibniz, 46, 69–74, 130, 150–152, 176, 183
Lenin, 115
Leo XIII, Pope, 39
Les Deux Magots, 158, 161
Leviathan, Hobbes', 50
Lewis, 67, 154
Lewis, C. I., 191
Lewis, David, 81, 181–186
Liar Paradox, 137, 140
liberalism, 189
libertarianism, 183
liberty, 98
Locke, 63, 77, 89, 90, 92, 93, 105, 119, 182
locus, 110, 111
Logic, Aristotle's, 19
logical positivism, 169
logical probability, 60, 169–173
Logos, Universal, 23
London, 101
London School of Economics, 150, 167, 175
Louis Napoleon, 102
Lucretius, 27, 97
Lyall, 111
Lyceum, 11, 15–17, 20

Madison, 96
Malcolm, 34
Malthus, 107
Manchester, 101
Manhattan project, 141
Marcus Aurelius, 24–28
marginal utility, 145
marginalist revolution, 146
Mars, retrograde movement, 18
Marx, 101–106, 115–120, 156, 175, 179
Marxism, 133, 150, 176, 179
masochism, 160
mass-action, 165
materialism, 21, 116, 118, 132
mathematical induction, 138
maximin criterion, 142, 192, 201, 202
maximin strategy, 143, 144
maximin value, 144
Mazda, 24
Medicis, 161
Meditations, Descartes', 49, 51
Mendel, 107–113
Meno, 9
Mercury, 178
Méré, Chevalier de, 55, 59, 60
Mersenne, 50, 51, 56, 57
Mersenne prime, 50
metamathematics, 138, 151
metaphysics, 118, 137, 139, 151, 156
Metaphysics, Aristotle's, 16, 18
methodological individualism, 103, 104
Metrodorus, 21, 23

Michigan, 170
Mill, James, 96
Mill, John Stuart, 30, 61, 95–99, 137, 142, 189, 191, 192, 198
Millikan, 112
mind, 9
mind-body problem, 51, 72
minimax strategy, 144
minimax theorem, 143, 144, 164
minimax value, 144
mixed strategy, 143
model, 9, 71, 72, 74, 117
monad, 71
monetarism, 112
Monroe, 90
Moral Commitment, 193
morality, 155, 193
Morgenstern, 141–147, 166, 171
Mouseion, 29
mutation, 112
Mytilene, 15, 21

Nash, 163–166
Nash equilibrium, 81, 102, 141, 163, 166
Nash program, 147, 167
Natural Duty, 193
Natural History Society of Brno, 111
natural laws, 67, 105, 155
natural philosophy, 97
Natural Rights, 95, 182, 193
natural selection, 111
natural theology, 39, 47
naturalism, 130, 131
Nebula Hypothesis, 83
neo-Darwinian synthesis, 107, 112
neoplatonism, 29
Nero, 26, 27
Neue Rheinische Zeitung, 103, 104
Newcomb, 181
Newcomb's problem, 181–183
Newcombmania, 181, 187
Newton, ix, 40, 56, 70, 85, 178–180
Nichomachean Ethics, Aristotle's 16
Nicomachus, 16, 20
Nietzsche, 55, 161
noble savage, 80
nominalism, 45, 47, 51
nomos, 1, 33, 51, 89, 132, 176, 198
non-cooperative game theory, 147
non-cooperative games, 146
normal science, 179
Normandy, 197
Nozick, 67, 176, 181–186

objective probability, 60, 172
Ockham's Razor, 46, 48
Ockham, William of, 45–48, 135

one-to-one correspondence, 125, 126
ontological argument, 33, 35, 49, 51, 52, 71, 153
Oracle, Delphic, 1, 3
ordinal number, 125
ordinal utility, 146
Orestes, 30
Origin of Species, Darwin's, 107, 116, 118, 120
original position, 189, 191, 192, 194, 199–201
original sin, 29, 56
Other, the, 156, 158, 159
outlier, 112
Owen, 117–119
Oxford, 197, 198
Oxyrhynchus Papyri, 132

Paine, 89–94, 120
pangenesis, 107, 108
pantheism, 72
paradox of rationality, 182
Paradox of the Twins, 185–187
paradoxes of the infinite, 127, 132, 147
Parallel Postulate, 52
Pareto principle, 43, 200
Parfit, 43, 197–202
Parmenides, 5, 7, 15, 57, 132, 151
Pascal, 55–60, 70, 72, 132, 164, 169
Pascal's Theorem, 56, 72
Pascal's Triangle, 56, 57
Pascal's Wager, 34, 35, 56, 60
Paton, 84
Peirce, 26, 129
Peloponnesian War, 93
Pericles, 93, 161
perihelion, procession of, 180
Peripatetics, 12
Pertinax, 26
phenomenology, 155, 156, 161
philosopher-king, 79
physis, 1, 33, 51, 90, 132, 176, 198
Picasso, 158
pin factory, 104
pineal gland, 51, 72
Plantinga, 34
Plato, viii, 1, 7–15, 17, 21, 24, 30, 33, 47, 57, 106, 153, 175
Platonic solids, 15, 180
Plotinus, 29
Poincaré, 137
Poker, 142, 144, 145, 147, 165, 166
political economy, 101, 117
Pompey, 30
Pope, Alexander, 97
Popper, 149–153, 175–179
possible world, 35, 71, 74, 152, 183
posterior probability, 173
practical reason, 131

pragmatism, 129, 131–133
preference, instrumental, 98
preference, intrinsic, 98
Princeton, 142, 163, 164
Principia Mathematica, Russell and Whitehead's, 123
Principle of Least Action, 56
Principle of No Contradiction, 73
Principle of Sufficient Reason, 73
prior probability, 172, 173
prioritarianism, 197–199, 201
Prisoners' Dilemma, 181, 182, 184, 185, 200
Prisoners' Dilemma, indefinitely repeated, 81, 185
Prisoners' Dilemma, one-shot, 81, 185
private property, 105
probability, 55, 56, 58–60, 111, 147, 164, 169, 171, 172
Problem of Evil, 31, 73
proletariat, 120
promise, 79, 80
property rights, 105
Proslogion, Anselm's, 34
Protagoras, 1–7, 10, 18, 21, 34, 49, 73
protectionism, 104
Proudhon, 105
pseudo-science, 177, 178
psychoanalysis, 150, 175, 178
Ptolemy, 16
Ptolemy Soter, 31
pure reason, 131
pure strategy, 143
Puritanism, 90
Pyrrho, 28
Pythagoras, 10, 15, 18, 154

quantum mechanics, 154, 173, 178

Ra, 24
racism, 109
Ramsey, 146, 147, 170–172
random, 59
Raphael, 11
rational learning, 173
rational solution, of a game, 165
rationalism, 51, 56, 70, 83, 90
rationality, 79, 80, 86, 144, 147, 166, 171
rationalization, 56
Rawls, 43, 67, 142, 182, 189–194, 197–202
realism, viii, 45, 47, 51, 132
Reason, 79
recessive gene, 108, 110, 111
reciprocity, 119, 182, 185
reflective equilibrium, 191, 192, 200, 201
refraction, 56
refutation, 175, 178
relativism, 2, 3, 14, 21, 116, 194

relativity, viii, 116, 173, 178
Rényi, 56
repeated game theory, 186
replication, 112
Republic, Plato's, 1, 12, 13, 79, 106
repugnant conclusion, 199
reputation, 80
reserve army, 104
revealed belief, 27
revealed preference, 28
revisionism, 175
Ricardian socialism, 105
Ricardo, 101, 103–105, 120
Robbins, 143, 146, 147
Robbins, Lionel, 150
Robespierre, 90
robot, 84, 87
Rodin, 131
romanticism, 78
Rousseau, 63, 77–81, 84–86, 90, 92, 115, 156, 160
Russell, 48, 71, 78, 123–125, 129–133, 135, 137, 139, 149, 154, 161, 170
Russell's Paradox, 127

Sade, Marquis de, 156, 158–161
sadism, 158, 159
Samson, 182
Sartre, 155–161
Savage, 147, 150, 169–171, 173, 191, 192
Schelling, 183
Schlick, 149, 170
Schmeidler, 202
science, viii, 39, 175, 177
scientific induction, 177
Scottish Enlightenment, 77, 85
Self, the, 156, 158, 159
Seneca, 24, 25, 27, 31
Septimius Severus, 26
set of all sets, 127
sex ratio, 186
Sextus Empiricus, 25–28
Sextus of Chaeronea, 26
Shelley, 91
skepticism, 10, 25, 28, 77, 87, 133
skyhook, 193, 194
Skyrms, 81
slavery, 109
Smith, Adam, 40, 83, 84, 86, 87, 89, 101, 103, 105, 119
Smith, John Maynard, 186
social contract, 63, 78–80, 89, 92, 93, 102, 119, 120, 183
Social Darwinism, 116
social insects, 119
socialism, 103–106, 115, 117, 118, 183
Socrates, 1–7, 9, 13, 18, 19, 22, 27, 30, 57, 73, 74, 97

solipsism, 73
sophist, 2
sophistry, 3
soul, 5, 8, 9, 21, 23, 27, 51, 87
Sparta, 3
Spencer, 107, 116
Spinoza, 69–74, 79, 191, 199
St Petersburg Paradox, 145, 147
St Thomas's, Abbey, 108
stability, 93
stag hunt, 78–81, 84–86
Stag Hunt Game, 81
state of nature, 50, 80, 105
Stewart, 69, 71
stimulus-response machine, 84, 87
Stoa, 22
Stoicism, 21, 22, 25, 97
strategy, 164
subjective probability, 60, 169–173
subsistence wage, 104
suicide, 27, 28
Summa Theologica, Aquinas's, 40, 106
syllogism, 73
synthesis, 118
synthetic a priori, 83

Tarski, 178
teleology, 116, 118, 120
Theaetetus, 8, 15, 180
Themista, 23
Theophrastus, 16, 17, 20
Theory of Justice, Rawls', 67, 189, 197, 198
theory of types, 127
thesis, 118
Tierra del Fuego, 109
Timocrates, 23
tit-for-tat, 185
Torricelli, 57, 132
Tory party, 80, 92
Tractatus Logico-Philosophicus, Wittgenstein's, 150
tradition, 77, 90, 130
trait, 110, 112
transferable utility, 146
transfinite, 46
transfinite number, 125, 141
transfinite ordinal, 126, 138
Trier, 116
trolley example, 199
Trotsky, 115
trust, 79
truth, 3, 5, 24, 25, 35, 36, 60, 71, 99, 126, 131–133, 139, 178, 179
Turing halting problem, 8

uniform circular motion, 18
Unitarianism, 108

University College London, 96
use-value, 42, 105
util, 145, 146
utilitarianism, 91, 95–99, 103, 119, 142, 143, 146, 189–192, 194, 198–201
utility, 79, 80, 95, 97, 98, 103, 142, 147, 171, 191
utopia, 91
utopian, 80
utopian socialism, 105, 116–118

veil of ignorance, 189, 192, 193
Venus throw, 59
Vickrey, 191
Victoria, Queen, 97
Vienna, 135, 142, 150, 169, 170
Vienna Circle, 149, 150, 169, 170, 176, 179
virtue, 2, 5, 23, 36
void, 5, 74, 132
Voltaire, 71, 78, 84, 85, 93, 152
von Mises, Richard, 61
von Neumann, 136, 141–147, 151, 163–166, 170, 171
von Neumann and Morgenstern, 142
von Neumann and Morgenstern utility, 147
von Westphalen, Jenny, 117

Wallace, 108
Watkins, 176
Wealth of Nations, Adam Smith's, 103
Wedgewood, Emma, 108, 117
Wedgewood, Josiah, 116–118
Weierstrass, 16
Whig party, 89, 91, 92
Wiles, 56
William Rufus, King, 33
William the Conqueror, King, 33
Wittgenstein, 135, 136, 139, 149–154, 177
Wollstonecraft, 91
Wordsworth, 97
workers' cooperative, 118
working class, 118, 119
World Health Organization (WHO), 197

Xenocrates, 21
Xenophon, 22

Young Hegelians, 116

Zeno of Citium, 21–24
Zeno of Elea, 5, 21
Zenobia, 30
zero, 151
zero-sum game, 141, 143, 144, 163, 164, 192
Zeus, 24

GPSR Compliance

The European Union's (EU) General Product Safety Regulation (GPSR) is a set of rules that requires consumer products to be safe and our obligations to ensure this.

If you have any concerns about our products, you can contact us on

ProductSafety@springernature.com

In case Publisher is established outside the EU, the EU authorized representative is:

Springer Nature Customer Service Center GmbH
Europaplatz 3
69115 Heidelberg, Germany

www.ingramcontent.com/pod-product-compliance
Lightning Source LLC
LaVergne TN
LVHW010341260326
834688LV00036B/812